The Clash of Generations

The Clash of Generations
Saving Ourselves, Our Kids, and Our Economy

Laurence J. Kotlikoff and Scott Burns

The MIT Press
Cambridge, Massachusetts
London, England

MIT Press books may be purchased at special quantity discounts for business or sales promotional use. For information, please email special_sales@mitpress.mit.edu or write to Special Sales Department, The MIT Press, 55 Hayward Street, Cambridge, MA 02142.

This book was set in Sabon by the MIT Press. Printed and bound in the United States of America.

Library of Congress Cataloging-in-Publication Data

Kotlikoff, Laurence J.
The clash of generations : saving ourselves, our kids, and our economy / Laurence J Kotlikoff and Scott Burns.
    p.   cm.
Includes bibliographical references and index.
ISBN 978-0-262-01672-8 (hardcover : alk. paper) 1. United States—Economic conditions—21st century. 2. Budgets deficits—United States. 3. Generational accounting—United States 4. Fiscal policy—United States. I. Burns, Scott. II. Title.
HC106.83.K68 2012
330.973—dc23
2011040596

10 9 8 7 6 5 4 3 2 1

For our children and yours

Contents

Acknowledgments

This book owes a great debt to Ellen Faran, director, and John Covell, economics editor, at the MIT Press. John pushed us to write the book, and Ellen provided critical and steadfast support for the project. Both were exceptionally patient as we tussled vigorously over the title, but finally converged on *The Clash of Generations*.

We're also extremely thankful to the rest of the highly professional staff at the MIT Press for their care and skill in preparing the manuscript and helping us make changes to create a better book, designing the book's cover, and bringing the book to market.

Larry is a professor of economics at Boston University and warmly thanks his beloved university for its steadfast support of his research and engagement with the public on key economic issues.

Scott thanks his business partner at AssetBuilder, Kennon Grose, for his amazing patience, and his wife, Carolyn, for her much appreciated support. He gives his biggest thanks to his five grandchildren who remind him by their smiles, hopes, and worries of why this amount of work, on this particular subject, is so important.

Prologue

The Last Straw

The day was coming—for years, decades, really.

Warnings had been sounded, loud, clear, and often.

Most heard, few listened. The problem was distant, its size unclear.

"No worries. We'll fix it. The next election, the next party, the next leader."

There was time.

There wasn't.

The contract was simple: 100,000 barrels of oil, delivered to this country, at this port, on this day. Payment in Chinese yuan.

The seller was big and always insisted on dollars.

Not that day.

Thanks to U.S. pressure, the yuan was floating free. You could buy and sell it anywhere.

The yuan was strong and rising. The dollar was weak and falling.

No wonder: America's economy was awful; over 30 million, mostly young, looking for work; and Uncle Sam was broke. But Sam's ace in the hole was the dollar—the world's reserve currency. If Sam needed money, he'd print it, and everyone would take it.

No longer.

"Our shareholders come first. The dollar's too risky. Let's settle in yuan."

And so the contract said yuan.

The medium of exchange was the message, and the message was broadcast, posted, e-mailed, tweeted, Facebook'd, and texted around the globe, in seconds.

"They switched. We should too."

Denominating contracts in anything but dollars became routine.

If only. If only that company had waited or kept it quiet. If only that company was smaller or foreign.

But there it was. A major U.S. oil company had publicly called it quits on the greenback.

America's economic death was quick and painful.

In short order, the dollar plunged. Interest rates soared. Bond and stock markets vaporized. Towns, cities, states, and businesses—large and small—started declaring bankruptcy.

And massive layoffs began. The young got the first pink slips.

The Fed rode to the rescue.

"Not to worry. We'll print more dollars, buy bonds, and lower rates."

"Worked before."

"You need a loan. Step right up. We've got money."

This time was not different.

This time, ancient economic law prevailed: more money begets higher prices.

With prices rising, the dollar became a hot potato. No wonder. The longer you held it, the less it would buy.

And faster money pushed prices even higher.

Next came the bank runs.

Deposit insurance didn't matter. Everyone wanted to get and spend their money before it became worthless.

Uncle Sam printed trillions of dollars to honor insurance and other guarantees to depositors, money market funds, bondholders—you name it.

Inflation reached double digits.

Per month, per week, per day, per hour.

The economy was unraveling.

And then the next generation took to the streets.

1

The United States Is Bankrupt

Economic meltdowns are as much psychological events as they are economic ones.[1] They hit when people panic—when they see enough evidence of private or public financial turmoil or malfeasance to realize it's time to take their remaining money and run. Before 2008, no one would have viewed a wholesale U.S. economic meltdown as remotely plausible. But that terrible year changed everything. It turned our economic world upside down.

In 2008, we discovered that Wall Street was no longer safe for Main Street, that it had systematically produced and sold trillions of dollars of fraudulent securities, and that it was aided and abetted in this racket by regulators on the make, politicians on the take, rating companies on the fake, and directors on a break.

Countrywide Financial, Bear Stearns, IndyMac Bank, Fannie Mae, Freddie Mac, Lehman Brothers, Merrill Lynch, AIG, Washington Mutual, Citigroup, and Wachovia—each of these financial behemoths trafficked in "toxic assets" and each failed, was "rescued" in a shotgun wedding, or became wards of the state. The specter of so many financial giants going under panicked our nation's leaders as well as the public. Everyone decided bad times were here and took steps to ensure that outcome.

Consumers stopped buying. Companies started firing. Unemployment skyrocketed, leaving 15 million Americans out of work, 1 million too discouraged to look for work, and millions more working fewer hours for less pay. The stock market plummeted. In only sixteen months, it stood at 44 percent of its October 2007 peak. The Fed printed $1.6 trillion, more than doubling the basic supply of money, hoping to keep the economy afloat. (After that, it printed another $600 billion.) And the Treasury expended vast sums to stimulate the economy, running massive deficits in the process. Through it all, the public and the rest of the world decided U.S. government bonds were the safest securities on earth.

Nothing was further from the truth. The United States was, and is, in worse fiscal shape than many other countries commonly regarded as basket cases.

We made this point in our 2004 book, *The Coming Generational Storm*, which laid out our nation's grave long-term demographic and fiscal problems and their extremely troubling implications for our children.[2] What was true then is triply true today. Rather than heed our warnings and those of many others, the government has taken one step after another to dig our nation a much deeper hole. Our fiscal problems are now so severe, our economic institutions so poorly structured, our financial system so fragile, our politicians so divided, our foreign competition so intense, and our countrymen so anxious, that major social strife could occur at any time. This book makes that clear. But it also offers a path forward for ourselves, our kids, and our economy. And Lord help us if we don't take it.

President Kennedy said, "Our problems are man-made. Therefore, they may be solved by man." Looking at our current situation, one might well add, "Man's solutions may become his and his children's problems." Indeed, many of our problems today can be described as cases of catastrophic success, where we've identified a problem and fixed it, but in so doing, we ignored the attendant and potentially worse problems the fixes themselves created. More important, this isn't just a financial engineering mess. It is a generational time bomb, which will explode as a terrible clash of generations.

Our most disastrous success has been turning retirement into a well-paid, long-term occupation. We've done this by trying to do right by our elders by expending ever-larger sums each year to keep them healthy and financially secure. These sums are now huge, amounting to more than $30,000 per retiree per year. That's three-fourths of annual U.S. per capita income. In the process, we've done terrible wrong by our children, grandchildren, and great-grandchildren. We've saddled them with massive government bills to pay for this largess. These bills stretch from here to eternity. They are far beyond our childrens' capacity to pay, just as they are far beyond our own capacity—and will—to pay.

When individuals can't pay their bills, they are bankrupt. When companies can't pay their bills, they are bankrupt. And when countries, even those that print their own money and can still get foreigners to accept it, can't pay their bills, they are bankrupt.

Thanks to six decades of incredibly profligate and irresponsible generational policy, we can declare, *The United States is bankrupt.*

And the United States isn't bankrupt ten, thirty, or fifty years from now. It's bankrupt right now. Indeed, the United States may be in worse fiscal shape than Portugal, Ireland, Italy, Greece, or Spain (referred to as PIIGS), which are generally viewed as the developed world's worst fiscal basket cases.

You won't learn this by looking at our nation's official debt.[3] Our 70 percent debt (held by the public) to gross domestic product (GDP) ratio is lower than that of any of the PIIGS. Actually, it's less than half of Greece's ratio—the PIIG that's supposedly in the hottest water.[4] Unfortunately, our $11 trillion official debt is but a small fraction of our nation's true $211 trillion indebtedness, known as the fiscal gap.

Yes, you read that number right. Our fiscal gap—the value in the present (the present value) of all our future spending obligations (including servicing the official debt), net of all our future tax receipts, is enormous. It is fourteen times our nation's GDP, its total output. It is twenty-two times the official debt that now has everyone's attention.

Since the fiscal gap equals $211 trillion and the official debt equals $11 trillion, it's clear that our unofficial IOUs (unofficial spending commitments) overwhelm our official ones. Worse, they are growing rapidly. Yet these unofficial liabilities have been carefully kept off the government's books in a system of duplicitous accounting that goes far beyond Enron's and Bernie Madoff's wildest dreams. That's why most people know little or nothing about the true size of our problem.

Unfortunately, our unofficial IOUs are as real as our official ones, and they cannot be escaped. These liabilities represent senior claims on our government. This is not a legal statement. It is a statement about economics and politics. Our unofficial IOUs represent senior claims on Uncle Sam because the claimants are, to a large extent, seniors. And our seniors exercise tremendous political clout in ensuring they get what they believe is "owed" them. This includes demanding that their benefits be fully adjusted for inflation.

Compared to cutting, say, the Social Security benefits of today's retirees, Uncle Sam can de facto default by paying his bills with freshly printed money, generating inflation. That way he can pay back principal plus interest in watered-down dollars. Unfortunately the Federal Reserve's recent massive increase in money creation suggests this is precisely what Uncle Sam intends to do, although the announced intention has been to save the economy.

But before considering the precise nature and timing of the developing clash of generations, we need to explain why our country is so utterly broke. Chapter 2 begins by focusing on our two major demographic achievements: extending life and limiting births. But as chapter 3 shows, sustaining our long lives on the backs of our relatively few children has produced a fundamental dilemma: too many old hands reaching into too few young pockets, taking amounts that are far too high.

It didn't need to be this way. We could have asked each generation to pay for itself or, at least, limit its fiscal child abuse. But instead our politicians chose to keep raising the standards of living of the elderly but at such a high cost that it has driven the country broke.

Chapter 3 quantifies why our wonderful goal of trying to keep retirees out of the grave is putting our economy into it. First, we're going to identify U.S. fiscal policy for what it is—a six-decade-and-counting Ponzi scheme. It takes ever larger sums from the young and gives them to the old. Each young generation is induced to participate in the chain letter with the promise of having its turn, in old age, to indenture the young to ever higher payments to the old. And because each generation pays when young, it feels entitled to take back when old without bothering to ask whether what it's taking back vastly exceeds what it put in—or whether those forced to pay have the jobs and income to do it.

Second, we'll suggest that Shakespeare had it wrong when he said, "The first thing we do, let's kill all the lawyers." The right statement is, "The first thing we do, let's kill all the accountants." Government accountants have concealed Uncle Sam's Ponzi scheme since its inception by focusing attention on the official debt. But they knew, or should have known, as a matter of economic theory, that official debt is a figment of our language, not a meaningful measure of our fiscal affairs. As a result, they've made sure, with the help of the politicians, that the public (and most economists) would ignore the rapidly metastasizing economic tumor associated with our living far beyond our children's means.

Finally, we're going to explain why the fiscal gap is so huge, not only on its own, but also in comparison with the fiscal gaps of other countries. In this, we'll be relying on budget projections from the U.S. Congressional Budget Office and the European Union.

Chapter 4 begins with the two scariest and least well-known facts there are about our economy: we're saving less than nothing and investing (adding to our stock of equipment, factories, and other capital) next to nothing. In 2010, the U.S. net national saving rate was 0.1 percent, and the U.S. net domestic investment rate was a paltry 4.4 percent. This is no aberration. Our country has been on a six-decade-long consumption spree that has slowly driven our nation's rate of saving from close to 15 percent to essentially zero. And because we aren't saving, we don't have the wherewithal to invest. Hence, our saving rate has pulled our domestic investment rate down the tubes.

So why aren't we saving? The answer is simple. It's due in large part to the Ponzi scheme we've been running. Almost all the decline in national saving reflects an increase in personal consumption. And among all our households the group whose consumption has risen most rapidly is, yes, *the elderly*. As we'll discuss, this is delivering a double whammy to our kids. First, they face very high current tax rates today. But they face much higher ones down the road. Second, they are working in an economy with much less capital than would otherwise have been the case. This means they are earning less and experiencing a lower living standard. It also means their capacity to pay taxes is lower.

Chapter 5 takes a close-up look at the fallout from modern demographics on our children. It shows how failing income and uncertainty are causing the young to defer marriage, home buying, and child bearing. These are deep social changes.

Chapter 6 takes a close look at four specific problems young adults face: the terrible risk of home ownership, once the assured path to modest wealth and security; the consequences of grossly inadequate primary and secondary education; how highly overpriced tertiary education is putting tens of millions of younger people into a modern debtors' prison; and how the intense competition from ever more productive hordes of workers from China, India, and all other parts of the world is limiting, if not eliminating, real wage growth for most workers. The result is increasing income inequality that is eviscerating the middle class. The young have also inherited a highly volatile asset market thanks to a financial system that can't be trusted.

Chapter 7 looks at the range of problems we've left our kids. It points out how we've largely failed to notice or understand how tenuous their situation is. How this youthanasia will play out is hard to say. We don't expect the young to take up arms against their parents and grandparents, but we also don't expect them to sit back and smile. They have options. They could form their own political party to oppose the miseries brought to them by our traditional but witless parties. They could riot like the Tunisian, Egyptian, Greek, and English youth have done. Or they could vote with their feet and leave the country. The United States is a nation of immigrants, but it could, like Uruguay, become a nation of emigrants. In recent decades, an estimated half-million Uruguayans, mostly young, have called it quits and moved to Spain, Argentina, and elsewhere. They did so for one reason: Uruguay didn't pay; given its oppressive tax rates needed to cover official and unofficial government obligations, it didn't offer as high a living standard as the competition.[5]

Net emigration arises in many countries. In 2008, eighty-seven countries saw more people say adios than hola.[6] Most of these countries are members of the third world, a status the United States may ultimately achieve, given our lack of saving, investment, and growth, not to mention jobs.

Chapters 8 through 11 move from problems to solutions, offering four dramatic but practical government-based solutions to the problems we face. The country's only real hope is quickly enacting simple, radical reforms of our financial, health care, tax, and Social Security systems. There's actually not much to discuss because each solution can fit on a postcard. While many people fear reform, the real risk is maintaining the status quo. In particular, there is an enormous upside to fixing the biggest single cause of our youth-devouring fiscal gap: health care. Spending half again as much in health care as many other industrialized nations, Americans still have lower life expectancies. Less could literally be more!

Chapters 12 and 13 deal with what we all may face since our government is unlikely to enact practical solutions. First, we explain how an investment nirvana is hidden inside our current investment hell. It provides our recommendations on investing in this very dangerous environment. If you are looking for a magic bullet that will make you rich while everyone else becomes poor, you can stop reading now. But if you're looking for practical steps that you can take that don't involve buying a large supply of freeze-dried food and learning how to use deadly weapons, our suggestions will help you do well in a world that only manages to muddle through.

Second, we lay out simple, and highly personal, decisions you can make to preserve, protect, and raise your living standard without incurring additional risk or relying on investment returns. We demonstrate how these decisions can be the equivalent of large amounts of saving.

The book ends in chapter 14 with a summary and appeal that we grownups start acting the part and stop arguing over blame or parties. Let's, at long last, fix things for our kids and the future of our country.

To do that, we have to understand the size of the mess we've made.

2

Catastrophic Success

Being alive shouldn't be a problem, let alone a catastrophe. But that's what it's coming to for more and more of us. The longevity we human beings have sought for millennia is now ours. But we weren't careful with our wishes. The fulfillment of our dream has produced perverse and unintended consequences that threaten virtually everything we hold dear. It threatens our economy. It threatens our standard of living. It threatens our health. It threatens our ability and capacity to care for those in need. It threatens our ability to nurture and educate the young. It threatens most of what we have come to think of as "modern life."

Most important, unless we learn how to manage the economics of longevity, it threatens all our hopes for our children and grandchildren.

It's no surprise that public conversations about Social Security and Medicare are now routinely framed in fear and failure. The two of us are no different. We're going to present most of this book with a focus on an impending, gigantic, and virtually inescapable failure that will change our lives. But we should never forget that this is the result of *catastrophic success*.

Let's start with the incredible longevity and fertility successes that produced this catastrophe. You probably don't think of actuarial tables as bedtime reading (or any other kind of reading), but demographic change, past, present, and future, as well as demographic differences across peoples and countries, are truly fascinating and, potentially, awfully scary. That's why demographics are featured so often, sometimes directly and sometimes subtly, in disaster books and horror movies.

"No One Here Gets Out Alive"—Jim Morrison

For centuries life was even harder than Napoleon's disastrous march to Moscow. Leaving Paris with 420,000 men, Napoleon's army marched to Moscow in 1812, losing troops all the way. Of the original army, only 30,000 returned.[1]

What a relentless march to death! But an early mortality table is more distressing. Although Napoleon's army suffered slow but constant attrition, there were some survivors. When John Graunt compiled his "Bill of Mortality" from London birth and death records in 1662, it was a forgone conclusion that there would be a death for each birth. The darker news was that the march through one's years was an unfolding disaster if you were lucky enough to survive birth.

Graunt found that 65 percent of those born were dead by age sixteen. A typical Londoner could expect to live only twenty-seven years. Even places like Afghanistan and Angola, where life is currently the shortest in the world, have life expectancies that are much higher, at forty-five and thirty-nine years, respectively.[2]

You can get some idea of how tough life is in such parts of the world by considering a few facts: seventeen countries have life expectancies today that are no greater than U.S. life expectancy in 1900, more than a century ago. Of the 222 countries listed in the CIA's *World Factbook,* seventy-seven have life expectancies equal to ours fifty years ago.

You can see our long and positive march over the past century in figure 2.1. The two curves represent the number surviving, each year, starting with 100,000 births. While 31 people (only 3/100ths of 1 percent) among those born between 1900 and 1902 could expect to survive to age one hundred, in 2005, a stunning 1,519 (1.5 percent) could expect to have a hundredth birthday party. More important, nearly 88,000 could expect to live to age sixty.

If you take the maximum human life span to be one hundred years and start with 100,000 births, the figure represents a total of 10 million potential life-years. We got to enjoy only 4.7 million of them in 1900, but we're now enjoying about 7.5 million of them. That means we've captured about 75 percent of our total possible life-years. If we ever capture 100 percent of our possible life-years, the top curve will be a straight horizontal line. It would drop straight down at the maximum age of life.

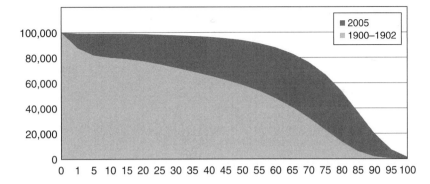

Figure 2.1

Gaining life: The enormous gains in life expectancy over the past 100 years *Source:* Elizabeth Arias, "United States Life Tables, 2006," *National Vital Statistics Reports,* June 28, 2010, http://www.cdc.gov/nchs/data/nvsr/nvsr58/nvsr58_21.pdf.

Such a "curve" would form the two sides of a rectangle. The prospect has been dubbed "the rectangular curve."

The limit to human life span and our prospects for achieving a rectangular curve is a long and divergent subject. At the radical extreme are people like futurist and inventor Ray Kurzweil. He believes that the growth of computing power is so fast that we are approaching the "singularity,"[3] the moment when computer power will make immortality possible by transferring all our memories and knowledge as a carbon-based life form onto an infinitely durable, silicon-based chip. When that happens, the only things we'll need to worry about are paying the electric bill and dealing with the inevitable bugs in the Windows Immortal Edition.

Preserving our personal software is one thing. Preserving our personal hardware is another. Here we do face the rectangular curve. For centuries our life expectancy has been lower due to disease, accidents, and mayhem. But modern medicine is advancing average life expectancy closer and closer to our natural life limit.

In their 1983 book, *Vitality and Aging: Implications of the Rectangular Curve,*[4] Dr. James Fries and Dr. Lawrence Crapo said that while our maximum life span may not change, the squaring of the mortality curve means that we had the prospect of a longer period of health and vitality followed by a briefer period of senescence and decline. Basically, we were approaching a golden age (of sorts) in which we might all live vital lives until we hit our maximum age. Like the replicants in the movie *Blade Runner*, we would live healthy lives until our genetic coding told us it was time to die. Then we would exit abruptly.

Moving the Curve

To whom do we owe our current good fortune? What, or who, did things that ballooned out the mortality curves so that each passing decade captured more years of life? Was it the heroic doctors we see in television programs, deftly cutting and stitching? Was it curmudgeons like House, in the TV series of that name, with brilliant insights into obscure symptom patterns that save patients' lives? Was it the creation of new drugs for chemotherapy that turn cancer victims into cancer survivors?

Yes, sometimes it is.

But more often it's not. A surprising portion of our life expectancy gains don't come from extreme medicine, practiced by heroic doctors in caring hospitals managed by warm-hearted insurance actuaries. Most of the gain can be traced to broad changes in how we live: as clean water to drink, toilets that flush, safer food, better houses, and the near extermination of diseases that once took millions of lives.

Rose Mahoney, Scott's maternal grandmother, died of tuberculosis in the 1920s. Death from tuberculosis, common then, is virtually unheard of today. Most of us believe the near eradication of tuberculosis is due to powerful antibiotics introduced by heroic pharmaceutical companies, but that isn't the case. As Dr. John Abramson points out in *Overdosed America*, the death rate from tuberculosis fell by 87 percent from 1900 to 1950 due to healthier living and working conditions and greater prosperity.[5] The first effective treatment drugs, in fact, weren't introduced until the 1950s.

The Centers for Disease Control (CDC) once estimated that twenty-five of the thirty years of life we gained over the past century were attributable to advances in public health.[6] That leaves only five years to what most would call modern medicine and pharmaceuticals.

Then again, modern medicine is about a lot more than adding years to our life expectancy. It provides us with new knee and hip joints, it lifts our sagging chins, it helps our athletes perform better and set new records, and it provides for the day-to-day needs of people who can no longer remember their names. As our lives have grown longer and more of us have experienced the decline (or ravages) of aging, the scope of medical concern has grown. Most of that concern has worked to improve the quality of our lives.

This is an important distinction: we are spending health care dollars on quality of lives as well as duration of lives. If we focused entirely on quantity of lives and let quality of life take care of itself, our experience of health care and its expense might be completely different from what we experience today.

The Other Mortality Curves

In some respects, life is much like money: it is not equally distributed. If we treat all human beings as part of one big happy family, we get the mortality curves in figure 2.1. But if we examine the lives of different members of that family, we get very different mortality curves. Most of us, for instance, know that women live longer than men. Girl babies born in 2005 have a life expectancy of 79.9 years, while boy babies born the same year have a life expectancy of 74.9 years.

There are reasons for this. Men have more accidents. Men are more likely to commit suicide. Men are more likely to commit murder, and when they do, they are more likely to kill another man. We men also don't take care of ourselves as well. We are heavier eaters, drinkers, smokers, and drug abusers.

Start dividing the human family by race, and the differences in mortality curves become even more dramatic. Here, for instance, is the life expectancy lineup for the major groups in America that the CDC follows:

White women: 80.4 years

Black women: 76.1 years

White men: 75.4 years

Black men: 69.3 years

At 69 years, the life expectancy of black men is about equal to the life expectancy of all Americans in 1960, a half-century ago. At 69 years, the life expectancy of black men is only slightly better than the 67.3-year expectancy of white women in 1940, seventy years ago. Divide the American family into more groups, and the differences become even larger.

Americans with more education live longer than Americans with less education. Americans with more income live longer than Americans with less income.

All this could be dismissed as living proof of the survival of the fittest, but it could also be used to make a damaging assessment about social inequality and about on whom public money is spent.

Longevity Marches On

Scott was born in 1940. For American men born that year, the life expectancy of a newborn was only 61.6 years. That's a bit short by today's standard of 74.9 years, but it was a nice improvement over the 47.9 years a man born in 1900 could expect.

Scott, now 71, can get a bit sensitive about this. After all, the mortality table used when he was born indicates he had a 55.4 percent chance of being dead by now. Larry is younger. He was born in 1951 with a life expectancy of 65.5 years. So he looks over his shoulder less often. He also knows that those tables have shown improvement every decade for more than a century.

Larry's sons, born less than twenty years ago, had life expectancies of about 72 at the time, but the expectancy of an American male newborn today is 74.9 years. Examine any group of Americans, born at any time, and you will find a continuous increase in life expectancy. The increases aren't evenly distributed, so some are doing better than others. But the basic fact is that most of us can expect to live longer than our parents and grandparents did.

In a bit more than a century, life expectancy at birth for American men has increased more than 50 percent, from 47.9 years to 74.9 years. That's a gain of 27 years. Women have enjoyed an even greater increase, from 50.7 years to 79.9 years, a gain of 29.2 years.

That's simply stunning, and the older you are, the more grateful you are likely to be. We like being alive. The last century has given us much to celebrate. Advances in public health and medicine have added literally millions of years to the experience of being human.

Many of those added years of life are young years. Fewer babies today die in childbirth. Fewer infants die during their first year of life. Fewer children die from childhood diseases. And fewer adults die from diseases that have been virtually eradicated, like tuberculosis and polio. If you add up all the years of life gained, you'll find that a slight majority went to people under the age of sixty. This was relief from the anguish and loss that death made commonplace in earlier times.

These are also productive years of life gained. More kids survived childhood and became workers. More workers paid taxes. And they paid them for more years. There was a gain in life and a corresponding gain in the means to support it.

But nearly half of the gain in years of life went to people who were at least sixty years old. Instead of dying at a rapid rate from age-related illnesses, more and more Americans are living for a very long time. While it was once common to refer to anyone over age sixty-five as "old," the older population is now commonly subdivided into four groups, the "young-old" who are age sixty-five to seventy-four, the "old" who are seventy-five to eighty-four, the "old-old" who are eighty-five and older, and the old old-old—the centenarians.

The gains might continue. If you examine life expectancies in other nations, it turns out we still have plenty of room for improvement. Life expectancy in the United States ranks forty-ninth among the 223 nations listed in the CIA's *World Factbook*.[7] In that book Americans have a life expectancy of 78.24 years, trailing Germany (79.41 years), Great Britain (79.92 years), France (81.09 years), Canada (81.29 years), and Japan (82.17 years),[8] even though each of these nations spends far less on health care than we do.

When Life's Not Cheap

The majority of our gain in life does not have a corresponding gain in the means to support it. This is what makes our success catastrophic. Most of the people over age sixty are retired, ready or not. They are living on their savings, if they have any; their home equity, if they have any; and their Social Security benefits. Similarly, they need an ever-increasing amount of medical care, and their own payments cover less than 25 percent of the bill.

It's already an extremely large bill, and it's rapidly growing. The cost of Medicare, which pays out 85 percent of its benefits to the elderly, and Medicaid, which pays out 70 percent of its benefits to the elderly, primarily for nursing home care, has grown roughly twice as fast as the economy for the past forty years. Recent reform notwithstanding, there is little to indicate that spending growth in these programs will slow. Indeed, much of it is already baked in as the boomers retire in larger and larger numbers over the next decade. At the same time, our economic and employment growth is slowing. Some estimate that it will be years before employment again reaches its 2006 peak.

The combination puts us in a gigantic squeeze that will be measured in decades, not years. It is a generational squeeze on the young. It is becoming a generational clash because the economy that supports the elderly and their medical care isn't growing as fast as the elderly population and their medical needs.

Centenarians, Left, Right, and Center

As one example of the lurking danger of the-really-long-retirement problem, consider America's fastest-growing population. We're not talking illegal immigrants. We're talking centenarians—those aged one hundred and over.[9] Today there are 79,000 members of the old old-old. By 2050 (when today's newborns are middle aged), this figure will reach 601,000.[10] That's enough centenarians to fill up Washington, D.C.[11] We can imagine movies being remade to suit an older demography, such as *Butch Cassidy and the Sundance Centenarian.* Coming soon.

Next, contemplate a much scarier vision: the annual health care costs, circa 2050, of these projected 601,000 residents of the new Century City.

Your Money or Your Life

We could solve the financial problem Social Security and Medicare represent simply by reducing life expectancy, but there is a remarkable lack of public enthusiasm for the idea. No politician has suggested a new program with special tickets to shorter lives. Unlike the 1973 science-fiction movie *Soylent Green,* there are no arrangements for a few glorious final moments before being turned into food for the young. And when palliative care was part of the 2010 health care reform bill, it was quickly labeled "death squads" and removed from the bill.

We like being alive, thank you, and aim to stay that way for as long as possible.

What we have never faced up to, however, is that we literally have a your-money-or-your-life decision. The operative word here is *or*—but we want both. We won't give up our growing years of life, but we don't want to pay for them. Politicians of both parties know this and act accordingly. They promise more public benefits because that's what we want. Then they hide the bill in the diaper of a newborn. This would be a minor issue if the advances in life expectancy were not so great and supporting the elderly at the style to which they've become accustomed so expensive.

But the life expectancy advances are major, and the cost per elderly is both staggering and exploding.

In most contexts, longer lives signal a successful society—something evoking pride, not panic. But for us, this success is starting to look catastrophic. An awful fear is starting to creep up the backs of our necks as we confront the longevity rub. *We aren't willing to pay for those extra years of life.* We don't want to save more as individuals. Our employers no longer want to take care of us when we retire. And we don't want to pay more as taxpayers.

The gap between what we are willing to do and what longevity actually costs has gone to the extreme due to an unrelenting political failure to deal with the issue. For several years now, the unfunded liabilities (the shortfall between benefits promised and expected tax revenue) of Social Security and Medicare alone have approached our entire net worth as households. These figures come from government documents. In 2009, for instance, the unfunded liabilities of Social Security and Medicare measured over the next seventy-five years were $43.5 trillion, and publicly held Treasury debt was $7.8 trillion, a total of $51.3 trillion. The total net worth of all households and nonprofits in America was $51.7 trillion, according to the Federal Reserve.[12]

The blame for our political failure cannot be put on a single political party. Both have been equally irresponsible in addressing the primary issue of living longer lives: they cost money, and that money has to come from somewhere.

Is There Death after Life?

Longevity—who's got it, who doesn't, and what it costs—isn't necessarily polite dinner conversation, but it does show up in literature and entertainment, generally with a frightening message.

In the 1726 novel *Gulliver's Travels,* Jonathan Swift reports on the unexpected fate of the Struldbruggs, rare individuals, born among the Luggnaggians, who appear to be immortal. When he learns of them, Gulliver is eager for a meeting, sure that the Struldbruggs will have acquired the wisdom of long history and enough wealth to make their lives comfortable. He imagines that if he was a Struldbrugg, he would "live in an honorable manner, but still on the saving side. I would entertain myself in forming and directing the minds of hopeful young men, by convincing them from my own remembrance, experience and observation, fortified by numerous examples, of the usefulness of virtue in public and private life."

Sadly, this is not how the Struldbruggs live. They may live forever, but they continue aging and no one wants to take care of them. To prevent them from dominating the lives of their shorter-lived brethren, their wealth, if any, is confiscated at age eighty. In fact, "they had not only all the infirmities of other old men, but many more which arose from the dreadful prospect of never dying. They were not only opinionative, peevish, covetous, morose, vain, talkative, but uncapable of friendship, and dead to all natural affection, which never descended below their grandchildren. Envy and impotent desires are their prevailing passions."

Yes, there can be too much of a good thing.[13]

That said, taking our leave from life isn't exactly easy. In his short story, "The Lotus Eater," W. Somerset Maugham tells of Thomas Wilson, a man who decides to retire from his life as a banker, sell his property, and go to live the rest of his life on the island of Capri.[14] To do this, he converts all of his financial assets into a fixed-term annuity—an income that will end precisely when he reaches sixty-five years old.

"I wanted," he told the storyteller, "to live the perfect life while I still had the energy and spirit to make the most of it. Twenty-five years seems a long time to me, and twenty-five years of happiness seemed worth paying something pretty substantial for."

His plan was to live his life to the fullest, living quietly amid the beauty of the island. Then, when he turned sixty-five, his intention was to die, paying with his life for those twenty-five perfect years. Many teenagers think this way. And most of us, even as young adults, imagine that it will be easy to give life up down the road. But then, like Steve Martin giving up material possessions in *The Jerk,* saying he needed nothing but grabbing at more and more as he headed for the door, we grasp for a few moments more. The only difference is that Steve Martin was grasping for things. We grasp for time.

Wilson does run out of money at age sixty-five, as planned, but he lacks the courage of his convictions. So he lives on, broke and homeless, and slowly goes mad. He is the gruesome literary version of "too much month at the end of the money."

Modern Aging and the Arrival of the Lupies

Science-fiction writer Richard Matheson offered a brand-new perspective on our terminal state. His 1956 novella, "I Am Legend,"[15] introduced us to the "living un-dead," otherwise known as "lupies," and death in life hasn't been the same since. As many sad newspaper stories tell it, the real death in life can be found in the Alzheimer's unit of any nursing home. This is simply too painful to bear, so our culture offers us the darkly comic movies that tell us about what might be called the Modern Zombie.

The first of those movies was the classic 1968 B flick directed by George Romero, *Night of the Living Dead*. Scott's favorite line from it is, "We may not enjoy living together, but dying isn't going to solve anything either."

So even as the baby boomers were coming of age and learning about birth control pills, some other part of the public imagination was worrying about what was going to happen when this crowd got to be really old. Imagination answered: it will be hell. The truly living young will be outnumbered, isolated, and besieged by the living undead. The actual situation of our young will be physically far less frightening and contain less visual drama, but in reality, young people will be defending themselves from the ever increasing demands of the elderly.

Achieving the Postmodern Dream: More Sex, Fewer Babies

Longevity was but one of our demographic victories that put us into our current quandary. Limiting procreation was the other. In the United States, we still like to have kids, albeit not as many and not right after we tie the knot. Consequently, our fertility rate is estimated at 2.06 for 2011, very close to the 2.10 rate needed to maintain the population. But go back to the baby boom years of the 1950s, and it was 3.7 children per woman. Our main demographic concern then was the population explosion.

Population explosion remains a huge, but barely mentioned, problem for the United States and the rest of the world. The population is simply growing less rapidly than it was in the 1950s. Still, the world's total population is scheduled to increase by a jaw-dropping one-third by midcentury, adding 2 billion people to the planet, with all their attendant needs and demands on our natural resources and environment.

The U.S. population is scheduled to increase by an even larger percentage, 42 percent, over the same period. The increase is due to births outstripping deaths (our population is still relatively young) and our high rate of immigration. Adding 42 percent more Americans will take us from 310 million inhabitants now to 439 million in 2050, an increase of 129 million mouths to feed, bodies to clothe, and minds to educate. To put 129 million in perspective, this projected people count exceeds Japan's entire current population. Imagine relocating every Japanese man, woman, and child to the United States right now, and you'll get a sense of how crowded our country is going to get. Given our proclivity for congestion rage, *bullet train* may take on a new meaning.

Although we have an exploding population, our retired population is growing much more rapidly than our working-age population. Between now and 2050, the number of oldsters (those over sixty-five years old) will increase by 120 percent, while the number of worksters (those ages eighteen to sixty-four) available to help support them will increase by only 28 percent. As a result, we'll go from 4.8 potential workers per oldster today to 2.8 in forty years, making the entire country substantially older than Florida is today.[16] Given the massive support the young are now providing the old, having relatively few young pockets to pick means the old hands will need to dig deeper and more often into those pockets.

Children of Men

If *Soylent Green* expressed our angst over unlimited population growth and its impact on the environment, a more recent movie addressed the other side of the dystopian coin, a total lack of newborns. In *Children of Men* (2006) actor Clive Owen seeks to protect and deliver a miraculously pregnant woman, the only pregnant woman on earth, to a place where she will be safe in a world that is disintegrating because it is literally a world without a future. No children have been born for years.

This is far less extreme than it sounds. Europe, Japan, and Russia are already older than Florida and aging much more rapidly and significantly than the United States. They're experiencing population implosion, not explosion. Germany, Spain, Italy, Poland, Greece, Japan, Ukraine, Romania, the Czech Republic, Russia, Bulgaria, Slovakia, Slovenia, Switzerland, Austria, Belarus, Bosnia and Herzegovina, Croatia, and Portugal all have fertility rates below 1.5.[17] Japan's rate of 1.2 is the lowest of the group. Since most of these countries are either witnessing emigration or are restricting immigration, they are gradually heading toward depopulation and possible oblivion.

Take Russia and Europe. Today they account for 22 percent of the world's population. By midcentury, their population share will fall to just 7 percent. By century's end, it will be just 4 percent. Think of Western civilization becoming a trace element in global population. Or consider Japan, whose population will shrink by 20 percent over the next forty years and by 50 percent by the end of the century. Or note that by 2100, only one of the now-developed countries, the United States, will rank among the twenty most populous nations.[18]

Next time you are in Italy, look at four out of every ten people. Imagine them gone. And while you're at it, make one of three of those you don't mentally eliminate an oldster. This will give you a good sense of where Italy and most other European countries are heading. Perhaps Europe's destiny is to become a giant historical amusement park, manned and womaned by elderly European ticket takers and chock full of tourists from Asia, Africa, and the Middle East.

When Aging Turns Economically Deadly

We'll tell you right now that we have no idea how this will turn out. But we're glad that the art, literature, and entertainment industry are providing some outlet for our demographic-economic angst. Whatever the limitations, we're dealing with the future a lot better on the media and art front than we are on the political and economic front.

This isn't just a national failure. This is a global failure. With a few notable exceptions, governments around the world continue to promise more in future benefits than they can possibly deliver.

In our case, there is a difference. As Greece has gone broke, it's been terrible for some financial institutions and millions of Greeks, but wishful thinking suggests that the disaster probably won't go much beyond that. But if the United States goes broke and descends into economic chaos and generational conflict, the whole world will suffer, probably in ways none of us can, or want, to imagine. If you do want to imagine that future, you'll find that Terry Southern has been reincarnated as a nonfiction writer in Dmitry Orlov. His sardonic and strangely comic book, *Reinventing Collapse: The Soviet Experience and American Prospects*,[19] will help you think about living in a world where the primary use of money is as a substitute for toilet paper.

3

Living beyond Our Children's Means

For those used to looking at long-term fiscal projections, our looming fiscal debacle is not news. What is news is that it can no longer be ignored; it's gotten dramatically worse, and it could easily touch off a financial collapse that would make 2008 look tame.

Bankruptcy is always in the eye of the creditor. So far, U.S. creditors seem blind to what's coming. One reason, as indicated earlier, is misplaced focus. They are concentrating on our country's official debt relative to its gross domestic product (GDP), thinking this actually says something about our country's fiscal condition. The other is distraction, in this case on the supposedly worse fiscal problems of the PIIGS—Portugal, Ireland, Italy, Greece, and Spain. The financial wolves have been circling these smaller countries for well over a year, thereby giving us a pass. Consequently, we can still borrow at remarkably low rates.

America's creditors should think again. Virtually all of Uncle Sam's IOUs are off the books. They are unofficial, informal, implicit, hidden away in odd places like an alcoholic's bottles. But call them what you will, paying 78 million baby boomers their Social Security, Medicare, and Medicaid benefits is a very real obligation.

To get a sense for how large these bills are going to be, note that we are now paying $30,000, on average, per oldster per year in Social Security, Medicare, and Medicaid benefits. In twenty years, when the boomers are fully retired and today's newborns are just entering the labor market, the average benefit will surely equal at least $40,000, measured in today's dollars. The total cost of these three programs, measured in today's dollars, will equal almost $3 trillion, or 13 percent of GDP, in 2030.[1] To put 13 percent of GDP in perspective, the Congressional Budget Office (CBO) projects that total revenues in 2030 will equal 19 percent of GDP.

Basically the CBO is telling us that expenditures on less than a quarter of the population will absorb two-thirds of the government's tax take.

Doing Ponzi Proud

The $30,000 combined Social Security, Medicare, and Medicaid payment that is being handed, on average, to each of today's elderly equals almost two-thirds of per capita GDP. By the time the boomers are fully retired, the figure will likely exceed 85 percent of per capita GDP. Whoever said America isn't a welfare state? It is a welfare state, but the welfare is for the elderly, not the poor. While our two parties argue over the haves and have-nots, we are blind to what the nows are doing to the laters.

Is this characterization fair? After all, many of today's elderly *are* very poor. According to the Social Security Administration, 22 percent of married couples and 43 percent of single retirees depend on Social Security for at least 90 percent of their income.[2] They also spent their entire working lives contributing FICA payroll taxes to Social Security and Medicare and paying regular income taxes to support Medicaid.[3] These payments could just as well have been saved and invested in the market and might have produced more income than the three programs provide in cash and in-kind health care benefits.

The first part of the last sentence in the previous paragraph—that they could have saved and invested—is true. The second part—that the savings might have produced more in benefits—is not. To date, successive generations of elderly have received more, or far more, from these programs than their accumulated past tax contributions.

This should come as no surprise. One postwar administration after another, from President Eisenhower to President Obama, has expanded these programs' benefits without asking retirees to pay for what they received. So who gets the bill? You guessed it: the next generation, the best people to tax because they have no representation. And when each generation becomes old, it turns around and extracts as much as possible from the following generation.

This taking from Peter to pay Paul and promising Peter that he can take from John, and on and on works just great right up to the point that it doesn't—when there is no one left to take from or the person left doesn't have enough to give. This is the sense in which U.S. generational policy has become a Ponzi scheme—a Ponzi scheme that's on the verge of collapse.

The most recent example is the introduction of Medicare Part D, the prescription drug benefit initiated by President George W. Bush. This new benefit, which started paying out in 2006, provides the elderly, on average, with over $1,500 per year.[4] Not a single older person, including senior billionaires like Warren Buffett, has been asked to pay a penny more in taxes to help defray the program's $16 trillion present value unfunded liability.[5] This fact didn't bypass David Walker, former comptroller general of the General Accountability Office. Walker described the enactment of Medicare Part D as "probably the most fiscally irresponsible piece of legislation since the 1960s."[6]

Walker's beef isn't with prescription drug insurance. It is with sticking the young with the bill. We're with Walker. We think prescription drug insurance is an important form of insurance that everyone should have. There are some prescription drugs, particularly biologics, administered by infusion, which can cost over $50,000 per year. The fact that a Republican president decided to take care of this problem using a massive government program speaks volumes for its importance. But leaving the bill for younger folks to pay was a cynical ploy to garner more votes in the 2004 election, particularly in Florida, which almost cost President Bush the 2000 election.

Unfortunately Medicare Part D was only part of President Bush's no-child-left-solvent policy. At the same time, he also massively expanded his intergenerational transfer by cutting taxes, including capital gains and dividend tax rates. These are taxes paid primarily by the elderly—the ones who hold most of the country's wealth. A regular examination of the distribution of wealth based on the Survey of Consumer Finance, for instance, shows that households of people in their sixties have about five times the net worth of households in their thirties.[7] While household wealth tends to decline after the sixties, households with members age eighty and over typically have more wealth than households in their twenties, thirties, and forties.

Firing the Messenger

Vice President Dick Cheney made the purchase of the next election clear when he told Treasury Secretary Paul O'Neill in November 2002, "You know, Paul, Reagan proved deficits don't matter. . . . We won the mid-terms. This [running deficits] is our due."[8]

Unlike Cheney, Secretary O'Neill didn't think Reagan proved anything of the kind. Instead, he was deeply concerned about the government's on-going fiscal child abuse and wasn't shy in making his views public. So in early 2002 O'Neill commissioned a major Treasury study to measure the size of the U.S. fiscal gap—the present value difference (the value in the present) between all projected future spending (including servicing the of-ficial debt) and all projected taxes. He intended to include the study in the president's 2003 budget document, to be released in February 2003. The study, which revealed a huge fiscal gap and would have derailed passage of Medicare Part D, never saw the light of day. On December 7, 2002, O'Neill was fired.

This wasn't a private firing. The White House announced it to the press at the same time Cheney was calling O'Neill, leaving the secretary no opportunity to resign gracefully. O'Neill immediately packed his be-longings, hopped in his car, and headed home to Pittsburgh. Two days later, the economists tasked with preparing the Treasury study, Jagadeesh Gokhale and Kent Smetters, learned that their fiscal gap calculations, which they'd worked on for the better part of a year, would not appear in the president's budget.[9] It had been censored.

Just to make the abuse of the young and the enrichment of the old and well-off complete, Bush then appointed John W. Snow to replace O'Neill as Treasury secretary. His immediate job was to sell a major tax cut to Congress.[10]

Muzzling Richard Foster

Richard Foster is the chief actuary for Medicare, a position that would normally grant him the media life of a Philadelphia gentleman—a person whose name would appear in a newspaper only three times: at birth, mar-riage, and death.

Foster, however, is a fighting actuary. He faithfully does the numbers and figures out what government programs will cost today and far, far into the future. His first conflict with political reality came when Medi-care Part D was about to be signed into law in 2003. Foster had figured that the prescription drug bill was going to cost much more than the

White House was saying it would. After the bill was passed, it came out that his job had been threatened if he made the larger numbers public.[11] Soon after the bill was passed, Foster disclosed his cost estimates.

We're not niggling over a few billion dollars here. Foster estimated that Part D's long-term unfunded liability would be about the same size as the unfunded liabilities of the entire Social Security system![12] In other words, the legislation, which many believe was designed to make life safer and better for the pharmaceutical and insurance industries by creating a third-party payment source, was going to create a liability as large as that of the country's most important income security program. Today the unfunded liabilities of Part D total $16 trillion. That's more than the $10 trillion of federal debt held by the public. It almost equals the $18 trillion of unfunded liabilities facing Social Security.[13]

Lying about Fiscal Child Abuse Is a Bipartisan Activity

In 2010, Richard Foster was still Medicare's chief actuary, but a new president, Barack Obama, was running the show. The change from a Republican to a Democrat as president didn't change the postwar generational game plan. The basic tasks were to keep our generational chain letter going and to do whatever was necessary to hide the truth about the bills we were leaving our kids. The Democrats, living up to their "kinder, gentler" image, chose a different tactic. Rather than shoot the messenger and censor the fiscal gap, the Obama team simply assumed it away—in both the president's budget and the Medicare trustees report.[14] They did so by pointing to provisions in the Affordable Care Act that established the Independent Payment Advisory Board, which is charged with recommending cuts to Medicare and Medicaid providers when their costs grow too fast.

We've had laws stipulating such cuts for years, and they are repealed with regularity. Indeed, President Obama signed a repeal in June 2010. But rather than laugh out loud at this so-called cost-control mechanism, the Medicare trustees, three-quarters of whom were appointed by the president, assumed in their 2010 report that these cuts will be made—and *to the dollar*. Then, in the president's 2012 budget, the report's fictional forecast was cited as its authoritative source for also showing a trivially small unfunded Medicare liability. From one year to the next, literally trillions of unfunded liability simply disappeared.

No one takes the 2010 Medicare trustees' report's long-run projections seriously, least of all Richard Foster. Foster added this statement to the end of the report: "The financial projections shown in this report for Medicare do not represent a reasonable expectation . . . in either the short range . . . or the long range."

This statement amounts to what a corporate auditor would call a "qualified opinion" in which the auditor informs you that the company in which you have invested is broke, soon to be delisted for public trading and then to be discreetly dismembered for legal fees.

This isn't the first Democratic administration to conceal our long-term fiscal problem. Back in 1993, Alice Rivlin, then deputy director of the Office of Management and Budget, asked one of us (Kotlikoff) and two other economists, Alan Auerbach and Jagadeesh Gokhale, to prepare a long-term fiscal gap/generational accounting for inclusion in President Bill Clinton's 1994 budget. The team worked for months on the analysis, but just two days before the budget's publication, the study was excised just as it happened eight years later in a Republican administration.

The censor was Gene Sperling, then deputy director of the National Economic Council. Why did Sperling knife the truth? Because the Clinton administration wanted to claim it was fiscally prudent. And this study showed that unofficial debt, unlike official debt, was growing at enormous rates.

Sperling is like a bad penny when it comes to our kids. Today he is top banana at the National Economic Council. He's the director, with plenty of say as to what does, and does not, appear in the president's budget and other administration fiscal statements.

What Goes Around, Comes Around

As long as they are alive, all the living presidents and their underlings should have real trouble looking their grandchildren in the eye. By giving the elderly so much more in benefits and taking so much less from them in taxes, our presidents have left their own descendants, and everyone else's, to pay for their largess. Many of the current elderly won't be around when taxes are ultimately raised to pay these bills. It appears that those in power, regardless of party, have taken an old Irish saying to heart: "Only a fool would die solvent."

When Ben Franklin said the only guarantees in life are death and taxes, he got it only half right. In postwar America, death lets each generation pass the generational buck. Each generation leaves much of its fair share of taxes for future generations to pay.

In taking from the young and giving to the old, year after year, decade after decade, in ever larger sums, Uncle Sam has, as indicated, run a massive Ponzi scheme. And he has sold his chain letter to the young with reassuring words that a Bernie Madoff might use: "Not to worry. Every dollar you hand over now in 'taxes' (wink, wink) will be repaid many times over when you hit retirement and collect the terrific benefits I've promised you."

Of course, our fiscal system doesn't sell explicit chain letters to current working generations that they can sell when old to their own children or, if need be, force them to buy. But the effect is the same. The most pernicious aspect of this generational buck-passing scheme is that it leaves every generation in a position of deniability: *Who says I'm getting back more than I put in? I worked my whole life and paid taxes year in and year out, and let me tell you, they were a lot of taxes, and now you are claiming these benefits for which I sweated bricks aren't mine, fair and square. Prove it!*

Proving anything to anyone isn't easy. But convincing someone that her lifetime benefits have, or will, far exceed her lifetime taxes requires an understanding of actuarial analysis on behalf of both the convincer and the convincee. Last we checked, almost all those over forty-five years old, that is, those on the receiving end of Uncle Sam's great transfer scheme (who can expect, going forward, to receive more than they pay), haven't had actuarial training. They aren't planning to get it either.

Uncle Sam's Fiscal Gap

When you add up all our unofficial future bills and net out all the future taxes that will be available to pay them, the difference, that is, the fiscal gap, is staggering. Since a dollar in the future is not the same as a dollar today, we have to make sure this adding up makes less of (discounts the value of) dollars paid or received down the road. Once you do so, using the government's preferred 3 percent real (inflation-adjusted) discount rate, you learn that the value in the present (the present value) of all the future bills, less all the future taxes, is $201 trillion. The icing on this enormous debt cake is the $10 trillion of official U.S. debt in the hands of the public. Add that with a deft hand, and you've got a fiscal gap of $211 trillion![15] Public discussion is all about the icing. It's never about the whole cake.

How can we wrap our brains around our $211 trillion fiscal gap? Clearly it's a huge number. And because we've done the proper discounting and netting, the fiscal gap is, in effect, the nation's credit card bill. It represents all the expenditures we've promised to make in the future but won't have the cash to pay. As with any credit card bill, if you don't pay it, it gets bigger.

We don't have to tell you that $211 trillion is a lot of money. It won't be raised, by either party, with $1,000-a-plate dinners. If you try to grasp it in collective terms, it is fourteen times our GDP. That's the amount of our wealth we'd need to hand Uncle Sam today if we wanted to discharge this bill today. But private sector net wealth is less than four times GDP. That leaves us far short. Broke, in fact. Like most people eying a new car, there is no way we can write a check and drive our new Solvent America off the dealer's lot. So let's see if we can do it the way we know best: in periodic payments.

How much would paying off the $211 trillion cost if we did so via annual payments that went on, well, forever, so we could really get the annual payment amount down? Those annual payments would take the form of tax hikes or spending cuts.

Brace yourself:

Paying off the fiscal gap with taxes requires an immediate and permanent 64 percent hike in all federal taxes.

We're talking federal personal income taxes, federal payroll (FICA) taxes (both employer and employee), federal corporate income taxes, federal excise taxes, and federal estate and gift taxes. Revenues from all of these taxes would have to be 1.64 times higher than what is now forecast in *every* future year starting this year to generate $211 trillion in present value.

Can't handle a new payment that high? We were afraid of that. The alternative is to eliminate the fiscal gap by spending less on other things, just as some folks give up food, clothing, and rent to make payments on their fancy new car. This is called balancing the government's intertemporal budge*t* using spending cuts. But just as the tax hikes are gigantic, the alternative requisite spending cuts are also enormous.

Paying off the fiscal gap by means of spending cuts requires an immediate and permanent 40 percent reduction in all federal expenditures apart from expenditures for principal plus interest on official debt.

Social Security, Medicaid, Medicaid, food stamps, health exchange subsidies, gas for *Air Force 1,* the president's lunch, Eisenhower-Class nuclear submarines, Supreme Court justices' salaries, and the CIA's budget—you name it. They would all have to be cut by two-fifths.

The Zero-Sum Generational Game

What if we don't immediately raise taxes by 64 percent or cut spending by 40 percent? What if we wait twenty years to change policy? Then these two figures become 77 percent and 46 percent, respectively. And if we wait forty years, until most of the baby boomers have taken their leave, the respective permanent tax hikes and spending cuts are 93 percent and 53 percent. In Maine, they call this a "can't get there from here" problem.

The longer we wait to address the problem, the larger the bill we force our children and grandchildren to pay. They will either pay higher taxes or have lower benefits. Whatever they choose, they are getting the short end of the stick. This is the awful zero-sum nature of our generational dilemma and the moral challenge of our day.

Voodoo Economics

Maybe we've missed something, but we've yet to hear any politician advocate raising all taxes by 64 percent for forever. Nor have we heard any politicians advocate a 40 percent immediate and permanent cut in federal outlays.

On the contrary, Republicans want to cut taxes and Democrats want to increase spending. Both groups are engaged in what President George H. W. Bush called *voodoo economics.* Republican supply siders are sure that every federal tax would produce more revenue if only it were cut. We think setting all tax rates to zero and forcing Republicans to announce each day's tax collections would change their tune, but maybe not.

Democrat demand siders are equally subject to magical thinking. They believe that raising federal spending, even if it entails paying people to dig ditches and fill them back up, will stimulate the economy so much it will pay for itself through extra taxes. We think providing all Americans a year's free vacation and forcing Democrats to provide daily revenue reports would alter their thinking, but who knows.

In the dream world of our political parties, their favorite action always "pays for itself." Republicans buy votes by reducing taxes and claiming they pay for themselves. Democrats buy votes by spending money and calling it an "investment." Setting just one set of these loonies loose on the economy would be damaging enough, but in recent years we've opened the asylum. We've watched them combine forces to both raise spending and cut tax rates. The bill goes to the kids who, conveniently, are never in the room.

Since 2000, federal non-interest, discretionary spending, as a share of GDP, has risen almost 50 percent. This spending includes all the outlays on the federal government's various departments—such as Agriculture, Commerce, Defense, Energy, Labor, and Justice. Simultaneously, federal taxes as a share of GDP have fallen by 25 percent. Neither move has accelerated economic growth. Neither move has paid for itself. Since 2000, real GDP growth has averaged a paltry 2 percent. With taxes lower and spending higher as a share of output, the ratio of publicly held federal debt to GDP has skyrocketed—from 35 percent to over 70 percent of GDP.

Nice job.

Unfortunately, we can't pay our bills by collecting less money to pay them. We can't pay our bills by making them bigger either. Members of Congress and the administration might check with fourth graders on this.

The last decade's experience is no outlier. There is no convincing evidence from any period in U.S. economic history that cutting tax rates (as opposed to changing the tax structure) will cause the economy to grow enough to generate more revenue, let alone 64 percent more revenue than is now forecast. Nor is there any convincing historical evidence that increasing spending will more than pay for itself.

On the contrary, standard economic growth models, even those in which households respond strongly to work and saving incentives, show that income tax cuts and spending hikes of the type we've been enacting will reduce rather than increase revenues. And simultaneously, they will wreak havoc on national saving, investment, economic growth, and real wages. We'll document this shortly.[16]

Oh, and By the Way

Uncle Sam is not the only government in our country that's utterly broke. It's just the biggest. State and local governments are also in very bad shape, and, according to the Government Accountability Office, they also face a massive long-term fiscal gap. Closing their fiscal gap would require an immediate and permanent 12.3 percent cut in expenditures or a roughly equivalent immediate and permanent hike in state and local taxes.[17] As a present value, the state and local fiscal gap appears to total some $38 trillion, bringing the U.S. total federal plus state and local fiscal gap to $249 trillion!

Is $211 Trillion an Underestimate of Uncle Sam's Fiscal Gap?

The source of the data used in the fiscal gap calculation is the CBO. Each year the CBO produces a seventy-five-year fiscal forecast. Actually it produces two such forecasts. One, which nobody, including the CBO, takes seriously, is called the extended baseline forecast. This forecast is produced by order of Congress—the CBO's boss. It pretends, among other things, that for the next ten years, the government will spend precisely the same number of dollars as its now spends when it comes to purchasing goods and services. In other words, there is no adjustment for inflation, let alone real economic growth. These and other heroic assumptions are then baked into all projections for all years after the next ten. The politicians force the CBO to forecast in this manner for a reason: they want to claim that our fiscal condition is far better than it is so they can justify spending more money and cutting more taxes.

The other forecast, called the alternative fiscal scenario, indicates what CBO really thinks will happen.[18] This projection is the source of the data used to calculate our $211 trillion fiscal gap. Although much more realistic than the extended baseline forecast, the alternative fiscal scenario also incorporates some highly optimistic assumptions, particularly about future federal health care spending. These assumption likely make the $211 trillion fiscal gap an underestimate.

Things That Can't Go On Will End Too Late

Let's look at Medicare and Medicaid. The CBO assumes a substantial decline in the growth rate in benefit levels in these programs without, it seems, any strong justification. Since 1975, benefit levels in these programs have grown at a 1.9 percentage point faster rate than has GDP per capita. But the CBO assumes this "excess cost" growth rate will gradually fall in half starting in 2020. Even with this assumption, the government's spending on Social Security and health care, including the new health exchange program, is projected to absorb every dollar of the nation's tax revenue by midcentury.

Herb Stein, President Nixon's chairman of the Council of Economic Advisors, had a favorite saying: "Things that can't go on will stop." That's true, but they can also stop too late. That's the concern with excess Medicare and Medicaid growth. There are millions upon millions of baby boomers waiting in the wings to collect sizable benefits from these programs. Indeed, they are no longer waiting. As we write, the oldest boomers, those born in 1946, have just reached age sixty-five and started receiving their Medicare benefits. Compared to the cohort that reached age sixty-five the previous year, this first cohort of boomers to hit 64 has almost 1 million more members![19]

The Potential True Cost of Obamacare(s)

The other heroic health care spending assumption in the alternative fiscal scenario concerns the cost of the new health exchanges legislated under the 2010 Patient Protection and Affordable Care Act. This bill, called Obamacare by its opponents and Obama Cares by its supporters, seeks to insure upward of 50 million Americans, including 8 million children, who don't have coverage. That's the very good part. The concern is with its costs.

Starting in 2014, the bill provides uninsured low- and middle-income households substantial annual subsidies to purchase a health exchange policy. The CBO expects about 20 million households to qualify for a subsidy.[20] To qualify, the household's income needs to be less than four times the poverty line. The current poverty line is $11,000 for singles and $22,000 for a family of four. So if the health exchanges were implemented today, the subsidies would extend to singles with incomes up to $44,000. A family of four would qualify with income up to $88,000.

How much extra could this cost Uncle Sam? Let's consider a family of four with a sole earner making $30,000. Such a family would pay only $960 for a plan that, we'll assume, costs $12,000. That leaves the government paying a subsidy of $11,040. If this family has employer-based health care, it won't qualify for the subsidy because its income exceeds the poverty line of $22,000. But if the employer shuts down his health insurance plan, the family will instantly become eligible to receive the $11,040, a very large chunk of change compared to what the family is earning.

Employers that shut down their plans face a $2,000 fine per employee. But this is small potatoes compared to the subsidy. If we subtract the $2,000 from the $11,040, we see that there is $9,040—over 30 percent of our hypothetical $30,000 earner's total compensation—effectively laying on the ground for the employee and employer to share at Uncle Sam's expense. The marketplace will determine how much of the $9,040 ultimately lands in the employee's versus the employer's lap.[21]

Competitive markets don't leave pots of money sitting on the sidewalk. They take steps to pick them up. This is no exception. Employers need only shut down their plans and tell their workers, "Hey, go to the health exchange for a great and really cheap policy."

The subsidy declines with earnings, but, on average, U.S. workers earn less than $35,000. This suggests a huge incentive for most employers to shut down their health plans.[22] If this happens, the U.S. fiscal gap will soar far beyond its already unimaginably high level.[23]

Why the Fiscal Gap Is Our Only True Compass: The Labeling Problem

Measuring a country's fiscal gap requires projecting highly uncertain government spending and taxes out to the distant future and properly valuing them in the present—heroic assumptions to make. Although hard to measure, the fiscal gap has something major going for it that the official debt does not: it is a conceptually well-defined measure of a country's true indebtedness. The same can't be said of the official debt.

In fact, trying to assess a country's fiscal position—its future spending commitments versus its expected future tax collections—by looking at its official debt is like the joke about the drunk looking for his car keys under a street lamp because the light is better. The reason we can't find the keys under the bright light of well-publicized official debt is called the *labeling problem* in economics. The problem is easy to understand once you accept that something you thought made complete sense, measurement of the government's debt, makes absolutely no sense.

Here's the deal. How we label government receipts and payments is, economically speaking, up for grabs. Nothing in economic theory says that monies that the government collects should be called "taxes" rather than "borrowing." And nothing in economic theory says that monies that the government pays should be called "transfer payments" rather than "repayment of principal plus interest on past borrowing."

In calling the money you give to or get from the government one thing or another, the government is choosing to use a particular fiscal language. This is no different from its choosing to communicate in French or English. The problem is that the government's choice of language dictates the size of the official debt it reports. This makes the reported debt a linguistic artifact rather than a meaningful fiscal policy indicator.

Language is extremely flexible. Every dollar the government takes in and pays out, whether the taking in and paying out was in the past, is occurring in the present, or will be occurring in the future, can be labeled with different words, producing whatever past, present, and future projected values of official government debt the government would like to report. Politicians may not think about this in the abstract, but you can be sure that they grasp the usefulness of careful labeling. All around the world, it allows politicians to reach into the pockets of tomorrow's children for cash to buy votes today. The same is not true of the fiscal gap. Its value is the same no matter the government's nomenclature.

Changing Policy or Changing Words?

Here's a concrete example: payroll taxes targeted to pay future pension and health care benefits. These receipts could just as well be labeled "borrowing." And the future benefits could be called (A) repayment (with interest) on this borrowing less (B) an old age tax (if the benefits fall short of full repayment). With this alternative, but no less natural, language, the U.S. deficit for 2011 is 15 percent, not 9 percent of GDP. And had we used these words for the past six decades to characterize FICA contributions, the United States would have tens of trillions of dollars more of official debt on its books.

The Chilean pension "reform" of the early 1980s entailed precisely this linguistic policy. It funneled receipts, which had been called payroll taxes, into private pension funds, which the government then borrowed to cover pension payments to Chilean retirees. The same money was still flowing from workers to retirees (at a terrifically high "investment" fee), but was now described by the Chilean government as having been "borrowed" from the workers' pension funds.[24]

Thanks to this pension "reform," Chile's reported surplus went down considerably. So the stock of debt changed with no real change in policy. What does that tell you about the usefulness of debt as a measure of policy?

Minding the Wrong Deficit

Our fiscal position is so dire that it is showing up even in our official deficit accounting. In 2010 the CBO projected that official U.S. federal debt in the hands of the public would exceed the supposedly critical 90 percent of GDP share in 2021.[25] This year, 2011, the CBO projects 2018 as that critical date. That's a three-year deterioration in just twelve months. When the debts of federal agencies to one another, such as those of the Treasury to the Federal Reserve, are included, the number has already passed 90 percent.

Ninety percent is viewed as a critical debt-to-GDP threshold because two prominent economists, Ken Rogoff of Harvard and Carmen Reinhart of the Peterson Institute for International Economics, have studied the historical record. They find that countries passing this threshold face sharply lower rates of economic growth.[26] Rogoff and Reinhart are outstanding scholars, and although we'd like more empirical support for the concerns we're raising, we actually have to take issue with their analysis. The reason is that we view their data as meaningless because of the labeling problem.[27]

The True Deficit

The true annual deficit we need to consider is the change in the fiscal gap from one year to the next. The fiscal gap as of June 2011 was $211 trillion.[28] In June 2010 it was $205 trillion, measured in 2011 dollars. So the country's true deficit over the year was $211 trillion minus $205 trillion, or $6 trillion. By contrast, the accumulated official debt held by the public in 2011 was "only" $10 trillion—$850 billion more than 2010 figure, after adjusting for inflation. Hence, the true deficit in 2011 ($6 trillion) exceeded the fake official deficit ($850 billion) by a factor of more than seven!

In this context, the battle in Washington over whether to extend the nation's official debt ceiling is ridiculous. Some members of Congress were called crazy for pushing to run a balanced budget starting immediately. This means cutting spending or raising taxes by $850 billion. As draconian as this sounds, and while doing it would create a balanced official budget, the nation's true indebtedness—its fiscal gap—would still have risen by $5.15 trillion.

What accounts for the extra $5.15 trillion? In part, the CBO projected somewhat smaller future tax revenue in June 2011 than it did in June 2010. But the main reason is that June 2011 brought us one year closer to having to pay 78 million baby boomers roughly $40,000, on average, per year in Social Security, Medicare, and Medicaid benefits. And since the fiscal gap is a discounted present value, one year makes a very big difference.

The General Relativity of Fiscal Language

The labeling problem is a matter of theory, not simply practice. Consider the equations of any economic model with rational agents, by which we mean agents who aren't fooled by language and who interact with governments that make decisions based on fundamentals.[29] Now discuss the equations of the model in French, English, and Chinese. Will the model's behavior be any different based on what language one uses for the discussion? Certainly not. The model's behavior is dictated by the math, not by the words or labels one uses to discuss the math—that is, not by what words, sounds, or noises we attach to the model's variables.

But in attaching particular fiscal labels or descriptions to the variables of this model, which one is perfectly free to do, one is simply choosing an internally consistent language for discussing the equations. But each internally consistent labeling choice produces a different measure of "the"

debt and its changes over time, "the" deficit. It also produces corresponding different measures of the government's implicit (unofficial) debts. And
since math isn't impressed by titles, whether a government IOU is explicit
and official or implicit and unofficial doesn't change the fact that it's an
obligation of the government. The math keeps track of the total obligations, no matter whether they are stamped official or not.

So just as Gertrude Stein once described Oakland, California, "there
is no there there" when it comes to the standard fiscal measures used to
evaluate the stance of fiscal policy. Instead, the emperor (traditional deficit accounting) has no clothes. The emperor will still be naked if his at-
tendants (most economists and policymakers and every politician) think
or pretend otherwise.[30]

In a recent paper, Harvard economist Jerry Green and one of us (Kotlikoff) referred to the labeling problem as "the general relativity of fiscal
language." This was done to emphasize that in economics, as in physics, certain concepts aren't well defined.[31] Time and distance aren't well
defined in physics insofar as two observers traveling through space at a
different speed and in different directions (with a different frame of reference or language) will record time and distance at a given spot differently.
Just so, government debt and the deficit aren't well defined in economics.
Nor, for that matter, are taxes, transfer payments, private net wealth, disposable income, private saving, and personal saving.[32] As with the deficit
and the debt, the size of these terms varies enormously, indeed from negative infinity to plus infinity, depending on one's labeling convention.

The consequence of this Alice-in-Wonderland practice is that meaningful discussion of where we are and where we are going never takes place.
And as we have already shown, both parties have no qualms about making sure the growing fiscal gap is never discussed. They censor it.

The Fiscal Gap Is the Only Label-Free Measure of Our Fiscal Policy

We've dwelled on the labeling problem to bring you around to the key
point: *the fiscal gap is the only proper way to assess a country's fiscal
solvency because it's unaffected by the choice of labels.* If the government
labels more of its current receipts "borrowing" and, accordingly, more of
its future receipts as "taxes," the present value of its taxes won't change,
and the fiscal gap, which depends on the difference between the present

value of spending and the present value of taxes, won't change. And if the government labels more of its current payments as "transfer payments" rather than loans and measures less of its future payments as transfers, the present value of its spending won't change—and neither will the fiscal gap.

Is the United States in the Worst Fiscal Shape?

Based on official debt figures, the United States appears to be in relatively good fiscal shape compared to other developed countries. Its 69 percent debt-to-GDP ratio is, for example, roughly half of the comparable ratio for Greece. But on a fiscal gap basis, the United States appears to be in either worse or much worse fiscal shape than its co-members in the Organization for Economic Cooperation and Development (OECD), the club for developed economies.

The U.S. fiscal gap now stands at fourteen times U.S. GDP. For Greece, this figure is roughly twelve times GDP. Compare the two numbers and you see the naked emperor: on a fiscal gap basis, the United States is in worse fiscal shape than Greece even though its ratio of official debt to GDP is roughly half that of Greece.[33]

A recent OECD study suggested that the U.S. fiscal gap, when measured as a share of GDP, was higher than in the other major developed economies: Japan, Germany, France, Italy, the United Kingdom, and Spain.[34] This is no accident. While U.S. demographics look either better or much better than in these other countries because the United States is aging less rapidly and significantly, Medicare and Medicaid benefit levels are so high and projected to continue to rise so rapidly that they have tipped the scale against the United States. This is not to lay all the blame on Medicare and Medicaid. The Social Security system is, based on its actuaries' own fiscal gap analysis, some 29 percent underfunded. Defense spending is also a major spending burden. The United States spends more on defense than the next thirteen countries combined and appears intent on continuing to do so for the conceivable future.[35]

The Short and Long Terms Are Inseparable

The government's fiscal gap is calculated as an infinite horizon present value. Some readers might ask, "The seventy-five years over which the government makes projections seems pretty long to me, so why not stick with that?" Unfortunately, we can't. The math tells us very clearly that over any finite horizon, we can produce any fiscal gap we want simply by choosing the right set of labels. The math also tells us that separating one fiscal program from others and considering its separate fiscal gap alone is misleading or meaningless. Which receipts and payments one calls part of one program versus another is also solely a matter of language.

The annual report produced by the trustees of the U.S. Social Security system presents both of these problems. Although it provides an infinite-horizon present value unfunded liability (fiscal gap) calculation, it buries this calculation in one table (IV.B6) deep in its innards. The report's main focus is on Social Security's seventy-five-year fiscal gap (unfunded liability) and the immediate and constant percentage tax hike needed to close that gap. Not surprising, the $18 trillion infinite-horizon unfunded liability is three times larger than the $6 trillion seventy-five-year fiscal gap. Were the trustees to use different labels, they could make the $6 trillion anything they'd want, but the $18 trillion would stay the same.

A Dollar's a Dollar

In addition, the trustees' separate calculation of Social Security's unfunded liability begs the question of whether this institution is itself well defined. For example, should we consider the federal income taxes assessed on Social Security benefits a source of Social Security revenue or a source of general revenue? Or maybe we should call only half of Social Security benefits part of Social Security and describe the other half as federal tax credits? Doing either of these things would dramatically change Social Security's seventy-five-year as well as infinite horizon liabilities.

Unfortunately, a dollar's a dollar, and nothing in economic theory determines the boundaries of fiscal programs. Stated differently, nothing in economics will ever resolve what are inherently rhetorical questions.

These are the bottom lines:

• The deficit is a number in search of a concept.

• Deficits of particular programs are no better defined that the overall deficit.

• Fiscal gaps over any finite horizon are entirely meaningless.

• The fiscal gap calculated over the infinite horizon provides the only economically meaningful way to assess fiscal sustainability.

• Fiscal gaps calculated for all government operations taken together are meaningful. Calculations for specific programs, like Social Security or Medicare, are not.

Fiscal Gap Accounting Isn't Perfect Either

One reason that we can't trust short-term fiscal gap measurements is that things that are terrible in the long run can be made to look very good in the short run. Suppose, for example, that Congress decided to reduce this year's deficit by selling every federal building in the country and leasing all the buildings back on a perpetual basis. The proceeds from this gigantic sale-and-leaseback arrangement would be called "receipts" and would greatly improve this year's reported cash flow, but the new rental payments would show up in the next and all subsequent years, reducing the cash flows in those years. Over the infinite horizon—taking into account all future rental payments—the fiscal gap wouldn't change. And it should not. Selling an asset just moves our asset holdings from their prior form to cash. It doesn't make us richer or give us more assets. Our net wealth remains the same.

The fact that the government's cash flow over any finite period is not well defined means that distinguishing short-run from long-run fiscal policy is impossible. A policy that looks good over the short run because it runs a huge "surplus" can readily be said to run a massive "deficit" over the same period by simply changing labels. This means that short-run fiscal policy cannot be studied independent of long-run fiscal policy.

The long run is, of course, very long. It's also highly uncertain. We know how to discount over the infinite horizon. But uncertainty is a much tougher nut. If we are really serious about marking the government's intertemporal budget to market, we need to properly discount the government's uncertain net cash flows using the appropriate risk-adjusted discount factors.[36] What that means, in practice, is that politicians get to sound like pragmatists for talking about seventy-five years while economists get to look goofy for talking about forever. Getting the fiscal gap precisely right is a daunting challenge. It leaves economists in the position of string theorists—knowing what they want to measure but unable to do so to the degree of accuracy they'd like. That said, there is no reasonable alternative discount rate that makes our fiscal gap disappear. Our fiscal gap is huge.[37]

Darkness at the End of the Tunnel

If you're not thoroughly bummed out at this point, we haven't done our job. You've learned that our country is in much worse fiscal shape than any politician has let on and that our official debt bears no intrinsic relationship to our nation's true indebtedness. But don't stop reading. The story gets worse. Our reckless, generationally immoral fiscal policy has done terrible damage to the underlying economy. Yet few economists, let alone politicians, have connected the dots.

4

Economic Fallout

America's scariest economic chart—figure 4.1—provides a snapshot of postwar American economic decline. It shows that our country is now saving nothing and investing next to nothing. This isn't anything new. Hop onto either the saving curve or the investment curve in 1950 and you'll take a ride downhill, with some uphill stretches, over the next sixty years.

Countries that don't save don't have the wherewithal to invest, so it's not surprising that our nation's net domestic investment rate has followed our national saving rate down the tubes. But there is one way for a spend-thrift country to experience investment: let other countries invest in our stead. That's what the bars show—the U.S. current account deficit (measured as a share of national income). They measure the difference between our rate of saving and our rate of investment. When our national saving is less than our domestic investment, as has been the case for decades, our current account is negative (a deficit). This means foreigners are investing more in the United States than we Americans are investing abroad.

What Makes This Chart So Scary

Saving nothing—just 0.1 percent of national income, as we did in 2010—is quite an achievement. Look around the developed world, and you'll find that no other country comes close to matching our profligacy. Saving nothing means that, collectively, we're eating everything we produce.[1] And this means we're failing to add to our nation's stock of wealth. Consequently, as other countries add to their wealth, the United States will become the poor kid on the block.[2]

Worse, saving nothing leaves our wealth fixed in absolute terms but not per American. Don't forget that we're experiencing population

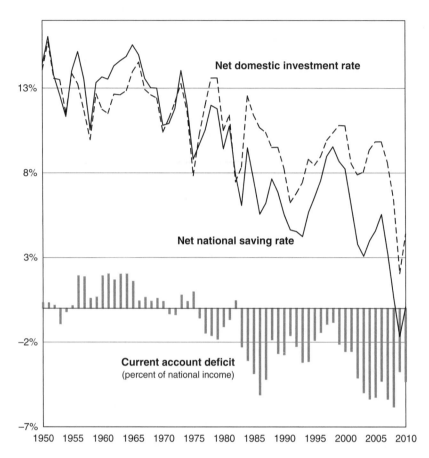

Figure 4.1   U.S. national saving and domestic investment rates, 1950–2010. Authors' calculations based on National Income and Product Account Data.

growth—indeed, dramatic population growth. Between now and the middle of this century, our population will expand by over 42 percent. Continuing to save nothing means less wealth per capita because our fixed stock of wealth will be divided across more people. And as technology improves, making workers more efficient, our fixed holding of wealth becomes smaller and smaller compared to our country's effective supply of labor.

In countries that can't import capital from abroad, a fixed stock of wealth means a fixed stock of capital. We're not in that group. We do import capital from abroad, but not enough to offset reductions in our saving, that is, in the amount we invest on our own. So as our labor force grows in terms of the number of workers and their capabilities, there is an ever-growing shortage of capital per worker. The flip side of having capital become ever more scarce compared to labor (measured in terms of its productive capacity) is that labor becomes ever more abundant compared to capital. This leads to downward pressure on real wages in the marketplace. In short, countries need to save enough to at least keep their capital stocks even with underlying forces of economic growth. If they don't, they'll see their workers' real wages either fall in absolute terms or grow at slower rates. This is the opposite of the take-off point that economic historian W. W. Rostow celebrated in *The Stages of Economic Growth: A Non-Communist Manifesto*.[3] While other nations are reaching the take-off point where their stock of capital is increasing faster than the number of workers, America is on a steep glide path in the opposite direction.

There's no question here. We're not saving enough to keep our capital growing in line with our population growth and technological change.

Our Postwar Party

We didn't reach this milestone overnight. It took six decades to consume more and save less. In 1951, our national saving rate hit a postwar peak of 16.1 percent. In 2010 it registered 0.1 percent. And 2010 wasn't even the bottom. In 2009 our national saving rate was a negative 1.7 percent. You have to go all the way back to the early years of the Great Depression to observe our country dissaving, that is, actually eating up its seed corn.

The Great Depression was a terrible time. Output fell by 29 percent, unemployment reached 25 percent, and 7,000 banks failed. It's no wonder the country had to dip into its savings to stay afloat. But 2009? It was a tough year for sure, with unemployment close to 10 percent. But output in 2009 was only a bit lower than in the prior three years. Yet we still managed to spend more than we made.

The fact that we went from saving less than nothing in 2009 to saving next to nothing in 2010 doesn't guarantee that our saving rate will stay slightly positive. The trend line suggests the opposite: that our national saving rate will again go negative and stay negative. When this happens, we can expect an even lower rate of domestic investment. In fact, our net investment rate could itself become negative. In this case, our new (gross) investment wouldn't suffice to make up for annual depreciation of the capital we already have.

Domestic investment is a country's addition to its stock of capital—the factories; machines; schools, and government buildings; apartment complexes; private homes; highways, bridges, and other infrastructure; software; inventories; and other capital goods used to produce goods and services. Think of capital as the tools that workers use on the job. When we invest at a lower rate, we add less to our workers' stock of tools. And since more tools make workers more productive, and since being more productive lets one earn more, we have this nasty economic fact of life:

Low saving → low investment → low productivity growth → low real wage growth.

This seems to say that not saving means not investing, not investing means less productivity growth, and less productivity growth means lower real wage growth.

Is this true?

Let's take a look at what's happened to U.S. real wages in recent decades. The answer is that average earnings per hour, adjusted for inflation, are no higher today than they were way back in 1964.

This real wage stagnation isn't the American dream. It's the American nightmare.

Imagine turning back the clock to Friday, January 20, 1961, and hearing President Kennedy, in his inaugural address, pronounce, "Let the world go forth from this time and place, to friend and foe alike, that we will bear any burden, pay any price, meet any hardship to assure our children's children earn no more than we now earn."

Actually, the real earnings growth picture isn't quite this bad. First, the data on average real earnings per hour don't incorporate salaries paid to management. So we're talking about what's been happening to production and nonsupervisory workers, not the big dogs and their sidekicks. Second, earnings per hour doesn't include fringe benefits, which constitute about 30 percent of total compensation and have grown rapidly in the postwar period. In fact, although take-home wages per hour, adjusted for inflation, are stuck back in the 1960s, the growth rate in total real compensation per hour has been similar to the growth rate in labor productivity per hour, which is what one would expect.

But research by economists Ian Dew-Becker and Robert Gordon suggests that almost all this productivity growth can be credited to the top 10 percent of earners, leaving the remaining 90 percent experiencing little or no improvements in productivity or real compensation.[4] Moreover, much of the increase in fringe benefits has come in the form of higher health care premiums, paid by our employers, to help us pay to the health care industry what are often highly inflated health care costs.

There is an active debate among economists as to the source of our growing inequality in productivity and labor earnings. Some believe top "management" has been increasingly "productive" in their ability to skim cream from their businesses, to the detriment of employees and shareholders. Some believe the Internet and other communications and information innovations are permitting superstars, whether they are a LeBron James or a Warren Buffett, to reach a larger, indeed global, market at very low cost and thereby squeeze out competitors. This creates an increasingly winner-take-all economy. Others believe that competition with billions of highly disciplined, productive, and energetic workers in China, India, and Southeast Asia has limited real wage growth for those not at the very top of the U.S. earnings distribution. And still others think that automation of services (self-checkout machines at the supermarket and automated toll booths, for example) is putting downward pressure on wages, particularly of low-skilled workers.

But Hasn't the Personal Saving Rate Risen?

One of the supposedly good effects of the Great Recession is a change in the spending behavior of the American public. The personal saving rate (personal saving divided by disposable income) is now running at 6 percent—three times higher than in 2007. Put in "personal saving" on your search engine and you'll find articles applauding Americans' newly found parsimony.

But when the two of us read these stories, we cringe. The personal saving rate, like the federal deficit, is a made-up accounting measure, with no economic content. Its value and changes through time are entirely dependent on how we classify things. For example, counting Social Security contributions as part of personal saving dramatically raises the personal saving rate—but it also dramatically lowers its recent growth.

Calling Social Security contributions part of personal saving seems as natural as not. After all, the system provides most Americans with the majority of their old-age income. And it has, until it ran out of the funds to do so, been sending all American workers who pay FICA tax an annual statement detailing what we've contributed and can expect to receive in retirement. That's pretty darn personal.

But why stop with Social Security? Medicare contributions can also be called personal saving. After all, we're buying an asset—an old-age health insurance policy—with those contributions.

Labeling contributions to Social Security as personal saving makes 2010's personal saving rate 9.8 percent, not 4.6 percent. Treating Medicare and Social Security contributions as personal saving raises the rate to 12.7 percent.

So which rate was it? Take your pick. Or classify some other "tax payments" as "personal saving" and make the rate even bigger. If you prefer to claim personal saving was negative, simply reclassify a good chunk of the funds the public receives in "transfer payments" from Uncle Sam as "borrowing from the government." (To be consistent, also designate part of the public's future tax payments as repayment of this borrowing.) So rather than taking in income, the public is taking on debt. And since it's consuming the same, its personal saving is lower.

John Mitchell, Richard Nixon's attorney general and a real expert on deception, put his finger on the labeling problem of economics. Before being jailed for perjury, Mitchell used to say, "Figures lie and liars figure." The personal saving rate is one of those figures. And the tailors of this emperor's new clothes work at the U.S. Department of Commerce.

The right saving rate to consider is the national saving rate (national saving divided by national income) shown in figure 4.1. National saving is a label-free measure because it references physical concepts. It's the value of a country's net output (national income) less its consumption. As we've seen, the national saving rate provides an entirely different picture of America's saving behavior. It didn't rise by a factor of three after 2007; it went negative. But do a Web search for "national saving rate," and you'll find nary an article on this topic. The government reports the values of national income and consumption but doesn't do the arithmetic to form a national saving rate. The result is that the press isn't provided the right saving rate and ends up writing about a senseless number that comes prepackaged.

Blame It on China

Whatever the precise reasons most American workers are flat-lining when it comes to their real pay, our low rate of domestic investment is surely a key one. As indicated, our rate of investment would equal zero without foreign investment in the country. What foreigners are investing, on net, in the United States is recorded as our current account deficit.

A current account deficit can't be a good thing, can it?

It can.

Come on! You mean it's okay to borrow billions from China and other countries?

Well, yes.

You can't be serious. The current account deficit is China's fault, not ours. They're taking away our jobs, putting us into hock, and are going to turn around and buy up the entire country. And don't forget, China's manipulating its currency. If they weren't underpricing their goods, we'd have balanced trade.

Blaming our problems on someone else is a popular national pastime, but the reason the United States is running a current account deficit is plain to see in figure 4.1. We're not saving; therefore we're not investing in our own country. Since there are good investment opportunities here, foreigners are coming in to take advantage of those opportunities.

China is doing this primarily in the form of buying U.S. government bonds. But because China is buying these bonds, others who might buy them are investing their savings in, for example, the bonds and stock of U.S. companies. Or they are investing directly in the United States by buying existing U.S. companies and running them, or setting up new companies in the United States from scratch. Everyone thinks of well-known brands like 7-Eleven, Budweiser, Holiday Inn, and Toll House Cookies as quintessential American companies, but they are all foreign owned. Here's the bottom line—every dollar that China invests in U.S. securities, no matter what their nature, ultimately leads to another dollar of capital available for American workers to use on the job.

Furthermore, if China invested nothing whatsoever in the United States and instead invested every dollar it was investing in the United States in, say, Europe, Europeans and others now investing in Europe would move their investments into the United States. We'd run the same size current account deficit, but a smaller one with China.

That's the nature of the global investment sea level. It stays at the same height all over the planet. Suppose ocean A flows into ocean B, which flows into ocean C, which flows into ocean A. Now take some water from ocean A and put it into ocean B. What happens? Water from B flows into C. And water from C flows back into A. How much goes back to A? Precisely what was taken out initially.

The oceans can't coexist at different heights. Water seeks a point of equilibrium where it can no longer fall. In the same way, global capital can't be allocated in different countries at different expected rates of return (after proper adjustment for risk). If it can earn more in country X than in country Y, it will move to X until expected returns are equalized. The bottom line is that our current account deficit is not due to China, and it would not likely go away if we banned China from holding U.S. bonds or otherwise investing in our country.

Where China invests is also immaterial to our competition with it and other countries when it comes to producing and selling goods and services. Regardless of where it invests its money, if China is able to produce toys, toasters, and, soon, jet engines at a much lower cost than we can, we will either cut costs or lose that business.[5] That means we'll have to pay our factors of production—labor and capital—less for their services. We're in a tough, globally competitive market. We're not competing just with China, and China is not competing just with us.

Finally, blaming our trade deficit on China and its exchange rate is yet another way to avoid facing the real problem: that our country is not saving. Were we saving 15 percent of national income, as we did in 1951, we'd be running a massive current account surplus. We'd be investing lots of our savings (our capital) in other countries, including China. In the process, we'd be physically taking capital goods produced in our country and placing them abroad. This would be recorded as a trade surplus. Indeed, a current account surplus is the sum of a country's trade surplus plus the net income earned abroad that it reinvests abroad.

In America, we're not saving enough to run a current account surplus. We're saving less than our own country's investment needs. So we're effectively asking the Chinese and nationals of other countries to bring their capital here and put it to work. When they do so, the physical movement of their capital into our country is recorded as the U.S. running a trade deficit—and properly so. We are importing tools for workers in addition to all those consumer goods that we buy.

So when we see the Chinese run a current account surplus with us we should say, *"That's great. They are bringing us more tools with which to work. Aren't we fortunate they are investing in our country and not in Iran, Mexico, Chile, or other places that won't help our workers find jobs and earn more!"* Instead we say that they are manipulating their currency and undercutting our markets.

China's "Currency Manipulation"

Yes, the Chinese peg their currency to the dollar, but that is not evidence of "currency manipulation," as *New York Times* columnist and economics Nobel laureate Paul Krugman and many politicians continue to claim.[6] As a result of the 1944 Bretton Woods agreement, the United States spent decades fixing its currency to those of other nations. No one accused it of unfair trade practices.

The same is true of our fifty states. They've been pegging their currencies, dollar for dollar, ever since they joined the Union. But when did you last hear the senator from Iowa excoriate the state of Virginia for manipulating its currency? But here's Senator Chuck Grassley on China: "Everyone knows China is manipulating the value of its currency to gain an unfair advantage in international trade."[7] And here's Treasury Secretary Timothy Geithner, back in 2009, in his campaign to secure Senate confirmation to the Treasury: "President Obama—backed by the conclusions of a broad range of economists—believes that China is manipulating its currency."[8]

The reason a fixed exchange rate is fully compatible with free trade and does not really represent currency manipulation is that the price that exporters set is the product of the exchange rate and the cost they face to produce the good. Getting the Chinese to reduce their money supply and make their currency more expensive (forcing us to pay more dollars for one yuan) won't make Chinese exports more expensive to American consumers because the internal yuan cost of producing these products in China will fall as the money supply falls.[9]

There is a good reason for this economic proposition. In the end, how many Chinese toasters swap for a Boeing 777 is not a matter of how many pieces of paper with pictures of American presidents are swapping for pieces of paper with pictures of Mao. Instead it depends on the underlying demand and supplies for toasters and 777s. Furthermore, if Chinese internal prices weren't flexible and the fixed exchange rate was making those toasters far too cheap relative to 777s, we'd see a major black market in China for its currency. But no such market exists.

What's amazing is how many economists seem to leave the basics of international trade behind when they calculate the "overvaluation" of China's currency. If you look closely, the typical study asks by how much China would have to revalue to dramatically lower its current account surplus. These studies forget that such a revaluation would reduce China's money supply and all domestic prices, including for toasters, leaving the net cost to Americans of this and other Chinese products unchanged.

Ultimately, forcing the Chinese to print less paper with pictures of Mao and thereby make their currency relatively scarce isn't going to make toasters relatively scarce compared to Boeing 777s. Nor will it change our national saving behavior, investment needs, or current account deficit.

Yelling at the Chinese, the Japanese, the Koreans, the Germans, and other foreigners for investing in our country is stupid. And it's stupid whether the yeller is Paul Krugman, President Obama, Secretary Geithner, or Senator Grassley. Instead of yelling, we should be trying to understand why our country isn't saving. Let's also realize that the analogy of global investment and global oceans is not perfect. If the United States saved more, the additional saving would not all flow abroad. Much of it would be invested at home and provide our kids with more jobs, more tools, and higher real wages.

Blame It on the Government

If our de minimis saving rate is the cause of our current account deficit and our miserably low rate of domestic investment and our current account deficit (the willingness of foreigners to invest in us) is not the reason we're saving so little, what is the reason?

Must be the damn government. It can't control its spending. Surely its higher rate of consumption explains most, if not all, of our rising consumption rate and falling saving rate.

Sorry, but government consumption is not to blame. In 1951, our national saving rate stood at 16.1 percent. As we write, it stands at 0.1 percent. This means that national consumption—the sum of consumption by households and government (federal, state, and local combined)—is now a 16.0 percentage point higher share of national income than it was in 1951. But back in 1951, government consumption stood at 18.8 percent of national income. It now stands at 19.4 percent of national income. So we can't blame government. Do the math, and only 3.75 percent (0.6 divided by 16.0) of the 16 percentage point increase in the nation's overall consumption rate reflects a higher propensity of governments to consume out of national income.

Virtually all the decline in our nation's rate of saving is due to increased consumption by the household sector.

One label-free measure of household consumption and saving behavior is the household saving rate. This is the share of national income left over after the government has eaten its slice of the pie that the household sector doesn't consume.[10] Think of national income as a stegosaurus that has just keeled over from a heart attack. Some raptors (federal, state, and local governments) run over and bite off a bunch of the meat. (We're throwing our right-wing readers some red meat. We'll get some to you lefties shortly.) Then the T-Rex (the household sector), which frightened the stegosaurus to death, ambles over. He has to decide how much to eat and how much to save for tomorrow. Back in 1951, that T-Rex (the household sector) ate 80.8 percent of what the raptors hadn't chewed and saved 19.2 percent. In 2010, that T-Rex (the household sector) ate 99.9 percent and saved just 0.1 percent, which, by coincidence, is the same as the national saving rate in 2010. In short, the household saving rate, properly measured, is now zero. The T-Rex (that is, us) is now eating everything he can get his mouth on.

Blame the Banks

The banks have been loading us up with credit cards for years. The country has been borrowing like mad from China and everyone else who would lend us money. It's obvious that borrowing is the reason we're spending so much and saving so little.

Not really. Remember, every dollar that someone borrows is a dollar someone else lends. Ignoring the rest of the world, we Americans cannot collectively borrow because we don't collectively have anyone to borrow from. Yes, Jim Jones, down the street, just borrowed $80,000 to buy his shiny new Porsche, even though he's making only $30,000 a year. But in a closed economy, he borrowed that $80,000 from Sally Smith, who lives either next door or in another part of the country. Sally, wherever she lives, is a lender. And the lending of all the Sallies offsets the borrowing of all the Jims. So on net, there is neither borrowing nor lending by Americans as a group.

Furthermore, before we start judging Jim, let's realize that he might have spent years saving up the $80,000 to buy the Porsche and actually used the $80,000 he borrows from Sally to invest in, say, blue chip stock.

The real issue is not the borrowing, which in a closed economy always nets to zero (so for every "bad" borrower there is a "good" lender), but the consumption of the people and the government. Jim, it turns out, is fifty years old. He spent the last thirty years working overtime and saving every nickel he could to buy his dream car. In keeping his income high and his consumption low for so long, Jim made an important contribution to national saving. And here we are, pointing a finger at the poor guy.

So what about foreign borrowing? We are borrowing from abroad, right? We must be borrowing from abroad to consume, right? Sorry, wrong on both counts. Think about America, including its various governments, as one big household that has income and wealth and is consuming all its income. It's not adding to its wealth or subtracting from it. It is neither saving nor dissaving. And it's not borrowing from abroad on net.

And yes, foreigners are investing some of their savings in the United States. That's often called foreign borrowing, but this language is highly misleading. And, yes, some of the investment that foreigners do in the United States entails their buying bonds from our governments, companies, and banks, but these entities may turn around and buy assets with this "borrowing."

The point is you can't look at particular transactions and get a true picture of what's really going on. What's clear, though, is that our country as a whole is not now in debt. Nor is it currently going deeper in debt. For now, there is no sense in which our country is collectively borrowing from abroad.

Although we're not adding to our wealth (we're not saving), our current wealth is still positive. Indeed, at the moment, we're pretty darn rich. According to the Federal Reserve's flow-of-funds data, we have some $48 trillion in national net wealth.[11] Since our consumption is running at $12 trillion per year, we could all go on vacation for four years, that is, produce no income whatsoever during those four years and still consume at our current rate without borrowing a penny. Hence, our country on the whole is not currently borrowing to consume. It may reach that point, but we're not there yet.

Blame the Boomers

Okay, if it's not the Chinese or Uncle Sam (and his state and local cousins) that have killed our national saving, and if we can't pin it on the banks, foreign lenders, or borrowing, why don't you authors stop wasting this reader's time and just find out who within the household sector is doing all the consumption?

It's got to be those baby boomers, right? Damn, if they aren't a self-indulgent lot. Look at the big fuss they made over Vietnam. They didn't call themselves the Me Generation for nothing. They must be doing all the extra spending. Sure it was a war we couldn't win and a huge waste of life [note the red meat for the lefties], but plenty of other generations wasted their lives in senseless wars without complaining. What makes them so special? If they just stopped smoking dope and had the values and backbone of the Greatest Generation—those who fought World War II—we'd have plenty of saving and investment.

Sorry, but it's not the boomers, at least not yet, who are consuming so much more. And it's not the young. So who does that leave?

Taking from Young Savers and Giving to Old Spenders

Remember that massive Ponzi scheme we already discussed—the scheme that's been taking more and more resources from the young each period and giving them to the old? Well, that scheme has been redistributing from young savers to old spenders. Youngsters (young adults) are savers because they have many years over which to spend. Knowing that they won't always be earning income, they defer some spending for the future, spreading their resources. When you give them money, they generally save a portion of it. But if you give the oldsters money, they have a much higher propensity to spend. They realize that you can't take it with you and have relatively few years over which to spend any windfalls.[12]

These findings make sense. If you can't take it with you and don't want to leave your wealth to your kids, you have to spend each dollar at a faster pace the closer you are to knocking on heaven's door, or that other destination.

Now what if the government takes lots of resources from the young and gives them to the old while telling the young, "Not to worry. When you're old, we'll take from your kids and give to you. In fact, we're going to take a whole lot more from the next generation when they're young than we took from you so that you'll get back far more than you pay in now"? This, by the way, is precisely what Social Security was designed to do. In addition to preventing starvation for millions of older Americans whose savings had been wiped out in the Great Depression, not to mention taking revolutionary fodder from the very real lefties of that era, Social Security took cash from young workers too scared to spend it and gave it to old people who had to spend it to survive. Small wonder our saving rate has declined: that's what has to happen if you transfer money from savers to spenders.

The condition of the elderly has improved greatly since the first Social Security check was sent out in 1940, but the system still encourages workers to save less while providing more spending power for the elderly.[13]

So the elderly consume more. They get resources, and since they are close to the end of their lives and have pretty high marginal consumption propensities, they spend like there was no tomorrow, or at least not many tomorrows. Not all of that spending is on frills; some of it may be on necessary medical treatment. Either way, it doesn't matter: the elderly have a high propensity to consume. How about the young? Well, they too may spend more. Why not? Don't they have a government promise to hand them back a lot of freebies when they're old?

But for argument's sake, let's assume the young don't spend any more or less than they had planned before the government transferred a large chunk of their resources to the oldsters. What about the losers from the Ponzi scheme—children not yet born? They, after all, will be at the end of this chain letter. Unfortunately, they aren't around yet to scream or vote or consume. The losers from this policy—the unborn—aren't in a position to reduce their consumption while the oldsters increase theirs. So overall consumption in the economy rises and national saving falls. As the government expands the Ponzi scheme decade after decade, consumption as a share of national income keeps rising and saving keeps falling. Moreover, if foreigners don't fully make up for the loss in saving, domestic investment falls, which lowers real wages or, at least, limits their growth.[14] We'll bet you've noticed. The unborn may be the ultimate bag holders in this scheme, but a lack of saving is a big negative for all the workers along the way.

The unfortunate children who end up getting stuck with the bill for the Ponzi scheme get hit with a double whammy. Unlike their parents and grandparents, they will pay much more in taxes than they get back in benefits over their lifetime. On top of that basic injustice, they are born into an economy with low or very slowly growing real wages.

The mechanism by which intergenerational redistribution arising from an ongoing Ponzi scheme reduces national saving and damages the welfare of our children and future generations was not one that the two of us cooked up. This is the clear prediction of the standard model of saving and growth in economics: the life cycle model. It was developed beginning in the 1920s by Irving Fisher of Yale. Franco Modigliani won a Nobel Prize in economics in 1985 for his work at MIT on the model, and in 1965, MIT's Peter Diamond, a 2010 Nobel laureate in economics, wrote a seminal article showing how taking from the young and giving to the old crowds out national saving in the life cycle model.[15]

Since Diamond's work, there has been a veritable explosion of research that uses this framework to understand how intergenerational policy affects the economy's consumption and saving behavior and its growth through time. Much of this work entails computer simulation of highly detailed life cycle models featuring millions of variables describing the interlinked economic behavior of overlapping cohorts in response to government policy over the span of hundreds of years.[16] Yes, it's complicated.

Computer simulations don't mince words in displaying their findings. The ones we're referencing show major damage—what can rightfully be called *fiscal child abuse*—arising from the Ponzi scheme our country has been running. The same simulations also show natural limits to these policies. If governments, in attempting to meet promises they've made to the old, try to take more from young generations than those generations earn, the young can't comply. The way a computer simulation model screams, "Enough already!" is that it refuses to converge to a solution.

The computer's message is this: *governments can take everything the young make, but not more.* And if they get close enough to that limit, they will send the economy to an early grave. The young will hand over everything they have to the old, the old will consume it all, and the young will bring no seed corn (no capital) into old age for the next set of young to work with.

Furthermore, foreigners won't necessarily be there to provide the seed corn. Foreigners witnessing generational theft are likely to presume that a country willing to steal from its kids is also one that is willing to steal from foreigners. It's easy enough to do: just expropriate the foreign-owned assets. In the past ten years alone, Venezuela has nationalized its oil industry, Argentina has defaulted on its debt, and Russia has taken over foreign investments. Such expropriations are some of the many unlawful "policies" routinely pursued over the years by third world countries. Retaliation for expropriation rarely restores the full amount that was taken. Unfortunately, when we Americans look at our financial system, our saving rate, our pronounced and growing inequality, and our state of fiscal insolvency, we are looking at a country that's doing its best to join the third world. Every passing year gives us more assets to expropriate, increases government temptation, and causes more worry for foreign investors.

What about Intergenerational Altruism?

While the life cycle model is the bread-and-butter framework of economics for considering national saving, there is a competing model that features economic love, which economists call *altruism*. Add enough altruism to a model and it will nullify all the adverse effects from Ponzi schemes.

How can this be? Simple. In the altruism model, parents and grandparents actually care about their children. They take steps to protect them from government policies that seek to redistribute from the young to the old.

Yes, economists may be cold-blooded realists who extol the virtues of self-interest. But they long ago realized that a parent's self-interest may include that of his or her child. This is formulated mathematically by saying that person A cares about (gets utility from) her own consumption (the goods and services she gets to consume) as well as her child's utility. Let's call the child B and assume the child cares about her child, C, who cares about her child, D, and so on, with each parent directly caring only about her own narrow self-interest as measured by what she gets to consume and the well-being (utility) of her child.

If you substitute B's utility into A's and C's into B's, and D's into C's, and continue this way, you find that person A, although she directly cares only about herself, ends up indirectly caring about the consumption of all her descendants. Consequently A won't be greedy and eat up all the resources she can before transiting to the afterlife. Doing so won't actually accord with A's being selfish because A, in effect, thinks of her kids, grandkids, great grandkids, and so on as future versions of herself. Their consumption, given this formulation of economic love, is her consumption. *Mi casa es su casa.* And in loving her kids economically and in their loving their kids economically and so forth and so on, the original parent ends up acting as if she's going to be around forever. She becomes, in the words of economists, *infinitely lived.* (Bet you never thought of economists as deeply spiritual mystics who have figured out how to overcome death and achieve immortality?)

Economic love also has the power to turn capitalism into communism! All one need assume is the presence of marriage. With marriage, if A economically loves B and B loves not only her own child C but also her spouse, call him X, A will start economically loving X, not because A does so directly but because B loves X and A loves B. If altruism runs in both directions—from the young to the old and from the old to the young, X will love his own parents, call them Y, and A will end up loving Y because he loves B who loves X who loves Y. A will also end up loving Y's other children if Y loves them.

Going down this path leads to John Lennon's dream:

Imagine all the people
Sharing all the world . . .

Talk about groovy. Everyone economically loves everyone else, and there is total agreement over who gets to consume what. With that one little assumption—that parents economically love their kids—we end up with economic heaven on earth as if by an invisible hand.

This notion of economic love (altruism) was conceived long ago by one of the great economists of all time, David Ricardo. Ricardo, who invented the theory of international trade known as *comparative advantage*, wrote economics tracts as a pastime in the early 1800s. In one of those tracts, he mentioned intergenerational altruism as a theoretical possibility, but he immediately rejected the proposition on empirical grounds because he didn't see any facts to support the theory.

Knowing whether intergenerational altruism holds is important for thinking about government Ponzi schemes. When you add such policies to an economic model of altruism, something funny happens: nothing. The Ponzi scheme has no effect. To see this, suppose the government takes money from son David and gives it to father Alex. And assume that Alex economically loves David. If so, Alex will hand all the money right back to David. Why? Because it's not in Alex's self-interest to personally do all the consuming. He gets more happiness (utility) by spreading his economic resources over himself and all his dependents, both now and later.

Alex can hand the money back to David (reverse the government's transfer) immediately as a gift. He can also give it back later as a bequest. But however the money's handed back, David's consumption doesn't change. Nor does Alex's. In effect, Alex and David are one big happy family that puts its collective resources on the table, ignoring who owns what. They simply share those resources. The fact that the government is pushing more of the resources on the table over to Alex doesn't matter. The only thing that matters is the total amount on the table.

Economists have had lots of fun playing with the altruism model. Indeed, it has become a mainstay of macroeconomics. Edward Prescott, 2004 corecipient of the Nobel Prize in economics, is the father of the real business cycle model, which considers how economies respond to technological and policy shocks. This model assumes intergenerational altruism because doing so makes things much more convenient mathematically.

The problem, as Ricardo sensed, is that people really aren't intergenerationally altruistic. If they were, we'd see Billy Joe Bob in Biloxi, Mississippi, mailing checks to Ahmad Nadeed Sahib in Karachi, Pakistan, because Billy's fifteenth cousin, fifty times removed, is married to Ahmad's great uncle's great nephew.

Sure, everyone "loves" his kids, but whether that caring boils down to effectively treating their kids' consumption as their own is a different matter. Say what you want about economists being heartless people who are good with numbers, they've come up with a formulation of love with some teeth that can be tested empirically.

And what happens when it is tested? Well, Ricardo was right to reject the possibility. At least in the United States, altruism fails miserably. Regardless of the data used, one study after another rejects this proposition.[17] The proposition is even rejected in the case of households in which the parents are already giving their kids money. If one takes some of the kids' money and gives it to their parents, the parents spend the vast majority of it.

Transferring to Oldsters

Figure 4.2 documents the major growth in benefits paid to the elderly relative to growth in per capita GDP. It compares, in 2010 dollars, the level of Social Security, Medicare, and Medicaid benefits paid out per person age sixty-five and older with the level of per capita GDP. The key message of the figure is that these benefit levels have grown much more rapidly than has per capita GDP. In 1970 benefits paid per oldster were 41 percent of per capita GDP. By 2010, they were 72 percent. Thus, the government's policy of transferring to the old is clear. The next question is whether this transfer led the elderly to increase their consumption relative to that of younger population. The answer is yes.

Exhibit A: The Relative Consumption of the Elderly

The strongest and simplest evidence about who's consuming more and how that relates to the war on our kids and the destruction of our economy is the age-consumption chart (figure 4.3). This chart shows average consumption by age at different points in time. If the government is taking more and more from the young and giving it to the old and the old are giving it back to the young to ensure that everyone's consumption remains unchanged, then the profile of average consumption by age shouldn't change, so the pattern of columns should be the same from one period to another. They should all be higher through time, but one column shouldn't grow relative to the others. The sets of columns should maintain their shape.

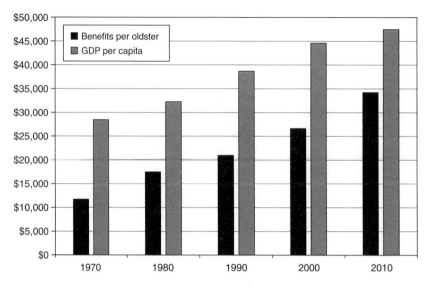

Figure 4.2 Real Social Security, Medicare, and Medicaid benefits per oldster compared with real per capita GDP, 1970–2010. Authors' calculations based on CBO and Social Security data.

But if intergenerational altruism doesn't hold, the elderly will consume what they receive and the pattern of the columns will change through time, reflecting the massive redistribution that has taken place and that continues. Specifically, consumption will rise as we go from younger to older age groups.

This is precisely what we see. The U.S. age-consumption profile has tilted dramatically over time in favor of the elderly. Hence, if you want to know whose consumption has risen the most during our six-decade consumption binge, the answer is *the consumption of the elderly.*

The numbers underlying figure 4.3 come from a highly detailed study of age-consumption patterns published in 1996 by Jagadeesh Gokhale, Laurence Kotlikoff (i.e., one of us), and John Sabelhaus. The three of us spent a year pulling together data from all available U.S. Consumer Expenditure Surveys, imputing consumption provided in kind in the form of Medicare, Medicaid, and other health care benefits, allocating consumption within households by age and sex, and benchmarking their calculations of average consumption by age and sex in specific years to the consumption totals reported in the national income and product accounts for those years.

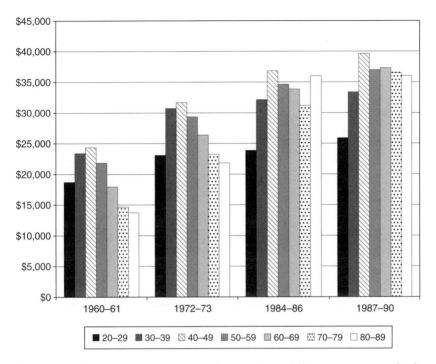

Figure 4.3   U.S. average consumption by age (2011 dollars). *Source:* Jagadeesh Gokhale, Laurence J. Kotlikoff, and John Sabelhaus, "Understanding the Postwar Decline in United States Saving: A Cohort Analysis," *The Brookings Papers on Economic Activity*, 1996.

The findings are quite dramatic. Consider the 38 percent growth in the average consumption of twenty year olds, measured in 2011 dollars, between the early 1960s and the late 1980s. This growth is paltry compared to the 164 percent increase enjoyed by eighty year olds! In the early 1960s, twenty year olds consumed, on average, 36 percent more than eighty year olds. By the late 1980s, this relationship was reversed: eighty year olds were, on average, consuming 39 percent more than twenty year olds. The relative consumption of the eighty year olds to the twenty year olds (the ratio of their average consumptions) almost doubled over the two decades. Sixty year olds and seventy year olds have also enjoyed much more rapid growth in their average consumption than younger age groups.

A recently published book by Ronald Lee of Berkeley and Andrew Mason of the University of Hawaii[18] shows that the average consumption of the elderly now dramatically exceeds that of all other age groups. No Surprise. Since 1990, real benefit levels per beneficiary under Medicare and Medicaid have grown at a rate that is more than three percentage points higher than the growth rate in per capita real GDP.[19] We've also expanded Medicaid coverage by roughly one-third, introduced Medicare Part D, provided tax breaks on capital gains and dividends (received disproportionately by the elderly), and cut federal income taxes.[20]

Wow. Hold on fellows. This is the AARP—the American Association of Retired Persons—jumping in to set the record straight. You guys are simply bashing the elderly. Don't you realize how poor the elderly were back in the early 1960s? What you are displaying in your chart is a great social achievement. We dramatically lowered poverty rates among retirees through the Social Security, Medicare, and Medicaid programs you seem to be denigrating. We'll take back your AARP cards, thank you! And you should thank your lucky stars we're here to protect your interests or you could be one of the millions of impoverished oldsters our organization has rescued.

The AARP has a point, but it's off target. First, we aren't bashing the elderly. Our mission here isn't about blaming. It is about identifying what has been happening and how seriously it threatens our children and our economy. We're trying to wake the elderly and the rest of the country up to the fiscal catastrophe and economic fallout facing young and future generations.

Like AARP's most ardent supporters, we're old. Some of our best friends are old. One of us, Larry, has a ninety-two-year-old mother whom he loves dearly and who is getting younger by the year, thanks to Medicare's assistance and her own spirit and exercise routine. And yes, the poverty rate among the elderly in 1960 was 35 percent. By 1995, it was down to 10 percent.[21] That's a fabulous achievement, and we give Social Security, Medicare, and Medicaid full credit for achieving this success.

But the achievement was not a free lunch. At the same time poverty rates were dramatically lowered for the elderly, they were little changed for the young. Today over one in five children live in poverty.[22] Among minorities, the child poverty rate is about one-third and 35 percent live in "food insecure households."[23] Back in 1960, one in four children lived in poverty.[24] So we've made some progress, again thanks in large part to Social Security, Medicaid, and Medicare (which covers disabled children), yet we're sitting here today with 13 million impoverished children. Another 16 million children live in households with very low levels of income, albeit that exceed the poverty threshold. To be clear, we consider the current distribution of wealth, income, and consumption to be outrageous. When some children go hungry while others are whisked to summer camp on the family private jet, you know the maldistribution of income has gone too far.[25] Yet how to reduce inequality is open to debate.

But our main point here is that most of the massive postwar redistribution from the young to the old has not been from rich young people to poor old people. It has mostly been from middle-class young people, who pay high employment taxes, to middle-class old people who receive them. And that redistribution has left the young with a fiscal sword of Damocles suspended over their heads. Furthermore, that redistribution has cut our national saving rate from 16 percent to 0 percent. It has cut our domestic investment rate from 16 percent to 4 percent, and it has contributed to the lack of real wage growth, which marks the death knell of the American dream. Reducing poverty among the elderly (or any other group) was a wonderful achievement, one that we should certainly preserve. But the means we've used has gone far beyond that narrow goal and is literally wrecking the country.

5

Beatings without Bruises

Every day terrible things happen to children. A child may be left in a car on a 100-degree day and die. Another may be locked in a closet, unfed for days at a time. Still others arrive at hospital emergency rooms with multiple fractures from parental rage. Others somehow survive the chaos of drug-addicted or alcoholic parents. It's a long and depressing list, yet a recent report shows that nearly 3 million children were abused or neglected in a single year.[1] If-it-bleeds-it-leads journalism makes these events public knowledge. That's a good thing.

We respond to stories of this kind of abuse with justified shock and outrage. But what about abuse that isn't so obvious? What about abuse that is so subtle it simply isn't noticed, abuse so common it is like part of the air we breathe? That abuse exists not so much in one family or another, but in our society as a whole. It is not physical abuse. It is economic abuse. It is built into government policies, right in front of our noses, and we say little about it. We don't learn of it through media reporting, we cannot see it, and we don't understand it because, well, it lacks blood. How many fingers do you need to count the times you have heard fellow subway riders or office workers discussing the implications of the growing fiscal gap? None.

We are accustomed to arguments over how much the rich have, today, and how much they should share with the poor, today. But we never ask about the fairness of taking from the young to give to the old. Yet it happens, day after day and year after year. We don't condemn it. We applaud it because it can seem to be a good thing. We know that millions of elderly people retired to live in poverty fifty years ago and couldn't afford basic health care. Today relatively few of the elderly live in poverty, and health

care in old age is an unquestioned right. No one on the receiving end of .
this largess is going to say it was a bad idea. But generational policy is
a zero-sum game, by and large. And improving the lot of the elderly has
come at a major price to the young. Indeed, we're starting to see terribly
troubling effects in how young people live and the decisions they make,
or avoid. Without knowing it or thinking about it, we've taken too much.

A Rare and Modern Wedding

To say the wedding was long awaited is an understatement. Beyond the
area where the bride and groom would exchange vows, a gentle creek
is backed by a dramatic escarpment. The location is Driftwood, Texas,
about twenty miles outside Austin. Behind the bucolic scene, a rustic
building is ready with a waiting band, servers, food, and champagne. The
slightly balding groom walks carefully with his arms held slightly ahead
of his body. He is cradling his six-month-old daughter. He is in his early forties, an executive with a rapidly growing Internet-based firm. The
bride follows with her father. The bride, dark haired, lovely, and in her
mid-thirties, is a court judge.

The ceremony is short, sweet, and serious. The groom promises to
cherish his bride forever, but hopes she will forgive his occasional lapse
from vegetarian meals. If there is a leitmotif here, it is intentionality and
consciousness. These two know exactly what they are doing. They have
waited a long time. They are sure. And they are telling the world they are
sure.

In an odd way, this wedding opens a window on how we have changed
over the past half-century and how much different our world looks to the
young than it did a few decades ago. For starters, weddings are getting
to be rare events. And this couple, unlike the many who don't dare these
days, can marry with confidence. Both have good jobs, both have good
educations, and they own a home. They are ready. No one can say they
were impulsive.

They are fortunate. And their child is particularly fortunate, or so it
would seem. Unlike more and more children, this child will grow up with
a decent living standard, excellent education, and, most important, two
parents to help her reach adulthood. But there's the rub. Once she's re-

leased into the world of grownups, things are likely to be very difficult as they are for so many young adults today.

Putting Our Kids at Risk: Let's Count the Ways

The title of our earlier book, *The Coming Generational Storm*, suggests that we are heading for a major intergenerational conflict as the young are handed the bills older Americans have been racking up for decades. So far, the conflict has been muted. One reason may be that so many young people have boomeranged. Instead of creating new households, they have had to move back in with their parents. It's hard to bite the hand that feeds and shelters you.

The conflict may also be muted because the young aren't alone in being afflicted by a failing economy. Many boomers, on the cusp of retirement, have had their financial prospects blow up as vitally important housing values tanked along with their 401(k) plans. Since the market crash of 2008, one of the main themes in financial planning trade journals has been getting people to adjust and rethink their plans. Often it involves a major scaling down. Sometimes it requires that retirement be put off altogether. The big worry is that retirement may come, ready or not, in the form of extended (and involuntary) unemployment. And if it happens before age sixty-five, the minefield of medical insurance premiums and coverage awaits.

The dilemma of aging boomers attracts much attention. The dilemma of the young, not so much. Worse, the attention is often derisive and demeaning. Junior is teased for still living at home. The reality is that our kids aren't where they thought they would be at twenty-five, thirty, or thirty-five years old. Compared to their parents at the same age, their real income is often lower, they may be more burdened with college debts, their job security is minimal, they may not have health insurance, and the company pension their parents might have has been frozen and closed to new employees. On top of that, they have the task of buying a home when home prices, even now, are much higher relative to wages than they were in 1970. All that, and the really hard part, higher future taxes and lower future government benefits, has yet to begin. Often the young don't feel secure enough to do basic things like marry, have a child, or buy a house.

Those are big differences.

Fragile Ties: The Decline of Marriage

Let's start with marriage. Or not. Half a century ago, college graduation and June brides were nearly synonymous. Today young people are
waiting longer to marry. Many aren't marrying at all. Examining Census
Bureau figures, for instance, the Population Reference Bureau found that
marriage rates have declined "precipitously" since the start of the recent
recession, particularly among young adults age twenty-five to thirty-four,
and have reached their lowest recorded level.[2] The recession decline continued a descent that began in 2000. And that decline, when you look
further back, is just an extension of one that began in the 1960s.

How steep was the drop? Very. In 2000 some 55.1 percent of all twenty-five to thirty-four year olds were married. Only 34.5 percent had never
married. By 2009 the percentage of marrieds dropped 10 full percentage
points to 44.9 percent. In demography, a change this large and this fast is
more like a tsunami than a tidal shift. Meanwhile, the percentage of never
marrieds rose more than 10 full percentage points to 46.3 percent. Indeed, in 2009 the never marrieds exceeded the marrieds for the first time.

A similar but less dramatic decline occurred in the broader population
of those eighteen and older: those married fell from 57 to 52 percent. If
we focus on women, the decade brought another dramatic change: the
percentage of married women fell below 50 percent for what may be the
first time in U.S. history. As of 2009, the number of women who were
separated, divorced, widowed, or never married exceeded the number of
women who were married: 59.8 million versus 59.5 million. Extrapolat-
ing this trend, one statistical wag has gone so far as to predict the end of
marriage. "If the current trend continues sometime between 2028 and
2034 the US marriage rate will reach zero. What will America look like in
year one AM?" he asks on his blog.[3]

We can't blame all of this on the economy over the past ten years. Marriage has been in decline for a long time. Nor does this mean we are all
living isolated and sex-free lives. People are marrying less when they are
younger but living together more. Not being married doesn't mean sleep-
ing alone. Even so, marriage is still a big deal in America because about
90 percent of all people eventually try it.

The shift here is dramatic. Where once it was assumed that virtually
everyone would marry and the worry was about the number of failed

marriages and the divorce rate, we now have an increasing number of people bypassing the institution altogether. Between 1987 and 2002, for instance, the percentage of women between the ages of thirty-five and thirty-nine who had ever cohabited ("lived in sin") rose from 30 to 61 percent. The same study also found that over half the marriages between 1990 and 1994 had been preceded by cohabitation.[4] But as any scan of the magazines at a supermarket checkout will tell you, choosing to marry or not marry has less and less to do with having children, particularly if you are among the millions of people who are Hollywood movie stars or wannabes. The study also indicated that the number of children born to cohabiting couples has risen dramatically in recent years, recently accounting for 52 percent of all nonmarital births. It is now estimated that about 40 percent of all children will spend some time in a cohabiting household before they are sixteen years old.

We're not going to moralize here about the blessing of marriage. There are plenty of people already doing that. What this sea-change in habits suggests for children is what concerns us. In practical terms, what rising cohabitation means is that an increasing number of children are likely to be poor, lack home stability, have health issues but lack health care, and have trouble in school. The same circumstances are also likely to reduce the odds that the kids will be able to sustain a durable marriage when they grow up.

Some will argue that living together is the same as marriage. We beg to differ. Even in highly dysfunctional marriages, there is a greater likelihood of shared purposes and shared risks. And while cohabiting may have some economic advantages over living alone (shared expenses), the sharing is very likely not as complete as it is in marriage.

Born "Out of Wedlock"

The percentage of children born out of wedlock has risen as marriage has declined. Today a stunning 40.6 percent of all children are born outside marriage. That's a massive increase, the Heritage Foundation notes, from the 6.4 percent rate back in 1964, the year Lyndon Johnson started the war on poverty. Even so the U.S. birthrate has declined with the decline in marriage and with the recent recession. But it would have declined still more without the rise of children born out of wedlock. In 2009, for instance, the birthrate fell to 13.5 per 1,000 population, the lowest level in at least a century, according to one report. This figure is also well under the birthrate during the Great Depression. Back then, demographers were shocked that it fell under 20 per 1,000.

As many young couples contemplate a huge hangover of student loans that need to be paid back from the earnings of uncertain jobs and the (still) high cost of buying a home in much of the United States (particularly in areas with good public schools), it gets much easier to have children later rather than sooner. Or possibly not at all.

Significantly, although the decline in marriage has been universal, it has been highest among the people facing the greatest employment uncertainty: those with a high school education or less. While people with limited educations once married and had children early and people with more education tended to marry later, positions have reversed in the past thirty years. From 1965 through the early 1990s, for instance, a smaller percentage of people age twenty-five to thirty-four with college degrees were married than those with high school diplomas or less. Since the early 1990s, however, the percentage of college graduates who are married has exceeded the percentage of those with high school degrees or less (figure 5.1).

Fewer Marriages Mean More Poor Babies

Another painful consequence of the decline in marriage is that although the birthrate is declining, the number of children born into poverty is increasing. No surprise. More children are being raised by cohabiting couples with marginal incomes or, more often, by single parents. According to Heritage Foundation figures, the odds that a child in a single-parent household will be poor are 71 percent.[5] For children in married households, the odds of being poor are much lower—only 26 percent.

Something well beyond a slow, painful economic recovery is happening. We are looking at events and circumstances that will change entire lives forever. If it were possible to measure cultural capital—the traditions, practices, and habits of behavior that help whole societies get through the day—we'd have to say it was in sharp decline. While the *Wall Street Journal* now has a full-time reporter to chronicle the lives of the very rich—that small percentage of the population that has accumulated major wealth—the bigger but more subtle change is in the widening distance between the everyday haves and the growing horde of everyday have-nots. Increasingly those have-nots are young.

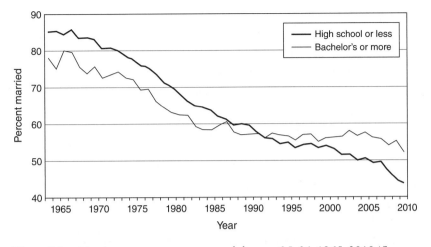

Figure 5.1   Marriage rates among young adults ages 25–34, 1965–2010 (*Source*: U.S. Census Bureau, 2000 Census; American Community Survey.

Women Are the New Men

Another challenge for our kids is the growing reversal of the ancient sexist order of things. A recent Pew Research Center study found dramatic changes between the roles of men and women in the family of 1970 and the family of 2007.[6]

While only 4 percent of women earned more than their husbands in 1970, more than five times as many—22 percent—earned more than their husbands in 2007. Another, and possibly related, major change is that husbands typically had more education than their wives in 1970. Then, 52 percent of couples had equal education levels, 28 percent of men had more education than their wives, and only 20 percent of women had more education than their husbands. By 2007 the figures had reversed. While 53 percent of all couples had equal education levels, 28 percent of women had more education than their husbands and only 19 percent of men had more education than their wives.

The rising number and proportion of women college graduates compared to men is regularly cited as a major reason for the fact that so many women are earning more than their husbands. One researcher, digging still deeper, found that the gender wage gap had actually reversed for a significant group of young women. He found that unmarried, childless women under age thirty who lived in cities are now earning a premium over men in their peer group. Indeed, in 147 of our 150 largest cities, the researcher found that full-time employed young women earned an average of 8 percent more than their male competitors. In some cities, like New York, Los Angeles, and San Diego, the gap is substantially larger—17 percent for New York, for example. Other working women still suffer a wage discount.[7]

With their rising earnings, women are discovering new economic power that allows them to make different decisions about how they manage their lives, such as if and when they marry and how long they remain married. The percentage of women who have no children nearly doubled from 10 percent in 1976 to 18 percent in 2008. During the same period, the proportion of women with advanced degrees who have no children fell sharply. According to another Pew Research Center study,[8] 34 percent of women with doctoral degrees had no children in 1992, but only 24 percent of women with doctoral degrees had no children in 2008. (And like the bride who followed her groom and newborn child to the altar at the beginning of this chapter, a woman with an advanced degree can be financially secure enough that there is little reason to marry until the decision to have a child has been made.)

Current education statistics indicate that this is the new order. For nearly a decade now, women have outnumbered men on college campuses and in earning an undergraduate degree. Recently men were trailing women by 43 percent to 57 percent. In Maine, the state with the highest proportion of women to men in college, men were trailing women by 40 percent to 60 percent. Say goodbye, Suzy Homemaker. Today the old joke of women going to college because of the marital guarantee—"A-ring-by-spring-or-double-your-money-back"—no longer applies.

Now the shoe is on a larger, and male, foot. "One way in which college-educated married men have gained financially is that they increasingly are likely to be married to the highest income wives," the Pew Research Center study notes.

The biggest gain women have enjoyed, however, is far more fundamental. When new jobs are created, women are getting them. In the first decade of this century, men have become the equivalent of a Sony Walkman in an iPod marketplace. From 2000 to 2010, according to Labor Department figures, men gained a piddling 54,000 new jobs. During the same period, women gained 2,119,000.[9] That's a whopping 97.5 percent of the total new jobs!

To be sure, it was a crummy decade for jobs: roughly nine times as many were created in both the 1990s and the 1980s. In the 1990s, men won 46 percent of the 18.4 million new jobs created. In the 1980s, they won 41 percent of the 19.5 million jobs created. In those two decades, it could be argued that women competed for new jobs and won a majority simply by accepting lower pay, the traditional route to gaining market share. But in the past decade, women vanquished men from the field, and they did it without wage concessions. The tenacity and smarts of Xena, the warrior princess of television fame, prevailed.

In addition to examining the rise in the number and income of women who work, it's also instructive to compare older men and women and younger men and women. The labor force participation rate for men ages fifty-five to sixty-four was 86.9 percent in 1950, but it fell to 67.7 percent by 1990 and 67.3 percent by 2000, before rising to 70.2 percent in 2009. The participation rate for women that age soared from 27 percent in 1950 to 45.3 percent in 1990, 51.9 percent in 2000, and 60 percent in 2009. The continuing increase for older women and the resurgence for older men indicate that older people are now holding onto their jobs due to economic uncertainty and inadequate (or lost) savings. Their reluctance to leave the labor force is one of the reasons the young are having more trouble joining it.

There are many reasons for the long decline in the labor participation rate for men. One is that they could retire earlier because they had early Social Security retirement benefits, generous pensions and severance, and rising home values during most of this period. Women, in contrast, often had to substitute for men who were no longer employed or who had divorced them, making work a necessity. Rising costs for housing and education also explained women's rush to work. The only way to cope was to abandon the Leave-It-to-Beaver family model and have both husband and wife work.

Whether women are commanding more of the job market in pursuit of personal fulfillment or out of financial necessity, the change may not be a plus for their children. Parental time gets squeezed when both parents work so there is less contact time, and tired-at-the-end-of-the-day parents are likely to use the television set as a substitute for personal communication. The kids can gain in some areas (there may be more money to spend on extracurricular activities and fun vacations), but both parent and child may wish for more time together.

The Two-Income Trap and Generation Debt

Change like this has not gone unnoticed, but it hasn't been front-page news either, even if its implications are greater than the homicide, fire, or multicar pileup of the day. Two women have written books trying to bring the change and its implications to our attention. In 2003 Harvard Law School professor Elizabeth Warren, with her daughter, Amelia Warren Tyagi, wrote *The Two-Income Trap: Why Middle-Class Mothers and Fathers Are Going Broke*.[10]

"This book," she writes, "is dedicated to all the parents who wake up with hearts thudding over the possibility that buying school shoes and Girl Scout uniforms will mean there won't be enough left over to pay the mortgage." The book is one, but just one, of the reasons that the banking industry did everything possible to keep Warren from being named head of the new consumer protection agency. While the bankers would like us to believe that personal bankruptcy is the result of foolish, careless, and dishonest people who misled otherwise kind but prudent lenders into providing the cash for Olympic-pool-size hot-tubs and casual trips to Las Vegas, Warren and Tyagi convincingly show that personal bankruptcy nearly always results from unfortunate events—things like medical bills without medical insurance coverage, divorce, and job loss, or some combination of all three disasters.

In their book, the authors note the illusion of security the two-earner family has and how two incomes, not one, are required to secure housing in better school districts. With the ever rising premium on education, the cost of houses in areas that have better schools (read: more of the town's high school graduates going on to college) is the product of competition among families trying to give their children a competitive advantage in an increasingly uncertain world. Add easy borrowing and bubble pricing, and you can see why so many young families now own homes that are worth less than what they owe the lender—23 percent of all home owners as we write this.[11]

How can this be? Easy. In the increasingly visible game of employment musical chairs, those with more education still have an advantage over those with less education. The chairs being removed just before the music stops are the ones for the less educated.

Anya Kamenetz, a young freelance writer and Yale graduate, adds a particularly impassioned voice for her generation. Her 2006 book, *Generation Debt: How Our Future Was Sold Out for Student Loans, Credit Cards, Bad Jobs, No Benefits, and Tax Cuts for Rich Geezers—and How to Fight Back,* crisscrosses the country to interview young people who are stymied by a world that seems to have turned against them. Combining anecdotes with broad statistics, she tells us bluntly just how bad things are for the young:

> What would you do if you grew up and realized that everything America has always promised its children no longer holds true for you?
>
> I am twenty-four years old, and I was born into a broke generation. I look around and I see people who have borrowed more to go to college than they can repay, who can't find a good job, can't save, can't afford basic necessities like health insurance, can't make solid plans. Their credit card bills mount every month, while their lives stall out on the first uphill slope. Born into a century of unimaginable prosperity, in the richest country in the world, those of us between the ages of eighteen and thirty-five have somehow been cheated out of our inheritance.[12]

Kamenetz is right. Her generation and those to come are increasingly being cheated out of two-parent, stable homes, decent elementary and secondary education, affordable college, a culture that values commitment, and reliable jobs that pay a decent wage. And those who make it through all the minefields she lists can look forward to the really big whammy—the government going under and talking the financial system and the economy down with it. Welcome to America!

6

Does It Pay to Grow Up?

Now let's take a closer look at three big parts of the American dream—three things we've enjoyed and naively assumed our kids would too:

- Ownership of a home that rises in value
- Access to a level of education that opens the door to a good income
- A growing job market that offers opportunity to all

The Decline in Home Ownership

Owning your home used to be a sign of financial stability. No longer. The housing market, which fell apart starting in 2007, continues to worsen. New housing starts remain close to the postwar low, and the Case-Shiller home price index, after a short and minor uptick, is again heading south.

For the young, the message is clear—homeownership is extremely risky. The minute they buy, they place a financial albatross around their neck—a house they may not be able to sell if they lose their job or have to move across country for a different job—a very real possibility given the state of our economy. So they aren't buying. Nor are the middle age and old.

From its peak at 69 percent in the third quarter of 2006, the percentage of households that own their home (however mortgaged) is down to 66.4 percent.[1] There has been no corresponding decline in the supply of homes. Given the broken hopes, the bad credit records, and the raw power of demography, it would not be surprising if the percentage of households that owned their own home fell to the 63 percent level of the mid-1960s, or lower. Indeed, the rate could fall much further due to an urbanizing and aging population. The western states, for instance, have always had a lower rate of home ownership than the rest of the country. Today the western states clock in at only 60.9 percent, about the same as in the mid-1960s. What happens in the West could be the new standard for home ownership across the country.

With fewer people owning houses and with home prices flat to declining, the single easiest way for middle-income households to build net worth has disappeared. It was easy because owning a home has a unique advantage over other forms of investing: when you own a home you are consuming, saving, and investing at the same time. If real appreciation is on your side, your investment will do well.

That's why home equity has routinely accounted for the largest share of personal wealth held by the majority of American households. Where else can you take money out of one pocket to make a mortgage payment and have it magically reappear as a higher home value on your personal net worth statement? During a good part of the past half-century, home values rose at rates that were often equal to or greater than the interest rate on their mortgages. That easy money has vaporized. Many believe it won't be coming back, and they are starting to act accordingly.

For the retirees hoping to sell their big old homes at high prices to the young and downsize to smaller quarters, using the equity extracted to finance the glorious retirement pictured in Viagra commercials, a decision by the young to stay clear of homeownership is an indirect decision to undermine the retirements of vast numbers of elderly. Housing has, thus, become radioactive for everyone.

House Prices are Still Ridiculously High

In 1970 housing was hot. Interest rates were rising, and home prices had risen to levels that made it nearly impossible for many households to buy a new house. The average new house in that year cost $26,600, a whopping 4.1 times the annual income of the average worker, $6,447.50.[2]

Back then, with mortgage rates just under 7 percent, lenders told home hunters to buy a home that cost about two and a half times their annual income. As a result, most workers could not qualify to buy a new home and had to hope they could buy an existing home at a lower price, a price they could qualify to finance.

This concern seems quaint today, but housing inflation was seen as a real problem at the time. The rate of home ownership declined for the first time since the end of World War II in 1970. Having risen modestly from 62.1 percent in 1960 to 64.3 percent in 1969, the fall to 64.2 percent in 1970 was troubling. Politicians of both parties worried publicly about access to the dream of home ownership.

Since then both circumstances and policies have conspired to turn homes into speculative capital gains vehicles. With the inflation of the 1970s, homes were seen as a sure inflation hedge. Buyers started bidding prices up. By 1980 the average new home sold for $76,400, nearly five times the average worker's $13,036 annual income. By 1990 new home prices had nearly doubled, rising to $149,800, while average income trailed at $17,994. That brought the ratio of home price to income to a staggering 8.3 times average annual income. New home prices didn't rise as rapidly in the 1990s, ending in 2000 at $207,000 while average earnings rose to $24,650. So it appeared that prices were stabilizing at a relatively high level of around 8.4 times average earnings.

That was before the bubble. In the housing bubble, the price of the average new home rose to $313,600, while the average worker's wages were $30,162. So houses were priced at an impossible 10.4 years of earnings for the average worker.

Today we're back to pre-bubble prices and ratios, about eight times average worker income. So even with a large percentage of home owners who owe more to their bank than their house is worth, houses still cost about twice as much in workers' wages as they did in 1970. As a consequence, millions of young workers can't afford to buy their parents' or anyone else's parents' homes.

What will those young workers who don't get to own houses lose? Quite a bit. Forget tax deductions. For most workers in most of the country, the tax benefits of home ownership are far smaller than commonly believed. But three more important things will be lost:

• Home ownership insures a household against higher rental costs in the future. As was true in the past, the out-of-pocket cost of shelter is likely to rise more slowly than rent and more slowly than the general cost of living.

• The burden of mortgage payments is a commitment to forced saving. Over thirty years, paying off the mortgage can involve building equity that is worth many years of income.

• The paid-off home can be a form of annuity, with the owner receiving housing services in untaxed noncash income. If the house is sold, the proceeds can buy a life annuity that will provide a genuine annuity income. A house that sells for four times annual income can become a joint life annuity that will replace about 24 percent of a worker's gross income before retirement.[3] A house that sells for eight times annual income can become a joint life annuity that will replace about 48 percent of a worker's gross income. At that level, home ownership can be as important as Social Security.

Older home owners have enjoyed all three of these benefits, and that's not counting the special benefit they received that was one of the primary drivers for the price bubble. In 1997 Congress passed the Taxpayer Relief Act. The bill made capital gains up to $500,000 on a home sale ($500,000 for a couple, $250,000 for a single home owner) tax free, opening a floodgate of speculative demand just as lenders were being urged to loosen their loan requirements and interest-only loans were becoming available. This worked to enrich older home owners, particularly if they sold their homes. Home buyers, anticipating price appreciation that was totally tax free, bid prices up to insane levels.

So here we have the elderly, who hold most of the financial asset wealth, enjoying legislation that increases their home equity, and simultaneously looking to the young to pay more taxes to cover their growing old age health care needs and desires. This is yet another clash of generations.

College, Sallie Mae, and the New "Company Store"

West Virginia became infamous late in the nineteenth century for its dangerous coal mines and their company stores. When the miners received a pay hike, which was rarely, prices at the company store were increased. If a miner fell into debt and borrowed from the company store, his life became an endless cycle of debt, work, repayment, and new debt. While the formal indentured servitude that had brought thousands upon thousands of workers to the United States and Australia was in decline, thousands of coal miners in West Virginia and Kentucky were effectively indentured to their coal mine and its company store. The miners' life was summarized in two lines from Tennessee Ernie Ford's 1955 hit song, "Sixteen Tons":

You load sixteen tons, what do you get
Another day older and deeper in debt.

Today millions of college graduates and holders of advanced degrees owe their souls to the company store, only the company store is Sallie Mae (the federal agency in charge of student loans) and the financial institutions that hold the debts young people have acquired in the course of getting an education. These are not small debts. During the summer of 2010, the total burden of student debt, at nearly $830 billion, surpassed the total of all consumer credit, at about $826 billion.

One reason student debt surpassed consumer debt (which is the total of all credit card and installment debt) is that households have either been defaulting on or paying down their consumer credit since it peaked at nearly a $1 trillion in late 2008. There's nothing like a recession and fear of job loss to motivate people to get out from under the debts that come so easily when the economy is expanding. Suddenly those giant 72-inch LCD television sets, Hawaiian vacations, and BMWs don't look so wonderful after you've had the thrill but now have to pay for them, at interest rates of 15 percent and higher, for as close to eternity as a lender is allowed to get.

Some would also argue that student debt is "good debt" because it is for education rather than consumer doodads. The argument has some merit, but the operative word is *some*. While education debt is acquired in the course of learning presumably valuable and marketable skills, increasing our human capital, millions of indebted former students are now wondering if they were sold a bill of goods because their new skills seem neither valuable nor marketable. So just as many once argued that mortgage debt was good debt because it gets you into owning an inflating or appreciating asset, the debt doesn't look so good when the house is sinking in value and your degree doesn't get you a job. In both cases, the debt is simply a burden, a deadweight.

Actually it's worse than that because there is a difference between student debt and mortgage debt. If you have a big mortgage debt that you can't handle, you can sell the house and pay off the mortgage. For some, particularly in real estate disaster states like California, Nevada, Arizona, and Florida, getting out from under will involve a short sale—getting the lender to agree to take a loss on the loan. For others, it will be a total disaster and go straight to foreclosure. Either way, the debt will go away.

Both events will injure future ability to borrow, but there are odd off-sets for those who take the short sale or foreclosure route. Some home owners, angry that their homes have turned into such bad deals, stop making payments but continue to live in the house. The lender, know-ing that the property will decline further in value if it is abandoned and vandalized, will go slow on the foreclosure process because taking pos-session of the house is the last thing they want. It will increase the bank's expenses, expose the house to vandalism, and increase the bank's liability. As a consequence, the disappointed owner may get to live, payment free, for periods approaching three years. The longer that owners stretch it out, the better the odds are that they will be able to save enough to have a generous down payment if they dare to buy a house again.

This happens even in homes that have reverse mortgages, the cash-ing-out vehicle for owners over sixty-five years old. Having taken out a reverse mortgage to obtain cash, an increasing number of owners then saved additional expenses by failing to pay their real estate tax and in-surance bills, exposing the lenders to loss and liability. This put the lend-ers between a rock and a hard place: they could do nothing and hope things somehow worked out, in spite of the home owner's failure to pay tax and insurance bills as required, or they could foreclose on the often aged occupants and suffer a public relations disaster. Early in 2011, both Wells Fargo and Bank of America withdrew from the reverse mortgage market.[4] They had provided 43 percent of all reverse mortgage loans in the country.

Education debt isn't so forgiving. In fact, it isn't forgiving at all. Like Br'er Rabbit's tar baby, once you touch education debt, you're stuck with it. Stop making payments, and the debt will continue growing. Declare personal bankruptcy, and your consumer debt may be wiped out, but your student debt will live on because it can't be discharged through bankruptcy.

Student debt is with you until you pay it off. It's a serious burden to those who overpaid for their educations by going to expensive private colleges but never got jobs with premium pay—or got a job with pre-mium pay, only to see it disappear in a corporate restructuring or merger. It's an even more serious burden for millions who have managed to find a job, but not one that requires (or pays for) their newly acquired skills.

And it's a still greater burden for the many recent graduates who are among the unemployed.

How Education Debt Crowds Out Consumer Spending and Home Buying

If you have student debt when you graduate from college, it will have a significant impact on your ability to take on other debt, including purchasing a car and buying a house. Although there are several measures for average student loan debt, the usual range of figures is about $23,000 to $28,000, with about two-thirds of all students graduating with debt.[5] This is about the cost of an average new car and the equivalent of about half a year of typical starting salaries for new college graduates. As we write this, the interest rate on these loans in repayment mode is 6.8 percent for Stafford Loans, the direct federal loans for students, and 7.9 percent for PLUS loans, the direct federal loans for parents of students.

If we assume a new college graduate with a starting salary of $48,000 and $24,000 of student debt at 7 percent interest, she will be committing 11.9 percent of income to loan repayment to pay off the debt in five years, 7 percent of income to pay off in ten years and 5.4 percent of income to pay off in fifteen years. Whatever schedule she chooses, it will reduce her ability to borrow for other consumer spending, and it will certainly reduce the amount she can borrow to buy a house.

Here's why. Lenders typically limit a home buyer's back-end ratio—the total amount of income committed to debt service—to 36 percent. The limit on the front-end ratio—the amount of income that can be committed to mortgage payments—is 28 percent. So no more than 8 percent of income can be committed to nonmortgage debt without reducing the amount available for home finance costs. Although a recent graduate is free to load up on car loans and credit card debt, virtually any such debt will get in the way of buying a house. If the graduate, for instance, owns a used car purchased for $18,000 and financed for four years at a typical 5 percent, the monthly payment will be $414, or $4,974 a year—10.4 percent of income all by itself. Add the student loan payments, and our recent graduate could be unable to buy a home for ten years or more, having committed at least 15 percent of income to education loans and a car.

Note that we're not talking about Beemers or Bentleys here, just average-cost new or used cars. According to recent census figures, only 4.7

percent of workers take public transportation to work. Nearly 90 percent of workers commuted by car, so we can't argue that a young college graduate with a car suffers from notions of entitlement.[6] A car is an essential tool for most people for getting to work.

The Education Racket

Since one of us is a university professor, it's a little painful to say that the value of education, particularly expensive education, has been oversold to our kids. But the reality is that we have more educated people in most areas than we have jobs requiring that amount of education. The operative word here is *most* since we also have areas, like science and engineering, where employers complain of ongoing shortages and job openings that can't be filled. The big mismatch, however, is another story. An increasing number of critics are calling higher education a scam. Type "Is college education a scam?" into your search engine, as we did, and you'll get millions of hits. That's a pretty good indication that questioning the value of education has gone mainstream.

An increasing number of observers are worried that young people are being damaged by the education bubble. Just as there was an Internet bubble and a housing bubble, the thesis goes, we've also gotten into an education bubble, with too many people borrowing too much money to get degrees that no longer bring the much-hyped income and security once synonymous with higher education. The only difference between the education bubble and the Internet and housing bubbles is that the education bubble hasn't yet burst. When it does, we'll have a new kind of problem: How do you foreclose on a college degree? Newly prudent lenders can foreclose on a defaulted NINJA loan, famously short for "No Income No Job or Assets," and someday may be able to sell the house to recover some of the money lent. But how does a lender recover money lent on a bachelor of arts degree that has no earning power? It can't and won't. But the lender can hold a perpetual lien against all future earnings, and even future Social Security benefits, as unpaid interest compounds and accumulates. That's pretty close to indentured servitude.

Is there some way the education bubble can be deflated slowly? Maybe, maybe not. One gesture in the right direction, but it is only a gesture, came from venture capitalist Peter Thiel in September 2010. At the TechCrunch Disrupt conference in San Francisco, he announced a

"Stop Out of School" program, offering up to $100,000 over two years to twenty high school graduates who would rather start a business than go to college.[7]

It's an interesting idea and a brilliant sound bite, but we doubt that it can be a general principle. Most people don't want to start or own a business. They want to be employees and have the security of employment as part of the foundation for exercising useful skills. Most people aren't Mark Zuckerberg. We might also mention that lenders like people more when they are employees than when they are self-employed.

So when it comes to education, most kids (and their parents) don't think there is much of a choice. Its college or the slow train wreck of a life spent hoping for a break at (insert fast-food franchise name here). Many jobs that don't require degrees now demand having one. Worse, educators regularly trot out the annual or lifetime income differences between people with higher and lower levels of education. College pays, they say, and less education is perilous.

Does College Really Pay?

Between 1970 and 2007, real incomes for men ages thirty to forty-four without college educations fell, with a decline of 21 percent for those who didn't complete high school (table 6.1). Only college graduates enjoyed gains, although those were only 13 percent over the thirty-seven-year period. Women did better, but the same general trend was in place: women with less than a high school education saw their real incomes decline by 2 percent, and those with college educations saw their incomes rise by 30 percent.

Even Bill Gates, arguably the best-known college dropout in the world, says college is essential. Writing in a recent publication celebrating the 150th anniversary of MIT, he lauded all that education can and has done for the world. And what he wrote was true enough.[8]

But the question most students face isn't quite so cosmic. It is more direct and personal: "Will I raise or lower my lifetime standard of living by seeking more education?" Increasingly, the answer is they may lower their lifetime standard of living, not raise it. Their lifetime standard of living won't be lower due to lower income; it may be lower due to the burden of debt service and the increasing uncertainty of employment. In such circumstances, it isn't difficult to imagine many former students feeling buyer's remorse, wishing they could trade their long hours in the library for the party time they lost. Today the cost of education carries significant credit risk. While some, even many, college graduates will enjoy the kind of security and income premium that the education establishment says they will enjoy, an increasing number seem to be betting on education and losing. They have the experience of a higher education but can't support the debt that goes along with it.

Let's take an extreme case: an elite college education at about $40,000 a year for tuition. We'll assume that our student somehow manages to cover room, board, and other living expenses and her parents cover the cost of textbooks. Graduating with total debt of $160,000 (excluding accrued interest), our graduate might enjoy about twice the income of only completing high school. Paying off that debt in ten years would take a monthly payment of nearly $1,700, much of it from after-tax income because it would be payment of principal, not tax-deductible interest. Basically our college graduate would have to forgo all of the presumed benefits of higher education for at least a decade before enjoying a higher standard of living than a high school graduate would. Add some uncertainty

Table 6.1
Median real annual earnings for full-year workers, by gender and education

	1970	2007	Percentage change, 1970–2007
Education level for men			
Less than high school	$35,250	$27,703	(21)
High school graduate	$42,750	$35,912	(16)
Some college	$50,250	$45,454	(10)
College graduate	$61,750	$69,772	+13
Education level for women			
Less than high school	$18,750	$18,469	(2)
High school graduate	$23,750	$24,830	+5
Some college	$26,250	$30,782	+17
College graduate	$37,750	$49,250	+30

Note: Includes only native-born thirty- to forty-four-year olds.
Source: D'Vera Cohn and Richard Fry, "Women, Men and the New Economics of Marriage," Pew Research Center, January 19, 2010, p. 8.

about getting a job that pays an income, rather than an internship that doesn't, and earning a real premium over the high school graduate, and higher education starts looking risky.

We have, of course, overstated the case. Lots of young people have parents who pay for their educations, and more people go to public colleges than to expensive private colleges, so the total debt accumulated can be a lot less than $160,000. And that's why so many still make the gamble. The problem is that fewer are winning the gamble.

One reason for the student debt bubble is the rapid rise in the cost of education. It is one of the few things whose prices have risen nearly as fast as the cost of health care. However you slice it, the cost of education has outpaced the general rate of inflation. Here's a personal example. When Scott went to MIT (class of 1962), a typical graduate would earn enough in his first eight or nine months after graduation to recoup all four years of tuition. That's a pretty fast payback. Today, with annual tuition at $39,212, or about $160,000 for four years, and an average starting salary for a recent graduate with a B.S. degree at $67,270 (a significant premium over the $48,633 average starting salary for all college graduates), it will take nearly 2.4 years of pretax income to get to payback. The higher payback period raises the risk. It could be argued, for instance, that the risk that comes along with the cost of education is more than three times what it was a half-century ago.

My Son the Plumber

Skeptics should consider an exercise we did on consumption smoothing. It takes a serious look at an old joke:

A home owner calls a plumber to fix a leaky pipe. The plumber arrives and fixes the leak. "That will be $150," the plumber tells the home owner.

The shocked home owner says, "Why that's more than I paid for our last trip to the doctor!"

"Yeah, I never made that much when I was a doctor, either," the plumber answers.

But what if it isn't a joke? What happens when we ask a simple question: Who will enjoy a higher lifetime standard of living, a doctor or a plumber? The conventional wisdom here is that the doctor will get to eat more caviar and drink more champagne than the plumber. Even those with a tendency to contrarian thinking would likely give the doctor an edge, though they might say, "Well, doctors earn more over their lifetime, but they also work more hours, so they could win on lifetime basis but lose on an hourly basis."

Using consumption smoothing software,[9] we found that the doctor did come out ahead, but by a very slender margin of only $423 a year. After paying income and employment taxes, paying off student loans, and all the other off-the-top expenses, it turned out that the doctor (who enjoyed peak earnings of $185,895) had a lifetime annual consumption of $33,666 while the plumber had lifetime annual consumption of $33,243.[10]

How could this be? Let us count the ways. A plumber doesn't need the years of education required to be a doctor, so he starts earning money earlier. He also doesn't start his profession with the mountain of debt that is attached to the typical M.D. degree. That same debt must be paid back out of dollars of income that have been taxed at relatively high rates, while the plumber, if married, can happily keep his maximum income tax rate at 15 percent. In addition, while the Social Security benefits the doctor receives will be somewhat higher than those the plumber gets, the doctor will have paid disproportionately more for them. This is thanks to the significant progressivity built into Social Security's benefit formula. The formula for calculating Social Security benefits credits low levels of past covered wages at a 90 percent clip, at the margin, and high levels of past covered wages at a 15 percent clip.

On top of that, the doctor will likely pay federal income taxes on her Social Security benefits, which the plumber may escape. Net it all out, and the plumber does nearly as well as the doctor. Indeed, we'll wager that any doctor would happily give up the $423 a year consumption advantage just to have a life that didn't involve daily dealings with insurance companies and Medicare.

There are, of course, other benefits to being a doctor. It's a respected profession, for one thing, usually held in higher esteem than plumbing, so it brings a lot of what some call psychic income. Of course, psychic income can't be used to buy food or make Mercedes payments, let alone make educational loan payments. A medical student can also tilt the odds in her favor by raising the educational ante: investing additional time in becoming a specialist. Then her income will certainly be higher than a general practitioner, internist—or plumber.

The Wolf at the Door: McJobs and Nojobs

Pop quiz question 1: You've just gotten a job as a Walmart greeter. Is there another way to describe your job?

Answer: Maitre'd at MickyD.

Since 1993 McDonald's, the only company razzed more for its "McJobs" than Walmart is for its greeters, has been installing small units of its restaurant inside Walmart stores. Greeters have abundant opportunities to direct customers to a convenient and fast meal.

Pop quiz question 2: How many McDonald's workers does it take to support one Social Security recipient? *Hint.* This is a variation on the old light bulb changing joke, so you know it's going to be a large number. You'll find the answer in the next chapter.

We can joke all we want, but at least McDonald's is hiring. Unlike most of the other largest companies in America, McDonald's has more employees working in this country today than it did five years ago. We don't have to tell you that the domestic job market hasn't looked good for a decade. Worse, the job market has been really bad for some and, as you'll soon see, isn't going to improve. So who got the shortest end of the job stick over the last decade? And why is this happening?

While the last decade worked very hard to be an equal opportunity disemployer, a close look at the figures reveals that the biggest part of the burden has been carried by the young and those with limited educations. Here are some figures:

• Between the beginning of 2000 and early 2011, the unemployment rate among workers at least twenty-five years old rose from 4.0 percent to 9.1 percent. The unemployment rate of workers age sixteen to twenty-four rose from 9.4 percent to 17.3 percent.[11]

• During the same period, the unemployment rate among college graduates rose from 1.8 percent to 4.5 percent.

• The unemployment rate among those twenty-five and over who hadn't completed high school soared from 6.4 percent to 14.7 percent.

A closer examination by the Employee Benefit Research Institute tells us that education level has been more important than age. The institute found, for instance, that the long decline in the labor force participation rate (the percentage of people in a group who have a job or are seeking one) ended in 1993. That's when only 29.4 percent of people fifty-five and over were in the labor force. Since then the participation rate has risen strongly, reaching 40.2 percent in 2010.[12] Indeed, this is the only age group whose participation rate has increased during the period. For other age groups, participation was flat to down.

It would be nice to argue that all those over age fifty-five continued working or rejoined the labor force because they realized that work was the only route to personal fulfillment or even that they had, say, exhausted the entertainment value of mah-jongg, but the real reasons are mostly related to uncertainty about financial security in retirement. So let's be clear about this: younger people didn't have such a bad time because older people had such a good time. The last decade was miserable for most people, but it was most miserable for the young.

Focus a bit closer on age, and you learn that the labor force participation rate for workers without a high school diploma declined slightly over the period, while the participation rate for more educated workers rose. An impressive 63.1 percent of workers age fifty-five and older with a graduate or professional degree were in the workforce, for instance, while only 22.4 percent of those without a high school diploma were still working or looking for work. That's quite a difference. Basically more educated workers are in demand and can hold on to their jobs longer. Less educated workers are less in demand and are more likely to lose their jobs or, worse, be in prison. The net effect is that the young are pushing against a job market where fewer older workers are giving up their jobs and the more educated workers, at all ages, are holding their own.

Being the logical, well-managed nation that we are, you would think that we would be looking for ways to increase the education and skill level of everyone of working age. But we're not. According to a 2007 National Academy of Sciences report:[13]

• We have fallen from first to eleventh place among the members states of the Organization for Economic Cooperation and Development (OECD) in the fraction of those twenty-five to thirty-four years old who have graduated from high school. The older portion of the U.S. workforce ranks first among OECD populations of the same age.

• We rank twentieth in high school completion rate among industrialized nations and sixteenth in the college completion rate.

- The World Economic Forum ranks the United States forty-eighth in quality of mathematics and science education.
- Sixty-nine percent of our public school students in fifth through eighth grades are taught mathematics by a teacher without a degree or certificate in mathematics.
- Ninety-three percent of our public school students in the fifth through eighth grades are taught the physical sciences by a teacher without a degree or certificate in the physical sciences.
- We rank twenty-seventh among developed nations in the proportion of college students receiving undergraduate degrees in science or engineering.
- We graduate more visual arts and performing arts majors than engineers.

This study was done in 2005, before the financial crisis and recession, so it was done before newspapers had daily stories about cutbacks in primary and secondary education, temporary school closings, reduced teaching staffs, higher student-to-teacher ratios in classrooms, and stiff increases for public university tuition. While it is inevitable that U.S.-educated scientists and engineers will become a smaller proportion of global higher education, these statistics are more indicative of a deliberate reduction to third world status. They also show that we are lagging in another form of saving and investment: the development of human capital. One dismal indication: a recent report by the Education Trust found that one in four who try to join the U.S. Army can't pass the entrance exam.[14]

Fortunately, there is some good news for young people entering the job market in this decade. The number of young people entering the job market will be virtually unchanged between 2010 and 2020, but the much anticipated boomer retirement rush means that the number of people in the sixty-five-and-over group will grow from 40 million to 54 million.[15] Since many of those people will have been employed, the young will be entering a job market with a great need to replace existing workers in existing jobs. This is different from hoping for newly created jobs, so the next ten years may be a lot easier for young people than the past ten.

But don't get too excited about the coming Good Times. American workers, whatever their age, are competing not just with other American workers. Like it or not, they are competing in a global job market. The job you have today in Akron, Ohio, could be outsourced tomorrow to China or any other country where the wages paid for any particular level of skills and education are lower than the corresponding skill set here.

That's why those patient souls who talk you through a computer problem or software installation problem could be in a call center in Phoenix—or in India or the Philippines.

We deal with this dismal situation a lot better as entertainment than as an actual event. "It's not personal, it's business" is a great movie line, but it doesn't feel so good when you are escorted out the door within minutes of termination, clutching your cubicle plant. Small wonder that a low-budget movie, *Outsourced,* was quickly turned into a TV show.[16] Lots of people can identify with it.

When we model the future, it looks like more of the same for the rest of this century. It's just a model, of course, and models shouldn't be confused with reality, but recent work by researchers Hans Fehr, Sabine Jokisch, and one of us (Kotlikoff) models the interaction of five regions—the United States, Europe, Northeast Asia, China, and India—over this century.[17] The model examines what can happen to wages and economic growth as the education level and productivity of workers outside the United States increase. The only truly good news is that change is a relatively slow process: building a productive workforce takes a long time.

The model gives us a number of messages. One is that low-wage, low-productivity workers in America will continue to have a tough time. Jobs will be scarce, and real wages are likely to decline while the real wages of high-productivity workers continue to rise. Basically our pool of low-productivity workers will be competing against an ever increasing army of similar workers in the rest of the world. The result will be stagnant or declining real wages—a continuation of what millions of workers have been experiencing since the 1970s.

This promises to create still more tension between the haves and have-less as top earners capture a still greater share of the income pie. The top 10 percent of earners in the United States, for instance, received 27 percent of the income pie in the 1960s but about 45 percent today. The most recent figure from the Internal Revenue Service, 45.77 percent, is for 2008, but it is down from a peak of 48.05 percent in 2007.[18]

While the model's high-skilled workers today earn about 5.8 times what low-skilled workers do, the model shows the ratio growing to over 10 times by the end of the century. This ensures the future of Starbucks and Whole Foods, although it may bring some grumbling from the baristas at Starbucks and the workers behind the esoteric and rare cheese counter at Whole Foods. Add the special skills of financial workers and bankers who continue to live in a government-sponsored "heads I win, tails you lose" world and the continuing ability of corporate managers to arrange high payments for egregious failure and still higher payments for success, and we'll bet that the distribution of income will be one of the leading issues of this century. While the previous century was notable for the rise of countervailing power—labor unions and antitrust laws, for example—this century is starting to look like a reversion to the nineteenth century.

This might have a slightly familiar sound to you. Competition with a growing and global horde of low-skilled workers has a scary resemblance to the old "reserve army of the unemployed" posited by Karl Marx.

Are there any cures for what appears to be a dark and dystopian future?

We think there are. Some of them are counterintuitive. One interesting result from the global model, for instance, is that if we can somehow increase the supply of high-skilled workers in China and the less developed world (as opposed to the current abundance of low-skilled workers compared to high-skilled workers), the rapid increase of skilled workers would blunt the increasing concentration of income. Sadly, this presupposes the United States could somehow help education systems in other countries when we're having trouble with our own education system.

7

The War on Our Children

Old age and treachery will overcome youth and skill.
Ancient Greek proverb

Not very many older people have gotten the message Anya Kamenetz was trying to deliver in *Generation Debt*. Sadly, the circumstances of the young have yet to become visible to many, perhaps most, older people. One indication is the regular stream of cartoons poking fun at recent graduates who have returned home to live with their parents. Only as the effects of the financial crisis drag on are we starting to see those in their twenties described as a new "lost generation."

And while older Americans worry about the future of Social Security and Medicare, the fact that both political parties have offered plans that reduce benefits only for those under the age of fifty has brought virtually no comments about generational equity. Yes, the derision and lack of empathy might qualify as a soft clash of generations, but reducing future benefits while maintaining current tax payments for workers is definitely a power play and a hard clash, yet it virtually never registers as such.

When it comes to generational equity, both political parties are tone deaf, and not by accident. Both, without a second's thought, promise to retain the current level of benefits for older people and to put the burden of reductions on younger people, and without a commensurate reduction in tax contributions. The promise of future benefits, paid for out of their own wages, is just one of the inheritances that Kamenetz sees disappearing from her generation's pocket. Moreover, many of the deductions that primarily reduce the taxes of middle-income working households (i.e., not retirees) are on the chopping block.

This, by the way, isn't new. Our friends in Washington have been taking from the young to buy the votes of the old for a long time. The Social Security reform of 1983, for instance, did nothing to reduce the benefits of those already retired or about to retire. It did, however, slowly raise the age for receiving full benefits from sixty-five to sixty-seven, effectively reducing the benefits those who are now young will receive when they retire by about 25 percent. Similarly, the same reform also instituted the taxation of Social Security benefits in the federal personal income tax and gave the states carte blanche to tax this income as well.[1] When the new tax went into effect, only about 3 percent of all retirees were affected. But the architect of this tax, David Stockman, director of the Office of Management and Budget under President Reagan, as well as members of Congress who supported it, purposely designed it as a tax time bomb that would blow up in the faces of future generations.

One of us (Kotlikoff) sat in on a meeting at the Office of Management and Budget in which Stockman gloated about having stuck this time bomb into a Social Security bill whose purported purpose was to immediately raise Social Security's retirement age. Stockman knew the retirement age change would be soundly defeated, which it was, but indicated that his real intention in proposing a rise in the retirement age was to divert attention from the time bomb.

The time bomb's fuse is lit by inflation. Thanks to inflation, each generation of retirees will have higher nominal incomes. But since the income thresholds beyond which retirees must pay income taxes on first 50 percent and then 85 percent of Social Security benefits aren't indexed for inflation, each successive generation of retirees can expect to see a larger share of its Social Security benefits lost to the income tax.[2] According to the formula for the taxation of benefits, for instance, half of benefits start becoming taxable when a couple's combined income (the couple's adjusted gross income, including nontaxable interest income, plus half of its Social Security benefits) hits $32,000. (The figure is $25,000 for single returns.) And when the couple's combined income exceeds $44,000 ($34,000 for single returns), 85 percent of each extra dollar of Social Security benefits is subject to federal, and, depending on the state, state income taxation.

The $32,000 and $44,000 couple thresholds ($25,000 and $34,000 for singles) aren't indexed (adjusted for inflation). Indeed, these are one of the few features of the federal income tax that aren't inflation indexed. Their purpose, though, is clear,: to impose a stealth tax on the young whose nominal incomes, including Social Security, will rise over time thanks to inflation, making these thresholds smaller and smaller in real terms.

Some 30 percent of all retirees now pay some federal income taxes on their Social Security benefits. When today's young people retire, virtually all will face taxation on 85 percent of their benefits. So the younger you are, the greater the reduction is in your real Social Security benefits through this mechanism.

The nonindexation of the Social Security income tax thresholds will cost Anya Kamenetz and her cohort roughly 20 percent of their benefits on average. Everyone in Washington who knows about Social Security and taxes knows about this time bomb, but no one is going out of their way to let young or middle-aged workers know it's coming. That would require encountering some sticky questions, like these:

Why are these thresholds one of the few elements in the tax code that aren't indexed for inflation? And why are you cutting our benefits in this stealth manner? And why are you leaving us at the mercy of inflation? If it's 2 percent for the next forty years, we'll get zapped badly enough, but what if it's 5 percent?

Basically the plight of the young has provoked no compassion at all in older Americans. Rather than face the differences and deal with the causes, boomers and greatest generation members take the easy path: they blame the victims, even though the victim is often their own adult child. Looking at his reader e-mail, for instance, Scott sees a lot of entitlement thinking, with boomers and older retirees holding that they paid taxes and therefore earned every dime of the benefits they receive.

If only they could accept the truth: the older you are, the greater the "return" on the taxes you paid. As regular studies have shown, the "return" on taxes paid for Social Security and Medicare has been falling from decade to decade, but it has always been positive. Until today. Now, many young people, unlike their parents, will pay more in taxes than they will ever receive in benefits.

So the entitlement thinking isn't being done by the young. It's the boomers and retirees who have a sense of entitlement. The young simply think they're being exploited, which they are.

Retirees assume that Medicare coverage of medical expenses is a right. Encouraged by the AARP, they complain about having no increase in their Social Security benefits even though there has been no inflation, even though 10 million of the workers who support them don't have jobs, and even though few of those still working have been getting raises of any kind and some had to agree to wage reductions. Retirees like to think that they paid in and therefore are entitled. They think that the young expect too much, too soon. They think that they, not their children, have led model lives of prudence, sacrifice, and good judgment because their homes have multiplied in value (if they have owned them long enough).

A closer look shows just how imperiled this entitlement is. Any morning in any McDonald's, you can find seniors gathered to drink coffee, have breakfast, and talk with their friends. They go for the "Senior Coffee," currently 55 cents a cup, and the $1 specials, like the sausage biscuit and the breakfast burrito.

The cost of gathering and eating together isn't high, and no one would call McDonald's a place of ostentation. But the reality is that it takes a lot of young workers to make that casual morning meeting possible. The average monthly Social Security retirement check is now $1,172. The average hourly wage for workers at McDonald's with one to four years of experience, according to payscale.com, is about $8.00. That worker pays a direct tax of 6.2 percent in employment taxes for retirement benefits, which amounts to almost 50 cents an hour. The employer's payment is another roughly 50 cents an hour. So it will take 1,172 hours of payroll tax time for typical McDonald's workers to pay a typical retiree her monthly Social Security check. If the typical worker puts in 120 hours a month (not 160 hours, or full time, requiring McDonald's to provide health insurance and other benefits), it will take almost ten minimum-wage McDonald's workers to support a typical retiree. Add in average Medicare and Medicaid benefits (and the Medicare tax) to the mix, and it takes seventeen McDonald's workers to support via payroll taxes a typical retiree.

Viewed this way, even a senior breakfast is a bit scary. Assuming customers spend $3 on breakfast, a McDonald's worker has to punch in for three hours just to cover the senior's cheap breakfast. It's fortunate for our elders that few minimum-wage workers see this connection.

Fighting the Fogies for Jobs

The latest area of generational collision is the reverse in the labor force participation rate for older workers, particularly men, that we pointed out in an earlier chapter. During most of the postwar era, older men were leaving the workforce. Some retired at younger ages because they had the wind at their backs in the 1950s, 1960s, 1970s, and 1980s. Between generous early retirement buyouts, good corporate pensions, the stunning rise in residential real estate values, and the allure of low-cost retirement destinations like Florida and Arizona, the labor force participation rate for men age fifty-five and over fell from 86.9 in 1950 to bottom at only 67.3 percent in 2000. Since then, older men have renewed their commitment to the workplace (or clung desperately to a job), probably because the alternative is pretty scary. Their participation rate rose to 69.3 percent by 2005. It continued rising through the recession, reaching 70.2 percent in 2009. During the same period, the participation rates for younger men—those twenty to twenty-four and twenty-five to thirty-four—declined, an indication that fogies were crowding out the young.[3] When youngsters meet oldsters on the battlefield of jobs, it is yet another clash of generations—but we hear little about it.

This was not just a man-against-man event. The participation rate for women of all ages held its own or rose during this period. The participation rate for women age fifty-five to sixty-four rose from 57 percent in 2005 to 60 percent in 2009. So women are displacing men, and fogies of both sexes are cheerfully stomping on the hands of the young as they try to grasp the employment ladder.

Locking Up the Young: A Major Growth Industry

In 2008 about 880,000 people still had jobs building cars in America. In the same year 770,000 people had jobs in our fast-growing corrections industry.[4] While the domestic automobile industry came to the point of collapse in 2008, with General Motors and Chrysler both seeking federal bailouts, the corrections industry has been in growth mode for decades.

Our land of the free now has the highest incarceration rate of any country in the world, and enforcement of drug laws has a lot to do with that. No other developed country comes close. Our imprisonment rate is six times that of Britain, seven times that of Germany, and nine times that of France. America's lockup rate is not only miles out of line with that of other countries; it's completely out of line with our own past practice. Today's rate is five times what it was in 1970. Over the same period, our violent crime rate has fallen by half. The increase in nonviolent criminal incarceration is concentrated among drug offenders, whose numbers have increased twelve-fold since 1980.

Among groups disproportionately involved in trafficking drugs, incarceration rates are staggering. Fifteen percent of white male high school dropouts and 69 percent of black male high school dropouts will spend time in jail by age thirty-five. These figures are four and five times higher, respectively, than they were in 1979.

As of 2008, more than 2.3 million Americans, roughly the population of our fourth-largest city, Houston, were locked up. China, with about four times the U.S. population, has 1.5 million people behind bars. Tally the number of Americans in jail, on parole, or on probation, and you're talking close to the populations of Los Angeles and Chicago combined.

These close to 7 million people are disproportionately young adults. This too is part of the war on our children.

The cost of putting so many people away is huge. Half of these expenditures are made by state governments, many of which are in terrible fiscal shape. Five states—Connecticut, Delaware, Michigan, Oregon, and Vermont—now spend more on prisons than on higher education. For those released from jail, legitimate jobs, let alone well-paying ones, are hard to find.

More than half of prison inmates have minor children. Consequently, millions of children are now growing up with at least one parent incarcerated, which helps explain why our country leads the developed world in child poverty.

But the business of America is business, and locking up people, even if they simply harm themselves, is good business. Today more than 30 percent of all inmates reside in private, for-profit prisons. Virtually every new prison built in recent years was developed by and for private jailers. Indeed, in the late 1990s prison real estate investment trusts were sold as safe investments, largely because the supply of tenants was assured.

Do you have the feeling something isn't quite right here? So do we. Perhaps these figures just represent a low point. Maybe the future will see a larger domestic automobile industry and a smaller prison population. Then again, we may see a smaller prison population in the future for the wrong reasons if more cities follow Oakland's lead in releasing prisoners or declining to prosecute people who have committed crimes short of homicide.[5] Indeed, the decline in prison population will be statewide in California following a recent Supreme Court decision that the overcrowded conditions of California prisons constitute "cruel and unusual punishment."[6] Burdened with one of the worst of the state budget crises, it's a pretty good bet that the California justice system will be reducing, not increasing, the number of prisoners over the next five or ten years.

How did it get this bad? This is America. How do you know when a country's best days are behind it? Decline is hard to spot. It tends to be subtle rather than dramatic. And since every country has some periods that are better than others, it's always possible to say the decline is temporary—just a short resting period on the long march to Better and Better.

When the last histories are written, we think most will date the beginning of American decline, or this period of decline, to the early 1970s. That's when real wages peaked for many workers. It's also when the decline in union membership (and bargaining power) was first noticed. And it's also when we suffered defeat in Vietnam and when the Organization of the Petroleum Exporting Countries decided to exercise its power to price oil a lot higher. Pick a personal hobbyhorse, and we're sure you'll find one in the wild herd of the 1970s.

As a practical matter, no single action can be identified as a flashpoint for decline. What happens instead is that many things change over a period of time. In our case, the pillars supporting a broad middle-class society were weakened—things like job security and pensions first, then negotiating power for wages and health insurance. During the same period, marriage declined. The number of children born out of wedlock into poorer households rose. Significantly, the one fundamental economic event was the decline and actual disappearance of saving.

How did we not notice? Actually it was pretty easy. Most of the decline was obscured by observing through a window of rising individualism, increasing personal freedom, and inflating asset values. Equally important, the decline in true spending power was masked by the growth of consumer credit. People who borrow more spend more, so the economy grew.

In 1970 the collateralized mortgage market did not exist. Money market mutual funds were just starting. Lending requirements were tight. Since then we've had a revolution in financial "innovation" that has massively expanded access to consumer credit. As former Federal Reserve chairman Alan "Bubbles" Greenspan put it in a tranquilizing speech to the Community Bankers annual convention in 2004, "In addition, improvements in lending practices driven by information technology have enabled lenders to reach out to households with previously unrecognized borrowing capacities."[7]

A staggering amount of "unrecognized borrowing capacity" was found and funded over the next few years as lenders boosted their loan volume by making loans to people who could not possibly pay the money back. Few asked awkward questions, like, "How can we have consumer spending be the engine for our economy's growth if workers aren't secure about their jobs, benefits, or future prospects?"

That's a really big question.

Rules for a Postconsumer Society

Demographers have called the period ahead "the demographic transition," noting that the next half-century will see the biggest demographic shift in human history. For the first time ever, the number of elderly people will be greater than the number of children in virtually the entire industrialized world. This is the shift from large families and high birthrates to small families (when we become families at all) and low birthrates. The supporting wave of new children simply won't exist.

This means that all the burdens that our legislators have so happily heaped on the next wavelet of children will be proportionately larger and certainly more than they can carry. That leaves us with a "can't get there from here" problem. If the young save more to provide the money to sustain the benefits government will need to welch on, they won't be the reliable consumers of what economist John Kenneth Galbraith once called "the new industrial state"—the orderly world of the 1950s where American corporations dominated world trade and did our saving and investing for us, much of it outside the country. In that world, households had their own specialized job: they worked assiduously at what they did best, which was to consume.

And we've done it quite well, taking the idea of consumer borrowing to its absolute limit. The miserable results are all around us. Declining home values, foreclosures, wrecked credit, unemployed graduates with loans they can't possibly repay, shrinking access to unaffordable health care, fewer marriages, more children born out of wedlock, and the highest rate of incarceration in the world. It's not a pretty picture. Now we have to turn it around. We need to start saving again. It's not going to be easy.

It could, however, be simple—as simple as our four purple postcard solutions.

8

Unsafe at Any Speed

The financial meltdown that's surely coming and will do more lasting damage to our kids won't be triggered, like the last one was, by the production and sale of trillions of dollars in fraudulent securities. It will be a run on the Treasury and the Fed triggered by the global realization that Uncle Sam is in far worse fiscal shape than ever imagined.

The moment of reckoning can come at any time. When the markets finally realize that our fiscal problem is enormous and cannot indefinitely be papered over by the Fed's money creation, things will change abruptly. We'll have a tremendous financial collapse, and not on a short-term basis. That will accelerate the fiscal collapse, reinforcing the financial collapse—in short, a vicious cycle. By design, our financial institutions have built no firewalls separating themselves from one another. Instead, there are only fire paths, including fire paths in Europe and other parts of the world waiting to ignite.

The hour is extremely late. We can no longer afford doing too little too late, putting off tough decisions for tomorrow, and enduring political gridlock. To fix America, we need to start from the ground up. Only radical, fundamental reforms of the financial system, the tax system, the health care system, and Social Security will solve our problems and get our country turned around. But it can be turned around.

The first in line for surgery is our financial system, which is unsafe at any speed. As you'll see, the needed reform is so simple that it can be conveyed on a postcard. We think postcard-length brevity is important. It matches the attention span of members of Congress.

We call our proposed reforms the *purple plans* because both Red Republicans and Blue Democrats will like what they see. Each of these reforms has been posted on the Web at www.thepurpleplans.org. Two of

the four plans have already been publicly endorsed by prominent economists, including economics Nobel laureates, and very high-level former
and current policymakers.[1] We hope you'll endorse them too.

The Purple Financial Plan Background

Let's face facts. Before it collapsed, our "trust-me" financial system manufactured and marketed trillions worth of securities we now call "toxic."
We call these securities toxic not because they were risky, but because
they were fraudulent. They were sold as one thing (relatively safe) but
were really another (hazardous).

To prevent a recollapse, Uncle Sam added his own fraudulent promises: "Don't worry. If the banks don't pay, I will." Sounds great, but Uncle
Sam doesn't have the income or assets to pay such bills. All Uncle Sam has
are us and our children to tax. That's it. But we "grownups" aren't about
to give up our tickets to the entitlement benefits "we paid for" throughout
our working lives. So we give the bill to our kids and grandkids to pay.
We don't do this face-to-face, of course. We do it through our elected representatives who know that what we always want are higher benefits and
lower taxes. The politicians, regardless of party, comply by lowering our
taxes, borrowing to cover formal deficits, and hiding the really big bills in
the future for our children to pay.

But our children will not be able to pay. The bill is far too high even taking into account the tax-paying capacity of everyone coming in the future.

So something has to give. As we've said, the easy out is printing money,
and that's what the Federal Reserve has been doing. It's been printing
money to cover the costs of the financial crisis and jump-start the economy. But the $1,800,000,000,000 the Fed printed in the past four years is
a pittance compared to our fiscal gap of $211,000,000,000,000. Yet what
has been printed already represents more than a tripling of the economy's
basic money supply (called the monetary base). Put that cash in motion,
in transactions, and prices could triple, moving us toward hyperinflation.
When inflation comes, as it surely will, everyone holding long-term nominal bonds will get paid back in watered-down dollars. So the stage is set
for a second, and larger, financial crisis.

Recall what happened when Standard & Poor's downgraded U.S.
Treasuries just one notch—from AAA to AA+ in August 2011. The

prospect and actual downgrade dropped the stock market by 20 percent and caused the markets to go completely nuts. Indeed, the daily swings in the market immediately following the downgrade were like nothing anyone had ever seen before. Remarkably, U.S. Treasuries rose during this episode as investors started worrying about another recession and the potential for short-term deflation. The market finally stabilized when the Fed promised to print enough money to keep short-term interest rates at record low levels for two years.

What the market clearly has yet to figure out is the true magnitude of the U.S. government's fiscal morass. This is the ongoing triumph of meaningless accounting over basic economics. The budget deal struck in August 2011 to reduce the official debt by $1.2 trillion over ten years occurred in a year when the fiscal gap rose by $6 trillion!

To date only a few "risk managers" on Wall Street and other financial centers have figured out what's going on and started dumping their long-term U.S. Treasuries. The most prominent is PIMCO's Bill Gross, who runs the world's largest mutual fund. So far, Gross has taken a hit. But others will surely follow. That, and the resulting stampede that will trample every financial institution, is what we need to stop by reforming our banking system. The rush out of Treasuries will cause a similar rush by depositors who will want to turn cash into closets full of canned soup, extra car tires, and any other physical good they expect to need.

When the herd starts to run, the stampede will be unstoppable. In dumping their U.S. bonds, they will raise interest rates dramatically and precipitate a tremendous crash in stock and other bond markets. The real economy will be greatly damaged, leaving our kids with fewer jobs paying even less, which means they will have less capacity to pay taxes to support their elders.

If Treasuries collapse and interest rates soar because everyone thinks Uncle Sam is insolvent, those same people will be no more willing to hold Uncle Sam's green pieces of paper—called currency—than they will be to hold his orange pieces of paper—the Treasury bills and bonds. This will turn the dollar into a hot potato, producing a crash of the dollar and inflation, if not hyperinflation, which everyone expects. Part and parcel of not holding green pieces of paper is not holding them here, there, or anywhere. You don't want to hold them in your pocket because they will lose value as prices rises, and you don't want to hold them in your checking account or savings account or money market account or life insurance cash-surrender policy or CD or, well, anywhere else. You want to get hold of that paper and quickly spend it on something real, like a mattress.

The point here is that the collapse of Treasuries—a fiscal collapse—can cause a run on the banks. Skeptics should talk to some Argentines about the run on their banks in 2002 when their government went broke. Fear of inflation will be part of the reason for our next bank run. The other part will be the dramatic collapse in the value of bank assets. U.S. banks hold about $9 trillion in different kinds of credit obligations such as long-term mortgages, corporate loans, consumer loans, and home equity loans.[2] Much of this credit is at fixed interest rates, so the value of these assets will be severely reduced when interest rates rise. When this happens, the banks' puny capital reserves, about 10 percent of total assets, won't be enough to cover the lost market value of their loans. Most banks will be bankrupt. This is what happened in the 1970s to the thrift industry and many commercial banks, but that crisis was small compared to the one coming.

As we write, this scenario appears ludicrous. After all, U.S. Treasury bonds are selling at historically high prices (interest rates are historically low) as partial default on Greek debt is transfixing the global financial world and riling global stock markets. But Greece's economy is the size of Ohio's. So it's not really Greece's default that has spooked the financial market. It's the potential for other weak calves—Ireland, Portugal, and even Spain and Italy—to get picked off one by one and also be forced to default. But if these countries go, they will put France and Belgium on the short financial hit list, followed by the U.K. and Japan, followed by, you guessed it, the United States.

The Fed to the "Rescue"

A run on the banks would force the Federal Reserve to print trillions of dollars to make good on its fraudulent Federal Deposit Insurance Corporation (FDIC) and other explicit and implicit guarantees to depositors and other bank creditors.[3] If it begins to fear hyperinflation, the public will first walk, then run, to get their money out of the banks, insurance companies, hedge funds, credit unions, savings and loans, and everywhere else. This will force the Fed to run its printing presses at hyperspeed to ensure a vast expansion of the money supply and, thus, hyperinflation.

When this happens, all those FDIC and other federal guarantees will be exposed for what they are—promises to pay green pieces of paper, not cans of soup. This is the sense in which Uncle Sam is making fraudulent financial guarantees. Uncle Sam is making nominal, not real, guarantees. He has never made clear to the public that his guarantees won't protect anyone in real terms. Depositors will get their money back, but whether it will buy much or even anything is not guaranteed.

The Purple Financial Plan: Limited-Purpose Banking

There is a better way to restore trust in our financial system and get our economy rolling. It isn't necessary to always have Uncle Sam standing by, pledged to clean up the mess. The better way is not to let the mess happen to begin with. Limited-purpose banking (LPB) is a simple and essentially costless change in our financial system. It limits banks to their legitimate purpose: connecting (intermediating between) borrowers and lenders and savers and investors.[4]

The list of notables who have publicly either strongly endorsed LPB or called for its serious consideration includes Mervyn King, governor of the Bank of England; George Shultz, former secretary of state and former secretary of treasury; former senator Bill Bradley; former secretary of labor Robert Reich; former head of the Cato Institute, the late William Niskanen; former vice chairman of the Joint Chiefs of Staff, Admiral William Owens; former chairmen of the President's Council of Economic Advisors, Michael Boskin and Murray Weidenbaum; economics Nobel laureates George Akerlof, Edmund Phelps, Robert Lucas, Robert Fogel, and Edward Prescott; former chief economists of the International Monetary Fund, Ken Rogoff and Simon Johnson; prominent economists Jeffrey Sachs, Stephen Ross, and Kevin Hassett; and economic historian Niall Ferguson. This list spans the political spectrum, from the far left to the far right. This plan can have broad public appeal.

A Safe Banking System

Under LPB, all financial companies that operate with limited liability[5] and engage in financial intermediation must operate in one way only: as mutual fund companies that market mutual funds to the public.[6] When we say *all* formally or effectively incorporated financial intermediaries, we mean all. Whether they call themselves commercial or investment banks, hedge funds, private equity firms, brokerages, credit unions, insurance companies, or securities exchanges—all must operate as nonleveraged mutual fund companies if they want to operate under the legal protection of limited liability.

A limited-liability bank means that the owners of the bank cannot themselves be personally sued for the bank's losses. Robert Rubin, the former secretary of treasury who helped weaken banking law before returning to the private sector where he proceeded to oversee (actually undersee) Citigroup's near collapse, was able to walk away from the fiasco with huge amounts of personal wealth. Rubin lost face but was still smiling after the crash of 2008. The same is true of all the other architects of our country's greatest financial collapse since the Great Depression. They took their companies and the economy down, they devastated the lives of millions of retirees who sold at the bottom of the market, they destroyed the jobs and job prospects of millions of young and middle-age workers, and they forced the government to borrow and print trillions to keep the economy afloat—but they saved themselves.

This doesn't happen under LPB.

Want to Gamble? Put Your Yacht on the Line!

Unlike Glass-Steagall (the banking law passed in 1932 and repealed in 1999 thanks to treasury secretaries Robert Rubin and Lawrence Summers and former senator Phil Gramm), which drew a line between commercial and investment banks, LPB draws a line based on limited liability. Bank owners, like Jimmy Cayne, former head of Bear Stearns, and Dick Fuld, former head of Lehman Brothers, who want their banks to borrow (take on leverage) must operate, under LPB, with unlimited liability.

With unlimited liability, if Jimmy's or Dick's fifty-to-one leveraged bank can't repay, their banks fail, but Jimmy and Dick also have a very bad day: they are personally liable for all the losses of all their bank's creditors. Consequently Jimmy and Dick lose all their villas, all their jets, all their yachts, and all their other toys. They go from riches to rags overnight.

LPB is tough love: you run your financial intermediary either in a way that is safe for the economy or that is extremely unsafe for you. There is no third option. The only shadow banks under LPB are unlimited-liability banks, and while the government might decide to rescue them under some circumstances if they get into trouble, it would not rescue their owners, who would find themselves financially ruined. We sense that such shadow banks would be so few in number and so small in scale as to literally get lost in the shadows.[7] We believe the only thing the general public would greet with more enthusiasm than LPB would be claw-back financial punishment for all those financial captains who took their personal lifeboats and let the *U.S.S. Economy* sink.

Mutual Funds

Most of us are familiar with mutual funds from participating in 401(k), 403(b), individual retirement account, Roth, simplified employee pension, Keogh, and other retirement plans. A mutual fund serves simply as a financial middleman: it takes in money by issuing shares of stock and invests these funds in the securities it is chartered to buy. The mutual funds in LPB don't borrow money. In fact, they aren't allowed to. They are never in a position to fail because they borrowed more than they were able to repay. And since the banks are restricted to sponsoring mutual funds, they too can never fail. Of course, the owners of mutual funds will lose money if the assets the fund buys lose value. But neither the mutual fund nor its holding company, the LPB banks, will ever go bust.[8] This gets government off the hook.

Is LPB a completely safe banking system? Yes. Financial intermediation isn't about risk taking; it's about facilitating financial exchange. And as we saw in 2008, letting financial intermediaries "manage" risk jeopardizes their critical mission of intermediation and everyone's economic future.

Gas Stations Aren't Allowed to Gamble; Why Should Banks?

Gas stations are a good role model for banks. They intermediate between refineries, which supply gas, and drivers, who demand it. Their job is boring but critical. Were all gas stations to close down due to gambling, our economy would literally screech to a halt.

Come again? Gas stations closing down due to gambling?

Yes. Suppose gas station owners started gambling not on personal account but through their gas stations. Specifically, suppose they had their stations sell gas price guarantees to their customers, specifying the maximum price per gallon the customer would need to pay in the future. The sale of these certificates would generate lots of cash flow to the stations in the short run, but if the refineries started charging much more than the gas station owners contemplated, the stations would go broke, leaving the nation with no gas to drive its 250 million vehicles.

Were this to happen, Congress would quickly pass a law saying, "No gas stations can engage in risky securities transactions because gas stations are critical intermediaries and their failure would greatly harm the economy." This law would not, of course, prohibit gas station owners from taking risky positions with their personal wealth, including speculating on the price of gas. But they wouldn't be able to put their businesses at risk.

Banks = Mutual Funds

The same is true of banks under LPB. Banks would let us gamble, but they wouldn't gamble themselves. Banks would be free to sell all manner of mutual funds, including the ten thousand or so now on the market. These mutual funds include stock funds, government bond funds, private equity funds, real estate investment trusts, commercial paper funds, private mortgage funds, credit card debt funds, junk bond funds, inflation-indexed bond funds, and you name it. In every case, the fund buyer, who is not "too big to fail," takes risk, but the bank—that is, the mutual fund company—is only an intermediary.

Cash Mutual Funds

Limited-purpose banking would include one additional type of mutual fund: cash mutual funds. Cash mutual funds would simply hold cash—no T-bills, no short-term commercial paper. As a result, cash funds would obviously be valued at $1 per share today, tomorrow, and every day thereafter. They could never break a buck, the problem that all money market funds face in difficult markets. All other funds could and would break or exceed the buck based on fluctuations in market valuations. No mutual fund holding company (the LPB) would be permitted to use its own assets to shore up money market or other funds that break the buck. Doing so conveys the implicit promise that these banks can back asset values to the buck in all circumstances, which they clearly cannot.

Fund shareholders would have the amount of risk they chose in their selected funds. *But they would never face the risk of having to bail out the bank itself.* That's what happened in the recent financial collapse. Americans who had nothing to do with excessive risks taken by bankers involuntarily bailed out the banks through new government debt. Much the same happened in Ireland, where the collapse of their banks was rescued by their government's guaranteeing to make good on debts to German banks. The Irish now face a situation similar to what the Germans faced with reparations payments after World War I, only they never started a war.

Owners of cash mutual funds would be free to write checks against their cash mutual fund holdings and use debit cards drawn on their cash mutual funds at ATM machines or in making purchases at stores. Hence, cash mutual funds would constitute our payment system. They would replace the checking accounts we now use for making payments.

In replacing partially backed checking accounts with cash mutual funds that are 100 percent backed by cash, there is no possibility that the payment system can get into trouble. So there would be no need for the FDIC. This is a good thing. In eliminating the FDIC, we eliminate its $6 trillion contingent liability. These days, every trillion counts. The only negative here is that you'd no longer earn paltry interest on your checking deposits and you'd probably have to pay something for the bank to hold your cash. We think that's a small price to pay to avoid being on the hook for every bank bailout.[9]

The Federal Financial Authority—Keep It Simple, Stupid

Mutual funds are legally required to engage third-party custodians to hold their funds' securities. Under LPB, a new federal regulatory authority, the Federal Financial Authority (FFA), would oversee these arrangements. It would ensure that no Bernard Madoff could ever again self-custody his clients' assets and spend their money illegally.

The FFA would be our nation's only financial regulator. We now have roughly 130 federal and state financial regulatory bodies, none of which can decide whether it is working for the public or Wall Street. Good regulation is simple regulation, and the FFA's mission would be very simple. In addition to overseeing custody, it would hire private companies to verify, appraise, rate, and disclose all aspects of all the financial securities held by LPB mutual funds. These rating companies would work only for the FFA so there would be no conflicts of interest.

Joe Smith Gets a Mortgage

Here's how the FFA would work. Joe Smith wants to get a mortgage to buy a house. He goes to Citigroup, which, under LPB is now a mutual fund company. Citigroup helps Joe fill out his mortgage application and sends it to the FFA for processing. The FFA assigns one or more of the rating companies that work just for it to verify Joe's employment, verify Joe's current and past earnings, appraise the value of the house Joe is buying, verify Joe's credit history, rate Joe's mortgage, and disclose all this information on the Web.

Joe is free to add information to this disclosure, including additional ratings of his mortgage that he is free to purchase from rating companies not working for the FFA. But it would be clear to all which information and ratings were being provided by the FFA and which Joe had bought.

Toxic assets, be they liar loans, no-document loans, NINJA loans, or overrated loans, would disappear. We'd have a reliable source of information on what any given financial security does, and doesn't, promise to deliver. This is a vastly different financial world from the one we now have. What we now have are people like Angelo Mozilo, who ran Countrywide Financial, still being able to manufacture liar loans by simply lying about Joe's employment, income, collateral (appraised value of the home he's buying), and credit score, and then sell the fraudulent securities to unsuspecting investors throughout the world. *Time* magazine, by the way, put Mozilo at the top of its list of "25 People to Blame for the Financial Crisis."[10]

This is no different from letting thieves bottle colored water and market it as a cure for cancer. The sale of such elixirs was perfectly legal in our country until the public got tired of being swindled, if not poisoned. In 1906, after Upton Sinclair and other muckrakers exposed plenty of what amounted to liar foods and liar medicines (including radioactive beverages, cosmetics that caused blindness, and purported cures for diabetes and tuberculosis), our government established the Food and Drug Administration to independently verify the safety of food and the safety and efficacy of medications.[11] This established the rule of law in the drug industry, permitting a functioning market.

Today few in our country would propose eliminating the FDA. But the FFA is simply an FDA for the financial services sector. It is a century late in coming.

LPB Auctions

Once Joe's mortgage is disclosed, Citigroup puts it up for auction to its own mutual funds investing in mortgages in Joe's part of the country as well as all other mutual funds investing in such mortgages. The auctioning of Joe's mortgage is no exception. Under LPB, all securities bought and sold by the mutual funds would be done at auction. This ensures that issuers of securities (Joe, in our example) receive the highest price (pay the lowest interest rate in the case of an IOU) for their paper. Moreover, the FFA would oversee ongoing, real-time, full disclosure of all holdings of all mutual funds.

Under LPB, households would do all types of borrowing from mutual funds, whether for auto loans, credit card lines of credit, mortgages, or student loans. Small businesses and large ones would also borrow from and sell stock to mutual funds. The combination of reliable disclosure by the FFA and the ability to sell one's paper at auction would afford American households and businesses much easier and reliable access to credit than now exists. This would be a tremendous boost to business, particularly small business.

Is LPB Feasible?

As a group, U.S. mutual fund companies hold roughly 30 percent of all U.S. financial assets. Hence, the glass is already 30 percent full when it comes to LPB. We know what it looks like. We know that it works. It has a long history. And cash mutual funds already exist, although they need to be restricted to hold only cash. As we suggested, mutual funds in the United States are already being used to fund home buyers, credit card holders, large and small governments, and large and small businesses. We can do this. The only impediment to making the change is the banking industry itself and all the politicians, of both parties, that it owns.

Moving to LPB is eminently feasible. Moreover, the transition is straightforward. Today's banks would be told to:

1. Stop borrowing and buying risky assets on their own account.

2. Convert their checking accounts to cash mutual funds and use their reserves, which are currently immense, to back their cash mutual funds dollar for dollar.

3. Begin marketing mutual funds.

4. Pay out the cash flow from the banks' remaining assets less liabilities as dividends.

These four steps would kill existing trust-me banking practices and jump-start LPB show-me banking practices.

Congress could also legislate the transition to LPB on an asset-by-asset basis. For example, it could start with home mortgages. Specifically, it could phase out Fannie Mae, Freddie Mac, and other federal housing lenders and restrict banks to financing mortgages only through mortgage mutual funds processed by the FFA and purchased at auction. In so doing, Congress would produce a mortgage-covered equities market, quite similar in many respects to the covered mortgage bond market that has been used very successfully, for over two centuries, in Denmark and Germany to finance home purchases.[12]

Cleaning Up Wall Street

Unlike the Dodd-Frank legislation, which represents a full-employment act for government bureaucrats and fails to fundamentally reform the financial system, LPB cleans up Wall Street directly. It uses the FFA to eliminate fraudulent initiation of securities. It makes the FFA's rating companies work exclusively for the public, not for the companies they rate. It limits regulators to a small number of tasks, like checking that Joe is employed—tasks the regulators can actually perform. It restricts the ability of boards of directors to conspire with top executives to steal from shareholders. It does so by turning bankers into mutual fund managers whose performance can be carefully monitored based on the returns of the assets they purchase on behalf of their mutual funds. It keeps the financial system extremely simple and transparent and thereby limits Wall

Street's ability to bribe politicians to change financial laws in their favor. Its use of auctions fosters standardization of securities and thereby limits the complexity of financial contracts, which is so often an invitation for deception. Finally, and most important, LPB puts a direct and bright light on Wall Street. Imagine a financial system in which the public can actually see, in real time and in fine detail, all aspects of their investments.

Making Bankers Unhappy

Limited-purpose banking is not something bankers will happily embrace. Thanks to the FFA, bankers would lose much of their ability to sell their "proprietary information," just as quacks, parading as doctors, lost, thanks to the Food and Drug Administration, much of their ability to sell magical elixirs.

"Invest with me. Only I have the Midas touch. Only I have the secret financial formula. Only I can cure your financial ills. And, no, I can't tell you my formula. If I do, everyone else will learn it, and I won't be able to beat the market, all on your behalf. So, trust me. Invest with me and do it today!"

This and much more of the financial industry's preying on the American public would end for good with limited-purpose banking.

The Limited-Purpose Banking Postcard

Limited-purpose banking is simple enough to put on a purple postcard:[13]

Box 8.1
The Purple Financial Plan: Limited-Purpose Banking

---

1. Financial companies protected by limited liability operate exclusively as mutual funds companies.
2. Mutual funds aren't allowed to borrow, and, thus, they never fail.
3. Checking accounts converted to cash mutual funds hold only cash and are backed to the buck.
4. Noncash mutual funds are not backed to the buck and can lose value.
5. The Federal Financial Authority (FFA) organizes verification, appraisal, rating, custody, and disclosure of securities.
6. Mutual funds purchase FFA-processed and -disclosed securities at auction.

9

Getting to Yes

Future growth in spending per beneficiary for Medicare and Medicaid—the federal government's major health care programs—will be the most important determinant of long-term trends in federal spending.
CBO director Peter Orszag[1]

Our health care system is a mess. It leaves one in six Americans uninsured, and its costs threaten our nation's solvency. The Affordable Care Act of 2010 introduced health exchanges to expand coverage to America's 50 million uninsured. But U.S. District Judge Henry Hudson ruled that forcing people to buy health insurance is unconstitutional.[2] This and related rulings may be the death knell for President Barack Obama's plan to cover the nation's uninsured.

Talk about literal interpretation of the Constitution. Had the health care law used different words and levied a tax on all uninsured Americans and used the proceeds to buy them a policy, nothing of substance would have changed, and the judge would have had no objection.

It's a sad legal system that confuses linguistics for principle. But adherence to original language may trump concern for original intent, even on appeal to the Supreme Court. If it doesn't, Republicans in the House of Representatives have a fail-safe plan to derail the law's implementation: block the program's funding.

If you're pleased by this prospect, think again. You or your loved ones may be next to join the ranks of the 50 million uninsured and learn firsthand that self-insurance doesn't substitute for actual insurance when it comes to paying potentially astronomical health care bills.

Everyone needs a health plan, but what we did in 2010 is add another health care system with a potentially huge and uncontrolled price tag to the three we already have: Medicare, Medicaid, and employer-based health care. Medicare and Medicaid costs are exploding and have been doing so for forty years. The same is true of the tax subsidy provided by the government for employer-paid health insurance premiums. Unless we get the direct and indirect costs of these existing systems, as well as the new health exchange system under control immediately, it's game over.

The big expense concern with the health exchange system is that employers with predominantly low-wage workers will shut down their plans en masse, sending their worker to the government-subsidized health exchanges. Employers will incur a penalty, but the penalty is small compared to the size of the subsidies. In short, the health exchange system to cover the uninsured is virtually designed to take down the employer-based health care system. In the process, it will raise overall costs.

The Purple Health Plan

The purple health plan that we present in this chapter is a better mousetrap. It has been endorsed at www.thepurplehealthplan.org by economics Nobel laureates George Akerlof, Edmund Phelps, Thomas Schelling, William Sharpe, and Vernon Smith, as well as hundreds of other folks of varying degrees of luminescence, but all of uncommon common sense.

The plan bears much in common with President Obama's health exchange; the Medicare reform plan advanced by former Congressional Budget Office (CBO) director and budget director Alice Rivlin and House Budget Committee chairman Paul Ryan, Medicare Part C; and the German, Dutch, Swiss, Israeli, and Canadian health care systems. No huge surprise here. There aren't fifty ways to properly design a health care system. But the purple health plan has one feature that is unique: it takes and keeps control of government health care spending, ensuring that no more than 10 percent of gross domestic product (GDP) is spent each year.

Staying at No

President Obama has urged that we disagree agreeably. This is good manners, but it doesn't get health care reformed; it only begets ongoing arguments. In fact, there is more agreement on what we need than you would think. If you look carefully at the positions people of all political persuasions are taking, you find that they are often saying the same thing as they scream at one another.

Health care is a good example. When Paul Ryan, Republican House budget director, proposed major Medicare reform in early 2011, it was roundly denounced by President Obama, a sign he was capable of disagreeing disagreeably. Yet Ryan proposed essentially the same Rivlin-Ryan plan that Ryan had proposed a few months earlier in concert with Alice Rivlin.

Alice Rivlin is a distinguished economist and a lifetime Democrat who served as CBO director and budget director under President Clinton. But Rivlin's cover didn't protect Ryan who heard this, in a public address, from the president: "I will not allow Medicare to become a voucher program that leaves seniors at the mercy of the insurance industry, with a shrinking benefit to pay for rising costs."[3]

This strikes us as over the top. The president's health care plan for uninsured young people is effectively a voucher program that involves full participation by the insurance industry. So is the president saying he's okay with leaving young people at the mercy of insurers, but not old people? And his health care bill, the Affordable Care Act, includes major cuts in Medicare, so it's providing a shrinking benefit to pay for rising costs.

In fact, the ACA has tight limits on what insurers can and can't do. In fact, Ryan has those same limits in his plan. So neither the President nor Ryan is proposing unleashing insurance companies on anyone.

For their part, the Republicans castigate Obamacare—the president's health exchange system. Here's Sarah Palin on the president's plan: "Next time he [the president] comes to us with another one of his harebrained proposals for a budget-busting federal power grab, let's make sure we remember the president's admission that he was lying all along when he told us his health care plan was going to cut costs."[4]

Perhaps Ms. Presidential-wannabe might consider that getting 50 million people a health plan when they are otherwise uninsured is hardly harebrained. And since we are covering these folks through the back door—actually, through the emergency room door—when they get sick and can't pay, this is hardly a federal power grab. As for cutting costs, we're with Ms. Palin: costs will exceed what the president forecasts. The

ACA is trying to cut costs along a variety of channels, but costs are still likely to rise.

We're Arguing Over What, Exactly?

Obamacare was designed to replicate Romneycare—the health care reform that former Republican governor Mitt Romney established for Massachusetts. But Romneycare, in terms of design, is essentially Medicare Part C—the Republican part of Medicare, which Democrats just love to hate. But Medicare Part C is simply Ryancare, except that Ryancare would cover all Medicare participants. But—and here's the cake's icing—in terms of its general architecture, Ryancare is Obamacare.

If you are following all this (and we're a bit lost ourselves), the Democrats hate Ryancare because it's Obamacare. And the Republicans hate Obamacare because it's Ryancare. Scratching your head? Starting to feel a strong itch to vote for a third-party candidate? Feeling this set of "leaders," regardless of party, may be doing too little for our own good? We're right there with you.

But let's suspend our disbelief for a moment. Let's assume that our leaders are capable of rational discourse and will eventually understand that if their opponents want what they want, they are to be hugged, not ridiculed.

Agreeing to Agree: Our Shared Health Care Values

Let's start with seven basic principles on which virtually all Americans agree:

1. Everyone needs a basic plan and should be free to purchase supplemental coverage.

2. Health care should be privately provided with free choice of doctors and hospitals.

3. All who can pay for their health plans should do so through taxes and copayments.

4. Government health care spending must be strictly capped relative to GDP so it doesn't drive the country broke.

5. Health plans should be affordable regardless of preexisting health conditions; people should not be penalized for bad genes or bad luck.

6. The system must provide strong incentives to prevent overuse of health care services.

7. Medical malpractice reform is needed to limit defensive medicine.

Hallelujah!

The purple health plan has many of the same features as all the previously mentioned plans. It's the plan we proposed in 2004 in *The Coming Generational Storm*. It was detailed in Kotlikoff's 2007 book, *The Healthcare Fix*.

Perhaps the best part of the plan is what it would end: *the government would immediately shut down Medicare, Medicaid, and the health exchanges, and it would eliminate the tax subsidy to employer-based health care.*

No more Medicare fee-for-service in which Uncle Sam nominally pays all bills but then lowers the fee to the point that doctors say, "Forget it. I'm not taking Medicare patients."

No more Medicaid that has trapped millions of people in poverty for decades by telling them if they earn or save too much money, they will lose their health care coverage.

No more health exchanges whose costs are poised to explode.

And no more employer-based health care, which locks us into our current jobs and permits our employer to decide what health care we do and don't get and how much taxes we pay.

Meeting Our Shared Objectives at Least Cost

Delivering on our objectives is straightforward. The purple health plan's nine features are shown in the postcard in box 9.1.

Each year all Americans would receive a voucher to buy a basic plan, which would cover that person for the entire year. The following year, the person would receive a new voucher. The size of each year's voucher would depend on the individual's objective health care status: those in worse shape will receive larger vouchers commensurate with their higher expected health care costs.

We'd have one efficient system, subject to a stringent 10 percent of GDP budget, which would provide an excellent basic plan for all Americans

Box 9.1
The Purple Health Plan

---

1. All Americans receive a voucher each year to purchase the basic plan.

2. Those with objectively measured preexisting conditions receive larger vouchers.

3. Insurance companies can't deny coverage and must offer the identical basic plan.

4. A panel sets the basic plan's coverages, keeping total voucher costs at 10 percent of GDP.

5. Insurance companies contract with private providers to cover their participants.

6. Americans choose their doctors and hospitals in the network of the plan they select.

7. Insurers provide incentives to improve participants' health.

8. Insurers offer supplemental plans to all participants priced independent of preexisting conditions.

9. Malpractice reform would limit judgments and, thereby, defensive medicine.

---

and not drive the country broke. As for funding this system, the roughly 10 percent of GDP now spent or allocated by federal and state government on health care as well as on the tax exclusion of employer-provided health insurance premiums, would be reallocated to pay for the vouchers.

But Obamacare(s) Includes a Mechanism to Limit Government Health Care Spending

True enough. And that mechanism is prayer or, more precisely, the Independent Payment Advisor Board (IPAB), which was included in the Affordable Care Act. Starting in 2015, IPAB is authorized to limit Medicare reimbursements if per capita spending in that program would otherwise be excessive. IPAB's dictates will go into effect provided Congress doesn't overrule its decisions, which it is very likely to do.

If you want to see a recent history of Congress's overriding provisions that would reduce physicians' and hospital reimbursement rates, just put this into your search engine: "Congress overrides reduction in doctors' reimbursement rates." The fact that IPAB won't even get to work until 2015 is itself indicative that IPAB is a charade.

IPAB is just the latest attempt to wrest control of Medicare spending. By our count, we've had nineteen different Medicare cost-control initiatives in the program's forty-five-year history, and costs are still exploding. From 2008 to 2009, for instance, Medicare spending rose by $40.9 billion, or 8.7 percent.[5]

Fee for Service

There's a reason that nineteen attempts to restrain Medicare spending have failed: fee-for-service, Medicare's method of compensating doctors and hospitals for care. Under fee-for-service, participants receive the service, and Uncle Sam pays the fee. When doctors order more tests or schedule more appointments, Uncle Sam receives more bills and pays them. In other words, Uncle Sam is a built-in customer. If the medical system needs or wants more income, it can, to a large extent, order it up by having its ultimate customer, Uncle Sam, buy more of its services. When Sam tries to limit what's paid for particular services, docs either scream foul or offer "new" services with higher prices.

Health Care Age Discrimination

We do not mean to dump on doctors, many of them general practitioners who are paid very poorly, as our comparison in chapter 6 of the doctor and the plumber shows. When it comes to Medicare, our doctors are stuck dealing with an inefficient, bureaucratic system that has driven many into a different field of work.

Our complaint is not with the doctors but with fee-for-service. Whatever its merits, it has been tried and tested for over forty years, and it has failed miserably. Given the magnitude of our fiscal gap, the proposition that we should maintain it is preposterous.

Yet this is precisely the position the president and the Democratic leadership have taken. "Let's keep it and fix it," they say. "If we can't fix it, IPAB will come to the rescue. We're not going to force the elderly to adapt to a different system."

Remarkably, when it comes to asking the elderly to adjust, the Republicans are just as terrified. Paul Ryan's plan, which is essentially the purple health plan but just for Medicare, changes nothing for those now over age fifty-five. He gives the current elderly a complete pass.

What part of our ethical principles leads us to believe that the elderly are more deserving than the middle aged and young when it comes to health care? If we all had to vote on it, would we vote to give our children inferior health care? We doubt even the elderly would endorse such health care age discrimination.

To be clear, the elderly are in need of more health care because they are older and have on average more medical problems than those in other age groups. But does this entitle them to their own health care system, let alone one that is fully capable on its own of driving the country broke?

The answer is no. Our shared health care values don't include giving sick older folk better care than sick children.

Malpractice Reform

The practice of defensive medicine leads to a similar outcome as fee-for-service in the private health insurance arena. Docs order up more care knowing that if they don't, they may be sued. They also know that the private insurer will pay for the extra care—also out of fear of being sued. Private insurers then shift the burden of this extra care onto their customers by charging them higher premiums. If the customer is an employer, the employer shifts the cost onto his or her employees in the form of providing employees with a smaller wage increase each year.

For the employee to exercise consumer sovereignty on her own, she needs to complain to her employer about the premium she is implicitly paying through the form of lower wage growth. Then the employer has to complain to the insurance company and request a different plan than the insurer is offering other employers and the insurer has to complain to the doctor. No wonder we don't see this happening.

Doctors, hospitals, insurers, and employers need to know that they can safely say no to doing more than they feel is really needed and not face a massive lawsuit if their honest judgment turns out to have been wrong. That's why medical malpractice reform is crucial.

Under the purple health plan, the government's liability is capped. Uncle Sam says to the medical sector, "Here's 10 percent of GDP. This is a huge sum. I'm paying it to you to provide a very generous basic health plan to all Americans. I'm talking the same high level of basic care that the Germans and Swiss receive for the roughly 10 percent of their GDP they are paying for all their health care. And let me be clear: this is all you're getting. You're not getting a penny more because if I pay more, the country goes broke."

Getting Employers Out of the Health Care Business

Our employers are not our parents or our friends. They should not be in the business of deciding what health care we do and don't receive. Nor should they be allowed to decide what taxes we end up paying by providing more or less tax-subsidized health care insurance.

Getting employers out of health care is a critical advantage of the purple health plan. It may also represents a major productivity improvement for the economy. No one knows how many workers have been stuck working in one job when they could be much more productive in another simply because the other job offered an inferior health care plan.

Is the Purple Health Plan Socialized Medicine?

We're not sure what the words *socialized medicine* mean. What we know is that having the government involved in health care is no sin. On the contrary, given the terrible information problems plaguing the health care industry, in which people know a hell of a lot more about their real health problems than the insurer does, government involvement is essential.

Without government involvement, health insurance markets can easily shut down. This is clear from the 50 million Americans now uninsured. The private market isn't providing them health insurance for a simple reason: the insurance companies can't tell who's really sick and who's not. Consequently the companies charge very high premiums to protect themselves against adverse selection by bad insurance risks—people with particularly high probabilities of needing a lot of care. But in charging such high premiums, the "evil" insurers discourage healthy people from buying their policies. Consequently, we end up with what economists call a lemons market.

The term *lemons market* is familiar from used cars, the worst of which are called lemons. People don't put their good used cars up for sale in the used car market because they know that they can't persuade buyers that their cars haven't been in multiple accidents or been driven with no oil in the crankcase. Buyers, since they can't tell what they are buying, presume that they are being sold a lemon and make low offers. As a consequence, only those with true lemons sell their used cars on the market. The good used car owners who can't prove their cars are good, like the good insurance risks who can't prove their health is good, end up priced out of the market. The good used car owners won't sell their baby for a "crappy" price and the good health risks won't buy insurance at an "outrageous" premium.

To deal with lemons markets (also known as cherry-picking) in health insurance, governments and employers create insurance pools and tell insurers they can't turn anyone away. This is like the government's forcing all used car owners to put their cars on the market. As a result, the average quality will rise and buyers will compete with each other and end up paying a higher price for a car that, on average, is of higher quality than without the government "interference" in the private market. In the case of health insurance, forcing everyone into the same pool can make everyone better off. The bad risks get insurance at a lower cost, and the good risks get insurance coverage they'd not otherwise receive.

Controlling Government Spending

Whether or not you like government involvement in health care, it's substantial and not going away. Our private employer-based health care system is heavily subsidized to the tune of $200 billion through federal and state income tax breaks.[6] Medicare and Medicaid cost federal and state governments another $962 billion. And the uninsured are now being covered, albeit poorly, through emergency room and other services, at another $323 billion in public expense.

Add it up, and government health care spending is $1.5 trillion, or almost exactly 10 percent of GDP. We're spending another $1 trillion privately, making our total bill 17 percent of GDP. Germany's population is older, but its total (basic plus extras) health care bill is only 11 percent of GDP. At an extra 55 percent cost, we're delivering unequal health care and worse outcomes. On average, Germans live longer and have lower infant mortality than Americans, who are paying an extra 6 percent of GDP for the privilege of living 1.7 years less than Germans. How's that for a great deal?

The usual response to this is that Germany has a relatively homogeneous population and we don't. But while black Americans have shorter life expectancies at birth than white Americans do, the U.S. white-only life expectancy at birth is only 0.5 years higher than the comparable figure for blacks. So, controlling for race, the United States is still shorter lived even though we spend 55 percent more on health care than Germany does. This sad reality opens an enormous opportunity to reform health care and make a gigantic dent in the fiscal gap.

We know the opportunities are there. So do you. We need only read a daily newspaper to be regaled with stories of spending that our children can't afford and that oldsters, when asked, agree: they wouldn't spend it either. Bob Svensson, an eighty-year-old patient with prostate cancer in Boston, received $93,000 of treatment with Provenge, a new drug. On average it extends life four months. Asked if he would spend the money if he did not have insurance, he said: "I would not spend that money."[7]

What most people fear in the discussion of health care is that they will lose something. But when you look at the life expectancy figures, it is more likely that getting control of health care spending will not only save our country, it may lengthen lives. More spending doesn't necessarily mean better care. It simply means more spending.

President Dwight Eisenhower once warned Americans about the military-industrial complex. Today we have another complex to worry about, the pharma-medical-insurance complex. It is the basis of the "supply-driven" health care that Dr. John E. Wennberg, cofounder of the Foundation for Informed Medical Decision Making, suggests is the cause for millions of Americans being overtreated.[8]

The purple health plan says let's spend at the government level the same 10 percent we're now spending on health care, but use it to give everyone in the country an excellent basic plan—comparable to what the Germans are getting. Moreover, let's make sure we keep government health care spending at no higher than 10 percent of GDP. The CBO forecasts this spending to rise to 24 percent of GDP over the next seventy-five years.[9] That can't happen. That's certain economic death.

The Purple Health Panel

To make sure that our economy doesn't die in the process of trying to keep everyone alive, the purple health plan establishes a panel of doctors—the purple health panel. (Call it the fiscal survival panel, if you like, or the death panel, if you must. We don't care. It's a panel.) The panel's job is to decide what coverages are included in the basic plan that everyone receives in exchange for her or his voucher. As the economy grows in real terms, the panel will be able to add more coverages to the basic plan—new medications, tests, procedures, and so on.

The key point, though, is that the panel will live within a completely firm lid of 10 percent of GDP on federal health care spending. Under the purple plan, Congress gives that much, and no more, to the panel to hand out in vouchers each year. The panel then determines what can be added to the basic plan's coverages each year so that the new vouchers being handed out for that year won't add up to more than 10 percent of GDP. In making these calculations, the panel will use individual risk adjustment software, which already exists, as well as electronic medical records that record our preexisting objective health conditions.

To illustrate what's involved here, suppose the panel considers including a new drug for diabetes in the basic plan. It then determines how much larger each diabetic's voucher will need to be to compensate insurance companies for covering this extra expense. If the resulting total increased cost of the vouchers doesn't break the 10 percent of GDP budget, it will be included. Otherwise it won't be included unless the panel chooses to scale back some other new coverage or eliminate something that has been covered thus far.

Private Provision

The purple health plan doesn't mess with our system of private provision of health care. Although the government gives each of us a voucher to buy the identical health plan, we get to choose the insurance provider. We may select a provider, like Kaiser Permanente, that hires doctors directly and builds and owns its own hospitals, and lets us select among its doctors and hospitals in seeking care.

Or we may choose an insurance provider, like Blue Cross Blue Shield, which has us choose our doctors and hospitals, which are operating independently and simply reimburses these health care providers. Either way, the purple health plan lets people see their own doctors and go to the hospitals they choose.

Commoditizing Health Care and Ending Insurance Abuse

The fact that the exact same plan is being provided by competing companies turns health insurance into a basic commodity. No one will need to read the fine print of a particular company's plan to know that this disease, test, or procedure is covered and those are not. Such games have been used over the years by insurance companies to try to cherry-pick their customers and skimp on what they covered.

Under the purple health plan, cherry picking is ended. Insurers are compensated up front for the extra costs associated with insuring people with preexisting conditions or simply higher objective probabilities (e.g., based on age) of incurring higher costs. Hence, insurers won't have an incentive to cherry-pick. Nor will they be able to do so since they aren't permitted to refuse full coverage in exchange for the voucher.

Since what's covered is crystal clear and the same for all health plans, there will be no, "Sorry, you missed reading paragraph 432 in section a, subchapter 14f, subsection 84231-aa7 that says your bursitis is not included." Finally, because we'll have a single health care policy with a single billing system, there will be a major reduction in insurance company administrative costs.

Why Private Vouchers? Just Have Uncle Sam Pay Insurers Directly

Obamacare(s), Ryancare, and Medicare Part C are effectively voucher plans, but ones that hand the insurance companies the vouchers directly: people simply choose a health plan and the government sends the insurer a check that differs depending on the person's expected health care cost. Premiums are assessed on a progressive basis in all three plans.

Under the purple health plan people, each of us receives a voucher in the mail or electronically. The goal here is to make each of us aware of exactly what our government is paying on our behalf before deciding which basic plan provider to choose. Furthermore, the government is not really paying for our vouchers. We are, so we should get to see how much *we* are spending before deciding how to spend it. This will make us think more carefully in selecting among plans. It will also help everyone see whether the system is delivering our money's worth.

Why Bother with Insurance Companies?

Everyone hates insurance companies. They aren't our favorites either. They've focused on cherry picking, have left a huge number of people uninsured, and have wasted massive amounts of money on administration and advertising. Worse yet, they've done far too little to help limit increases in the prices of medical goods and services and have not provided badly needed carrots and sticks to get us to improve our health.

So why bother with insurance companies?

The advantage of having private insurers is they can compete with one another to provide the best health care per voucher dollar. They can also experiment to give us the best financial incentives to improve our health. The financial incentives would include paying those who are overweight to lower their weight, paying those who smoke to lower their nicotine levels, paying those who drink to lower their breathalizer scores, paying those who use drugs for testing drug free, and so on.

We're not talking here about taking the patient's word for it. We're talking about objective medical tests done in the doctor's office and in the lab. It's also important to realize that a carrot can always be described as a stick, and vice versa. Thus, the insurers could tell their patients with condition X that can be improved with behavior Y, "Hey. Here's this money I'm going to give you at the end of the year. It's yours. But if you screw up and don't improve health measures A, B, and C in the testing we're going to do over the course of the year, we're taking this money away."

Economists refer to these kinds of incentives or penalties, if you prefer that language, as "getting the prices right." The Medicare system is an example of getting the prices wrong. Our private insurance system, focused on using prices (premium charges) to cherry-pick, gets prices wrong too. The purple health plan naturally leads insurers to get the prices right. First, it precludes their cherry picking. Second, it makes them bear, in terms of lost profits, the costs of every extra dollar spent on providing basic health care. Consequently they have the right incentives to control costs.

Now imagine basic health care evolving under the purple health plan to large health maintenance organizations (HMOs) that dominate the insurance market. Since HMOs pay their doctors an annual fixed salary, HMO doctors have no direct financial incentive to provide too much care. But if they provide too little care, their patients will take next year's vouchers and go elsewhere the next year. So the HMO fully internalizes the incentives against both over- and underproviding health care.

This also holds true when it comes to hospital utilization. Since HMOs own their own hospitals, they have no incentive to keep people in the hospital longer than needed. But since they will be competing with other HMOs as well as non-HMO insurers, they also have strong incentives to make sure no one is released too soon from a hospital.

As we write, we are anticipating getting lots of e-mail from people who have had bad or really bad experiences with HMOs. Not all that's gold glitters. Nothing in life is perfect, and the purple health plan will fall short in some areas compared to what we have. But the best we can do is set up a system that clearly meets our shared social values with respect to health care, eliminates cherry picking, gets prices right (provides the right incentives for neither over or underuse of the system), and puts the government on a strict health care spending budget.

Finally, private insurers can form very important buffers between the panel, Congress, and voters, who want the system to cover more than it can afford.

Supplemental Policies

Under the purple health plan, we'd all be free, if we can afford it, to buy supplemental insurance. Our insurance plans are required to offer supplemental plans. In so doing, they can't turn us down or kick us out. Nor can they set the premiums for supplemental coverage based on preexisting conditions.

The reason for these restrictions is to eliminate cherry picking by insurers in the market for supplemental policies. If need be, the panel could specify a menu of supplemental policies that each insurer would need to offer as well as the prices they could charge. If this feels like too much of a deviation from a free market in health care, all we can say is that free markets in health care don't work because of the severe information problem discussed above. Health care is not wheat. If it were, the private sector would be providing it with no problem.

10

There Must Be Some Way Out of Here

When Winston Churchill famously said, "Americans can always be counted on to do the right thing . . . after they have exhausted all the other possibilities," he might have been thinking of the American tax system. Unfortunately we're still working on all the wrong possibilities and doing the wrong thing.

Our tax system is well beyond the need for reform. Today it needs to be reinvented. The existing system is terribly inefficient, highly inequitable, and horribly complex. It also discourages work and saving. Thanks to a virtual encyclopedia of tax loopholes, the system generates remarkably little revenue. It is also surprisingly less progressive than is commonly believed. Indeed, our panoply of positive and negative taxes, called tax exemptions, credits, and transfer payments, leaves many of the poor in very high tax brackets—higher than many of the rich. When all our tax rules and taxes are put together, it turns out that, with the exception of those earning the minimum wage, we all pay taxes at a remarkably high, and flat, rate. So if you think taxes aren't fair, tax rates are too high, and tax revenue is too low, you're right.

Complexity beyond Measure

Our system of taxes and transfers has so many interconnected parts that it's virtually impossible to assimilate them all. That's why, with only two exceptions, no economists have dared try to assess their collective impact. It's also why we can safely say that *no one in Congress understands the combined impact of these different programs on our incentives to work and save, let alone whom the system rewards and penalizes on balance.* Unfortunately, that doesn't keep them from talking about taxes as though they did understand how taxpayers were going to be affected.

For starters, let's just name the biggest elements of our tax and transfer system: the federal income tax, the federal corporate income tax, the Social Security FICA tax, the Medicare FICA tax, federal excise taxes, the federal estate and gift tax, state income taxes, state corporate income taxes, state sales taxes, state estate taxes, the Food Stamps program, the Transitional Aid to Families with Dependent Children program, Medicaid benefits, Medicare benefits, and Social Security benefits. You probably don't think of the last five programs as part of our tax system, but they are in the most fundamental way. Our collective cost burden of government isn't just the things we call taxes; it's what we pay in taxes net of what we receive in transfer payments that really hits our pocketbooks. Right-wing politicians who want to claim that taxes are too high focus on gross taxes and ignore transfer payments. Left-wing politicians do the same things when discussing Social Security's payroll tax, which, taken by itself (i.e., ignoring the system's progressive benefit formula) is regressive. Choosing whether to discuss gross or net taxes is part of the labeling game discussed earlier. It also lets politicians engage in economically ridiculous fights over whether taxes should be cut or spending on transfer payments increased. Cutting a person's taxes is no different from raising her transfer payments since both reduce net taxes.

Look carefully at our fourteen fiscal programs, and you'll find that each of these systems has a tax schedule. Some have more than one. For example, the federal income tax has exemptions, deductions, and tax credits. It also has the beloved alternative minimum tax.[1] Any, or all, of these items can kick in or kick out depending on the household's adjusted gross income, number and ages of children, and marital status.

If you want to know why so many Americans are so angry with Washington, just spend a few hours with the IRS 1040 form and its pages of worksheets, side calculations, and eight separate tax schedules. And if you find this daunting, the IRS provides a handy instruction booklet that runs a scant 179 pages, not counting actual tax forms.

More recently our Washington representatives have taken the complexity of taxation to the next level. They did this by way of two recent tax-transfer system changes: Medicare Part B premiums and the Medicare FICA tax.[2] Starting in 2007, Medicare assessed its premiums on a progressive basis using a two-year look-back formula with respect to modified adjusted gross income (MAGI). The early documentation brags that only 5 percent of all Medicare beneficiaries will be subject to these higher premiums.

But there's a catch: the thresholds for getting hit with the extra premium, which can be really large, aren't indexed for inflation.[3] Washington, having learned that a delayed tax is a good tax from the taxation of Social Security benefits initiated in 1983, has set the same delayed ire trap.

Our children, poor and rich alike, can look forward to paying much higher premiums than we pay, adjusted for both inflation and growth (we hope) in the level of real wages. How much higher? Well, if you're now thirty years old and trying to plan for retirement and want to understand the size of the premiums you'll face at, say, age seventy-five, you'll need to consider what inflation will be over the next forty-five years. You'll also need to know what your MAGI will be at ages seventy-four and seventy-three. Good luck. This is essentially impossible to get right without advanced life cycle planning technology.

But, wait! There's more. In 2010, as part of the Affordable Care Act (ACA), Uncle Sam instituted two new Medicare taxes. One is a weasely shiv of an additional tax: 0.9 percent for single workers making more than $200,000 and married workers making more than $250,000. The other is no shiv; it's more like a shot from Dirty Harry's 357 magnum. It's a 3.8 percent asset income tax for single and married households with MAGIs above these same thresholds. Again, these thresholds aren't indexed for inflation, so the politicians get to pass the most popular kind of tax today—any tax paid by someone else—knowing that almost everyone will pay it in a tomorrow that is quite a few elections removed. What's the bottom line to these base provisions? Our kids can expect to pay an extra 3.8 percent tax on their asset income.

These two new Medicare taxes take effect in 2013. They were buried deep in the 2,700 pages of the ACA, so it's no surprise that most American workers and savers have no idea these taxes exist. Our forefathers fought the War of Independence to eliminate taxation without representation. And our representatives have given us *taxation without cognition.*

If our elected officials had the vaguest idea what they were doing to the overall level and distribution of net tax burdens, we'd have to give them credit for being smart, albeit in a really devious way. But even the representation part is questionable. Members of Congress were handed the complex and highly detailed ACA within seventy-two hours of being forced to vote on it. Nancy Pelosi, then Speaker of the House, famously told the members they could read the bill after they approved it.[4] This is a little like clicking Accept to a software license you haven't read only to discover you've agreed to sacrifice your firstborn to get tech support.

Our guess is that even Nancy Pelosi had no clue about the failure to inflation-index the two new Medicare taxes. This was likely the brainstorm of some Congressional staffers charged by their bosses to come up with enough money to make the numbers work for the President's health bill.

Marginal Tax Brackets—Neither Rhyme nor Reason

The only two truly comprehensive studies of our total marginal effective tax rates are those of one of us (Kotlikoff) and his coauthors.[5] The most recent of these, based on 2005 tax-transfer provisions, took a year to complete.[6] That's how much time is involved if you want to carefully include each of the tax-transfer programs and their abstruse interactions in a single computer program.

The findings can be described in one word: *insane.*

Take a married couple, both thirty years old and earning $30,000 in today's dollars, with two children. Assume the couple makes the same amount in the future. This couple is living at the poverty line, but their marginal tax bracket is a daunting 42 percent. The reason, in large part, is the earned income tax credit, which claws back the subsidy it provides very low earners to the tune of roughly 20 cents on the dollar for every dollar earned above a specified threshold.

Now suppose the same couple makes not $30,000 but $50,000 a year. Their tax bracket is much lower: only 24 percent.

Can this really be what Nancy Pelosi, House minority leader, and other Democrats who advocate tax progressivity have in mind? We doubt it. Table 10.1 shows how remarkably flat (and high) our tax burden is across all levels of income from $20,000 to $500,000.

When we raise the couple's earnings to $150,000, the tax bracket is 46 percent. At $500,000, it's 44 percent. At the other extreme, at $10,000 in earnings, the marginal tax bracket is minus 14 percent. So the marginal tax rate starts negative, immediately rises dramatically, then falls dramatically, rises dramatically again, and then falls again, albeit slightly.[7]

Table 10.1
The tax rate we really pay: The de facto flat tax

Age	$20,000	$30,000	$50,000	$75,000	$100,000	$150,000	$200,000	$300,000	$500,000
30	42.5%	42.3%	24.4%	36.9%	37.0%	45.9%	36.8%	43.9%	44.0%
45	41.7	41.8	35.8	36.1	36.1	45.1	35.9	40.9	43.2
60	32.0	36.3	36.5	45.5	45.5	47.7	43.2	45.8	45.0

Note: This table shows the all-tax marginal tax rate for couples, as calculated by Kotlikoff and Rapson.
Source: Laurence J. Kotlikoff and David Rapson, "Does It Pay, at the Margin, to Work and Save?" NBER working paper no. 12533 (Cambridge, MA: NBER, 2006).

If this same couple were sixty years old in 2005, they'd be in a 51 percent (not a negative 14 percent) bracket at $10,000 in earnings, a 36 percent (not a 42 percent) tax bracket at $30,000 in earnings, a 36 percent (not a 24 percent) bracket at $50,000 in earnings, a 48 percent (not a 46 percent) bracket at $150,000 in earnings, and a 45 percent (not a 44 percent) bracket at $500,000.

Why is government (federal and state combined) placing the thirty-year-old married couple who is earning $30,000 in a 6 percentage point higher tax bracket than the thirty-year-older version of the same couple? And why is it sticking the sixty-year-old $50,000 couple in a 12 percent higher tax bracket than the corresponding thirty-year-younger version? We doubt Dave Camp, chairman of the House Ways and Means Committee, has an answer, because this discriminatory treatment will surely be as new to Dave as it will be to Nancy Pelosi.

Whether the public itself correctly perceives the marginal taxes it faces is an interesting question. If not, people may be working much less or much more than they would if they really understood the work incentives they face. Either way, there's potentially a significant economic cost arising from such mistakes.

Who Said the United States Is a Low-Tax Country?

For my (Kotlikoff) coauthor and me, students of public finance for our entire professional careers, discovering precisely what the tax-transfer system really looks like, in all its combined glory, was both exciting and somewhat surprising. Leaving aside the anomalies, our tax-transfer system puts virtually all American workers into 35 to 45 percent tax brackets. This means that on every extra dollar earned, typical American workers, including virtually all welfare recipients, pay the government 35 to 45 cents in extra taxes net of what they receive back (which is typically negative) in extra benefits.

For the poor (except those making less than $10,000 per year), the generally high marginal tax brackets primarily reflect the 15.3 percent (employer plus employee) FICA tax plus the loss, on extra dollars earned, of two things—tax credits and welfare payments, including food stamps, Medicaid, and other benefits. For the middle class, the generally high marginal tax brackets reflect the FICA tax and middling-level federal marginal tax rates. And for the rich, the generally high marginal tax brackets reflect their position in the highest (35 percent) bracket of the federal income tax. The two Medicare taxes, at 0.9 percent and 3.8 percent, effectively erase the much reviled Bush tax cuts for the wealthy of 2004.

Taxing Our Saving

Our tax and transfer system does more than penalize work. It also discourages saving. If there were no taxation of saving, we could sock away an extra dollar and get to spend that dollar plus interest in the future. Measured in present value, our future spending would equal one dollar. So whether we spent the money now or in the future, the present value of our spending would always be one dollar.

But with taxes on saving, the present value of what we get to spend if we spend in the future is less than one dollar. The reason is simple: we don't receive the full return on our saving. Why? Because federal and state governments take a chunk of that return from us in the form of taxes on corporate income, noncorporate business income, dividends, capital, interest income, rental income, and other types of investment returns.

The marginal taxation of saving, when you combine all the different forms of this taxation, also produces crazy patterns by age and income. But in the main, we face a 20 to 35 percent tax on saving, regardless of whether we are poor or rich. In other words, that extra dollar of spending you forgo this year and save affords you only between 65 and 80 cents in future consumption when measured as the value today (the present value) of that future consumption.

A 20 to 35 percent effective tax on saving is pretty big—big enough to get us to think seriously about how much we really want to save. As we have already shown, Americans don't want to save. Given that our country is spending like mad, penalizing people for saving compounds the problem.

The Purple Tax Plan

The current tax system, in addition to being a monster, has encouraged borrowing and discouraged saving, exactly the opposite of what we need to be doing given the benefits we've promised everyone as they become old. We can no longer afford a dysfunctional and distortive tax system. Most politicians, whether from red or blue states, agree. Then they go on and fiddle some more with the existing monster.

We say time's up. It's time to reinvent our tax system altogether. The tax-paying public is ready. Sadly, the biggest impediment to reinventing our tax system is the army of accountants and lawyers who make their living adding new warts to an already ugly machine.

The purple tax plan is a simple, transparent, efficient, and progressive tax system that should appeal to both parties. In conjunction with the other reforms presented here, the plan will help the economy save, grow, produce jobs, and deliver higher wages.

As the postcard in box 10.1 indicates, the purple tax plan replaces the federal personal and corporate income taxes as well as the estate and gift tax with a broad-based, low-rate, progressive consumption tax and a low-rate, progressive inheritance tax. It also makes the highly regressive FICA payroll tax highly progressive. The plan eliminates the need for households to file tax returns and enormously simplifies business tax compliance. It also eliminates all taxation of saving.

As described at www.thepurpletaxplan.org, the purple tax plan taxes all of consumption, including the consumption services enjoyed from homes, boats, planes, cars, and other major durables that households own. But households in economic distress are permitted to defer their tax payments on the services from their homes. Also, to make certain that low-income households have a low tax burden, it provides a grant that

Box 10.1
The Purple Tax Plan

---

1. Replaces federal personal and corporate income taxes with a 17.5 percent retail sales tax.

2. Taxes all consumption purchases plus consumption services from homes, boats, planes, cars, and other major durables.

3. Taxes annual consumption purchased abroad above $5,000.

4. Provides an option to pay a consumption tax up front as a 15 percent tax on wages and wealth.

5. Demogrant based on family composition set high enough to ensure that the poor pay no sales tax on net.

6. Exempts first $40,000 of earnings from the employee portion of FICA payroll tax. Uses FICA tax to provide EITC and child tax credits.

7. Eliminates the ceiling on the FICA payroll tax.

8. Subjects to FICA taxation all income from ownership rights in businesses for which one works.

9. Taxes inheritances (accumulated gifts and bequests received) over $1 million at 15 percent. Eliminates estate and gift taxes.

10. In transition, taxes at 15 percent all tax-deferred assets, pensions, and capital gains.

---

rebates expected consumption sales tax payments up to a certain level of spending.

The tax base includes all consumption, whether by households, governments, nonprofits, or businesses. But its revenues are sufficient to permit governments to cover their sales tax payments.

Paying Sales Taxes Up Front

To clarify the equivalence between taxing consumption and taxing current wealth and current and future wages, the purple tax plan could, if desired, be modified to let us to pay our "consumption tax" at the time we purchase consumption goods and services or up front, as a direct tax on our current wealth and current and future wages. Taxes paid up front would give us electronic sales tax credits, for use when shopping. This would leave us indifferent between paying taxes up front or at the store. A simple mechanism for providing this credit is at time of purchase when we use our debit cards and credit cards. Unused sales tax credits would earn interest so there would be no disadvantage to waiting to spend.

Why the Plan Is Progressive

One of the surprises in the purple tax plan is that we can have a highly progressive tax system without high marginal tax rates. The plan features much lower marginal tax rates than the current system. Yet it achieves, we believe, a much more progressive distribution of tax burdens. It should also generate substantially more revenue. This is due not to supply-side, trickle-down effects, but simply to the very broad base of the plan's consumption tax.

Many people view consumption taxation, imposed as a fixed-rate retail sales tax, as regressive. The same people tend to view the taxation of wealth, in addition to wages, at a fixed rate as progressive. Since doing one is mathematically and functionally equivalent to doing the other, both views can't be correct. In fact, both are wrong.

Taxing consumption, or, equivalently, the resources used to pay for consumption at a fixed rate, is neither progressive nor regressive. It is proportional: if you double economic resources (current wealth plus current and future wages), you double the consumption that those resources will finance when both quantities are properly measured as present values. Hence, with a fixed consumption tax rate, doubling economic resources will double consumption and the associated taxes.

Regardless of how one pays the purple tax plan's sales tax—at the store or up front based on one's wages and wealth—the *demogrant*,[8] a rebate of consumption taxes up to a certain level of spending, makes it progressive. The demogrant is large enough to ensure that those living at or below the poverty line pay no tax, on net, on their consumption.[9]

The purple tax plan also makes the FICA tax highly progressive by eliminating the employee half of the tax on the first $40,000 of earnings and getting rid of the ceiling on taxable earnings. Finally, the plan includes a tax on inheritance (in the form of either gifts received or bequests) above $1 million. In combination, these three elements will make the purple tax plan, in our view, more progressive, when properly measured, than the current tax system.

Taxing inheritance rather than estates is something long overdue. If Joe has $10 million, drops dead, and leaves it to all to one person, Joe's wealth remains highly concentrated. If Joe leaves his money uniformly to 1,000 people, each inherits $10,000 and it's not a big deal. In taxing inheritance above $1 million, the purple tax plan gives the wealthy an incentive to spread out their bequests and gifts over more recipients. The more people they spread their money over, the lower will be the average inheritance tax paid on what they leave because each new recipient comes with a $1 million exemption from the inheritance tax.

Can the Rich Avoid the Sales Tax by Not Spending?

You've claimed that facing a sales tax is the same as immediately paying taxes on your wages and your wealth. But how can that be? I can avoid paying the sales tax simply by not spending.

No, you can't. To see why, consider a very rich man. Midas has $30 billion. His favorite food is steak. Before the sales tax is levied, Midas can purchase 30 billion steaks at $1 per steak. (He wrangled a special price with the local restaurant.) After the sales tax is levied, the price of steak rises by 17.5 percent, so Midas's $30 billion will no longer buy 30 billion steaks. Now his $30 billion will buy only 25.5 billion steaks—15 percent fewer.

This is terribly upsetting to Midas, who relishes his meat. So he says to himself, "I can avoid this tax by waiting a year, investing my money, and buying more steak next year."

But then he realizes that he's going to face the same sales tax a year from now. Waiting to spend his money doesn't avoid the tax; it just postpones chow time. Whenever he buys steak, he's going to end up with 15 percent less than he would if there were no tax.

Midas puts it this way: "I'm sitting here with the same 30 billion pieces of green paper marked $1 dollar on each, but if the prices of what I want to buy rise immediately by 17.5 percent and stay there forever, I'm immediately hurt. My purchasing power is cut by 15 percent immediately. This is no different from Uncle Sam's just taking $4.5 billion from me today and not imposing the sales tax. It's also no different from Uncle Sam's telling me, 'Midas, you owe us $4.5 billion right now, but we'll give you the option of paying the $4.5 billion with interest at any point down the road. If you want, give your money to your kids, either now or in the future. But just realize that 15 percent of what you give is ours.'"

Work, Saving, and Investment Incentives

Note that all three taxes—the sales tax, the FICA tax, and the inheritance tax—are levied at 15 percent rates. It's true that we'll pay 17.5 percent on our purchases at the store, but that's equivalent to a 15 percent tax on our wages and wealth. Here's how that works. If we start with $1 and spend it at the store, we end up with 85 cents of consumption. The other 15 cents goes to pay for the sales tax. To spend 85 cents at the store after the sales tax, the sales tax rate must be 15 cents divided by your 85 cents of consumption or 17.5 percent.

For low-income workers, paying an effective 15 percent tax on their wages via the sales tax plus 7.5 percent in FICA equates to a 22.5 percent total marginal tax rate. That's lower than what many low-income workers now pay at the margin. For middle- and higher-income workers, the marginal tax is 15 percent plus 15 percent, or 30 percent. It too is lower than most of these workers pay if they aren't cheating on their taxes or using loopholes to avoid them. Both low- and middle-income earners will pay less in taxes overall, since the purple tax shifts more of the tax burden on the wealthy.

How about the federal marginal tax on saving? Well, it's zero. Recall that the purple tax plan eliminates the personal and corporate income taxes. Both of these taxes are levied on asset income. Hence, if you give up a dollar of current consumption in favor of future consumption, you get to consume the full dollar when measured as a present value.

It's true that if you save to leave money to others and they are subject to the inheritance tax, this use of your dollar will entail a 15 percent present value cost. But this constitutes a significantly lower tax on saving than exists under the current system. In addition, much of the money that ends up being inherited does not reflect intentional bequests. Instead, many people die with positive wealth out of fear that they won't die on time: they don't spend their wealth because they don't know how long they will live, and they choose not to purchase annuities that can help hedge this risk.

As we showed in figure 4.1, raising national saving is critical to increasing domestic investment. By improving saving incentives and in taxing wealth, which is owned primarily by the elderly, who have higher propensities to spend than the young, the purple tax plan should lead to substantially more saving and investment than the current system does. But the biggest immediate stimulus to investment will be the elimination of the corporate income tax. Multinational companies choose where to invest based in part on the tax environment where they intend to invest. If it is too high, they will invest elsewhere. By eliminating the corporate income tax, the United States will move immediately to becoming the lowest-tax country. It should garner an extraordinarily large increase in foreign investment. It should also lead to the repatriation of billions in corporate profits that have been retained overseas to avoid domestic taxation. America will be open for investment to all.

Treatment of Social Security Recipients

Social Security recipients would be fully insulated from the increase in prices associated with the purple tax plan's sales tax. The reason is that their benefits are indexed to the consumer price index. In addition, since Social Security recipients, like everyone else, would receive the monthly demogrant (tax rebate), those living solely on Social Security would end up with more purchasing power under the purple tax plan than under the existing system.

Tax Compliance, Administration, and Avoidance

Under the purple tax plan, we can pay our federal sales tax at the store and have our employer submit our FICA taxes and, bingo, no more tax compliance costs[10] for America's 113 million households.[11]

Although there are no precise figures for what it's costing to comply with our current tax system, our sense is that we're talking 1 to 2 percent of GDP—a considerable sum. Just think of all the accountants and tax attorneys you know. Now think about the kind of cars they drive, and you'll get sense of the amount of money, not to mention lives, being wasted complying with a tax system that no one can fully follow. Rather than spend their lives helping us pay as little as possible in taxes, all of these often extremely talented people will be freed up to make more positive social contributions.

But what about tax avoidance? Aren't people always doing a lot to avoid sales taxes? The major concern with tax avoidance in the purple tax plan involves Americans' spending their wages and wealth overseas, thereby avoiding the retail sales tax. The purple tax plan requires Americans to pay taxes on overseas purchases of consumption goods and services in excess of $5,000 per year. This includes enjoying the services of homes, cars, yachts, planes, and other durables purchased abroad.

Getting people to pay taxes on their overseas consumption may not be simple, but the broad reform will free up huge numbers of IRS employees to work on this issue. Keeping the tax low at the 15 percent effective rate and making a few examples of high-profile tax avoiders, and also levying very stiff fines on overseas tax evasion can make this a minor rather than a major problem for the purple tax plan.

Is this a big change? You bet. But the reality is that we need major change if we are to become a nation that saves and invests as well as spends and borrows.

Transition Rules

In moving to the new system, the purple tax plan would tax at a 15 percent rate pensions and 401(k), regular individual retirement account, and other tax-deferred retirement account assets on which future taxes are due under the current tax system. The 15 percent tax would also be applied to unrealized capital gains on existing business and private assets, calculated as of the date of the reform.

These transition taxes are based on actions people have taken in the past: they don't affect the improved incentives to work and save at the margin that the purple tax plan would provide.

11

Time to Retire

Social Security is old. In 2010, it celebrated its seventy-fifth birthday. Love it or hate it, it has done its job. We think it should retire. We need a new system, the purple social security plan (see www.thepurplesocialsecurityplan.org). The new system will retain Social Security's best features, scrap the rest, and cover its costs.

Don't Toss the Baby Out with the Bathwater

Social Security's objective—forcing people to save for retirement—is not only legitimate; it's extremely important. Otherwise millions of us would seek handouts in our old age. Without Social Security millions of Americans would be gerontological versions of Tennessee Williams's Blanche DuBois, depending "on the kindness of strangers."

Even libertarians, the folks who hate government rules, regulations, and taxes, support compulsion when it comes to saving for retirement. The Cato Institute in Washington, D.C., is the leading libertarian organization in the United States, but its proposals for Social Security reform march hand in hand with those from the political left: they require people to save.

The reason is not political expediency. Libertarians, like most of the rest of us, actually care about more than just themselves. So their pursuit of self-interest entails helping others, particularly elderly poor who have little means of self-support. They opt for compulsory saving because they know that unless people are forced to save when young, they will under-save, knowing that others will help take care of them when old.

This doesn't require differences across people. Imagine a country consisting of 10 million identical strict libertarians, but all with a soft spot for oldsters who are poor. Then with no requirement that they need to save, each of the 10 million will have an incentive, when young, to save less, knowing that he or she can turn to others when old for a handout.

This is called the *Samaritan's dilemma*. A good Samaritan faces a problem. If she follows Jesus's advice and helps the wretched person she encounters on the road, that same person is likely to find her tomorrow and ask for more help, and do the same the day after. To protect herself from such future requests, the good Samaritan forces her donee to take steps to help himself.

The fact that Social Security is essential doesn't mean we need to retain it in its current form for all eternity. Despite its many virtues, Social Security has morphed into something of a monster over the past seventy-five years. Although it has lifted the elderly out of poverty, it has also played a central role in the fiscal child abuse that is better known as postwar U.S. fiscal policy. All those 10 million libertarians in our hypothetical libertarian Mecca may care about each other, but if they don't care much or enough about the next generation, they will, out of self-interest, likely seek to exploit it, their principles notwithstanding.

The System Is Broke

In 1983, the Greenspan Commission supposedly put Social Security on a firm long-term financial footing. It was, they said, good for another seventy-five years. But that's not even close to how it has worked out. Now, a scant twenty-eight years later, the system is running cash flow deficits. Benefit outlays now exceed tax receipts. Today it is in worse long-term fiscal shape than it was then. Indeed, Social Security is so broke that it can no longer afford to mail us our annual benefit statements, something it's been doing since the mid-1980s. This isn't just a matter of paying for the mailings. The system can't even afford to put our benefit statements online.

Think what this means. For the vast majority of us, Social Security is our primary form of retirement saving. And this system, to which we are contributing 12.4 cents out of every dollar we earn, is telling us we can't see what we've contributed, we can't verify that our contributions have been properly recorded, and we can't double-check that we're receiving the right benefits. Any private sector pension system that stopped sending annual benefit statements would be violating the Employee Retirement Income Security Act, the law governing private pensions. But Social Security isn't a private pension, it is a public pension, so it is free to make up its own law.

But let's return to our main question. How broke is Social Security? Very!

To get a precise measure of the financial debacle Social Security faces, take a look at table IV.B6 on page 66 of the *Social Security Trustees Report for 2011*.[1] This table reports the infinite horizon fiscal gap for the system. It shows that the system is 29 percent underfunded, meaning it needs an immediate and permanent 29 percent hike in its payroll tax rate to ensure it can pay all its bills over time.

The Social Security payroll tax rate is 12.4 percent. Increasing that rate by 29 percent requires raising the payroll tax rate starting today by 3.6 percentage points and keeping the rate at 16.0 percent forever. A 3.6 percentage point tax hike may seem small at first thought, but at second thought it's huge. We only have 100 pennies of every dollar to hand over to the various governments that are picking our pockets. And with virtually all of us in 35 to 45 percent marginal tax brackets, adding another 3.6 percentage points is a big deal.

You can get an idea how big a deal this distortion is by turning to a rule of thumb that economists use: the economic damage done by a tax distortion rises with the square of the tax rate. If you square a 40 percent marginal tax rate, you get 0.16. If you square a 43.6 percent marginal tax rate, you get 0.19. This means we're talking about a 19 percent [(0.19–0.16)/.16] higher distortion.

And that's just the issue of economic inefficiency. There's also the thing so nasty that neither party ever speaks of it: generational justice.

Thomas Jefferson on Generational Equity

Should today's twenty year olds be forced to surrender an extra 3.3 percent of every dollar they make each year, for the rest of their lives, in order to maintain all the benefits going to older generations? Mind now, these benefits were legislated before today's twenty year olds were born, so they had absolutely no say over their size.

Let's look at what Thomas Jefferson thought about this issue:

The earth belongs to each of these generations during its course, fully and in its own right. The second generation receives it clear of the debts and incumbrances of the first, the third of the second, and so on. For if the first could charge it with a debt, then the earth would belong to the dead and not to the living generation. Then, no generation can contract debts greater than may be paid during the course of its own existence.[2]

Jefferson wouldn't be welcome at an AARP meeting. Nor do we subscribe entirely to Jefferson's view. Clearly encumbrances go in both directions. Older generations do a great deal for their children and grandchildren. They feed, clothe, shelter, and educate them when young and help many of them receive higher educations. The generations are also here to help each other insure against cohort-specific risks, be it from a depression or a world war.

The real question is not whether debts incurred by older generations should be paid by the younger ones. The real question is whether older generations have been using the fiscal system, wittingly or not, to pile on those debts. Have the older generations taken far more from the young than is their due? Has modern politics found a form of taxation without representation that King George would have envied? The answer is unequivocal: the old have been stealing from the young, and that generational theft continues in full force.

Who, then, should pay to fix Social Security? Most public discussions proceed, without a second thought, from the proposition that middle-aged and young generations should pay. It is somehow a given that today's elderly should be left entirely off the hook. That's why there are proposals for gradually raising the retirement age, gradually cutting benefits by changing Social Security's wage-indexing benefit formula, and gradually increasing the taxation of Social Security benefits. The word *gradually* sounds benign, but its actual effect is brutal. Passing the buck from the old to the young leaves oldsters off the hook and puts youngsters on the hook.

In addition to their troubling generational ethics, these proposals would repeat the Greenspan Commission's mistake of doing too little too late. For example, raising the full retirement age from sixty-seven to seventy for those now age fifty or younger would translate into a 20 percent benefit cut for new cohorts as they gradually reach retirement age. That's a big hit for them, but it's also far too small a change to deal with the system's insolvency.

Cutting Everyone's Benefits to Balance Social Security's Budget: What's Required

An alternative to raising taxes immediately and permanently by 29 percent is cutting benefits right now and keeping them lower forever. Based on table IV.B6, the requisite benefit cut is 22 percent.

Imagine going to each of today's elderly Social Security recipients and saying, "Gee, remember that check you've been getting each month? Well, um, it's still going to come, but it will be a bit smaller. Well, to tell you the truth, it will be a bunch smaller. How much smaller? Well, uh, gee, um, it will be a tad more than one-fifth smaller from here on out. Oh, and one other thing. Sorry." Or imagine telling those about to retire that their benefits will be only 78 percent of what they'd planned on receiving.

Social Security's Solvency Myth

While we were writing this book, we came across a *New York Times* column written by Richard Thaler, a well-respected (for very good reasons) economist at the University of Chicago. Thaler wrote: "The [Social Security] system has to be tweaked to keep it self-sufficient, but economists of every stripe agree that this is a relatively easy fix."[3]

We can't think of a single economist who really understands the system's finances who would remotely agree with this statement. Thaler is not a long-term student of Social Security, so we aren't trying to give him grief here. Instead, we're trying to illustrate the mistakes even superb economists make in considering the system's finances.

Thaler's statement surely represents his reliance on the short-term projections of the trustees, which show that Social Security can pay for all scheduled benefits through 2036. This is true. But in 2036, Social Security's trust fund will be exhausted and benefits will need to be cut by more and more over time given the projected path of revenue. Recall that a 22 percent cut is needed to equate benefits to taxes in present value *if* the benefit cut occurs *immediately*. Waiting until 2036 to start cutting benefits will require much bigger cuts than 22 percent when the cuts begin, assuming all future benefits are cut proportionality starting then.

Thaler is also clearly focusing on Social Security's more sanguine seventy-five-year fiscal gap analysis. This analysis shows only about two-thirds the size of the underfunding that arises when you look truly long term. But thanks to economics' labeling problem, the cash flows of the federal government in general, and Social Security in particular, are not well defined. Hence, the seventy-five-year fiscal gap reported by the trustees is just one of many such seventy-five-year fiscal gaps one could manufacture with the proper choice of labels. Social Security's short run can't, in fact, be distinguished from its long run. The fact that the next seventy-five years look better than the period thereafter is illustrative of the fact that the federal government has, not surprisingly, used language (chosen labels) that makes the short term look better than the long term. Only the infinite horizon fiscal gap is label free.

Finally, Thaler seems to be falling victim to the comparison that many have made between Social Security's financial condition and Medicare's. Medicare's long-term outlook is indeed much graver than Social Security's. But this doesn't mean that Social Security can be fixed with a tweak or two. Far from it.

Thinking outside the Box

Running Social Security on a pay-as-you-go basis since its inception and not planning for the true long term has painted us into a zero-sum corner. If we maintain the current system, the choices are clear: we can hurt the young (some more), or we can hurt the old, or we can hurt both the young and the old, but each to a lesser degree. The only thing that's certain is that a lot of people will get hurt.

In fact, there is an alternative way forward. It involves capitalizing on the fact that the current system is so poorly designed, so inefficient, so inequitable, and so incredibly complex that we can actually provide something much more valuable at a lower cost.

Yes, we know that many people think the current system is the best government program ever instituted and that modifying even the smallest feature of the system would represent a sacrilege. All we can say to such folks is this: *You can't possibly understand how Social Security really works. You cannot possibly have spent time poring over the 2,728 rules in* Social Security Handbook, *a large share of which are completely indecipherable, without forming the belief that this is a bureaucrat's dream and a user's nightmare. Nor could you possibly have torn out your hair trying* to make sense of Social Security's Program Operating Manual System's thousands of equally opaque rules that are supposed to clarify the handbook's 2,728 rules. Nor can you possibly understand how much unequal treatment the system is generating or what labor supply and saving distortions it's generating. The reason is that no mortal human can do so. The system, as designed, is far too complex.

For married supporters of the current system, we recommend trying to determine how much your spouse's retirement benefit will be if one or both of you retire early. That's a pretty straightforward question, but the answer is anything but straightforward.

Without knowing much about the system's provisions, married couples would think they face 9 raised to the power 4, or 6,561 different possible combinations of when to take retirement and spousal benefits. Got that? Again, we're only talking about just one of many questions with which we are confronted in the normal course of choosing when and how to retire.

In fact, the system's spousal and retirement benefit collection so-called deeming as well as other provisions reduce the list of choices dramatically. But unless you understand these rules in fine detail, as well as the fact that the spousal benefit formula differs depending on when you take your benefit, you can easily do what millions of retirees over the years have surely done: take the wrong benefits from Social Security at the wrong times.

If you are single and you think Social Security is just fine as is, take a look at its delayed retirement credit, which gives claimants larger benefits if they wait to collect. (This applies to married as well as single people.) Social Security's delayed retirement credit is becoming increasingly well known as more and more people try to sort out how they are going to finance what will likely be a very long retirement with very few assets in the bank or the 401(k) plan.

Learning that there is a delayed retirement credit is one thing. Knowing precisely how it works is something else. The handbook's rule #720.1 has this little sentence about this credit that we doubt most of Social Security's most ardent fans know about, let alone have inculcated into their planning. "Delayed retirement credit increases apply for benefits beginning January of the year following the year you reach full retirement age."

This means is that if you become age sixty-nine on, say, February 1 rather than, say, December 1, and apply for benefits on your sixty-ninth birthday, you'll have to wait eleven months in the former case, but only one month in the later case, to start receiving your delayed retirement credit as part of your benefit. Furthermore, Social Security does not provide the person with the February 1 birthday who is forced to wait ten months more than the person with the December 1 birthday with any larger benefit for having to wait the extra ten months.

If you read rule #720.1 several times, this point will be clear, but it's just one of the far too many rules that most people, including, we venture, almost all financial advisors, don't know and can't easily learn.

Yes, there are online tools that provide advice on when it's best to take Social Security. One of us (Kotlikoff) has a company, Economic Security Planning, Inc., which provides such a tool at www.maximizemysocialsecurity.com. But knowing what each of these tools is doing under the hood and whether it's making the highly complex calculations correctly presupposes excellent working knowledge of the system's benefit provisions—something essentially no one has.

We also doubt that Social Security's most ardent supporters have made or read careful actuarial studies to determine how much redistribution the system is doing from the young to the old, from single to married folks, from married couples with two earners to married couples with one earner, from those who are childless to those with children, from those who have old spouses to those who have young spouses, from those born with bad genes who have short life expectancies to those born with good genes who have long life expectancies, and from those who contribute more when young and less when old to those who do the opposite.[4]

We won't take your time to lay out all these different forms of redistribution, some of which are truly egregious. Suffice it to say that when you have a system as complex as Social Security and you make piecemeal reforms for seventy-five years, you can produce lots of winners and losers that are not readily apparent.

Putting Labor Economists Out of Business

Our most important retirement saving system should not require superhuman effort and a lifetime of study to understand its provisions or see whom it really helps and hurts. Nor should it require complex calculations to sort out the incentive one faces for earning more money.

This work incentive issue is worth a few comments. As indicated, Social Security's payroll tax rate is 12.4 percent for those earning less than the taxable maximum—the case for the vast majority of American workers. But to understand how the system affects our incentives to work, we need to consider not just the marginal (extra) tax we pay to Social Security when we earn more money. We also need to understand how much more in benefits we receive back from the system.

As indicated, Social Security's benefit formula is extremely complex. But even if one understood all its provisions, including those governing the ancillary spousal, child, parent, survivor, divorce, and disability benefits available from contributing more, the system is still designed to make it literally impossible to understand one's total marginal tax bracket.

Here's the story. The benefits that Social Security provides are based on your earnings history. Specifically, Social Security considers your highest thirty-five years of earnings after they have been indexed for economy-wide real wage growth. If you are, say, age fifty-seven and considering whether to work more this year, all the earnings you made each year in the past enter into your decision. For example, if you started work at age twenty, you need to know whether working this year, or for more hours this year, will produce enough earnings to replace one of the prior top thirty-five years of earnings with this year's earnings. Solving this problem is, computationally speaking, literally impossible.[5] Basically Social Security has become the Oscar Wilde's Dorian Gray of social programs. On the surface it is handsome, useful, and benign. But hidden away in a dark and obscure place, far from close observation, seventy-five years of political gift giving and bureaucratic rule making have created a monster.

The Purple Personal Security Plan

Let's retire Social Security and replace it with a version—the personal security system—that achieves all its legitimate purposes but that's financially sound and extremely simple. We propose doing this by freezing the current system in place. This means paying today's retirees their benefits, while paying workers, in retirement, only what they have accrued up to now. To make sure today's workers receive all their accrued benefits when they retire, we'd fill zeros in their earnings record for each year in the future. Although no one would accrue additional benefit claims from the current system, everyone would get what's now owed them in the form of annual benefits. So the current system would remain in place, but pay out less and less in the way of benefits over time compared with the current design.

Next we'd have all workers, though age sixty, contribute 8 percent of their pay to their own personal security account, with half of their contribution going to their own account and half to the personal account of their spouse or legal partner. This ensures that if a married or legally partnered couple splits up, each party will have the same-size personal security account. The federal government would make matching contributions for the poor, the disabled, and the unemployed, permitting the system to be as progressive as desired.

Keeping Wall Street Out of the Picture

Unlike other proposals to "privatize" Social Security, notably that of President George W. Bush, the purple personal security plan doesn't let Wall Street loose on an unsuspecting public. The goal of the plan is to force people to save, not to drive them into a casino and have them throw dice to see who ends up with the best retirement. If the government is going to be involved in using compulsion to achieve a social objective, it needs to ensure that the objective is in fact achieved. That objective does not include enriching Wall Street or enhancing the public's ability to get taken to the cleaners by fast-talking financial product reps.

Going Global

Under the personal security system, all contributions would be invested in one way and one way only: in a single global, market-weighted index of stocks, bonds, and real estate. This ensures that all Americans earn the same rate of return on their personal security accounts. It also ensures broad diversification. Basically it puts us all in the same boat. The big difference is that it is a real boat built with real assets, not with promises to get the money by taxing the next generation.

A single government computer—a small laptop is all that's needed—would do all the investing at zero cost. Participants would also be guaranteed that their account balances at retirement would equal at least what they contributed, adjusted for inflation. The reason this investing job can be done by a single computer is that everyone will have the same portfolio, namely the global index, and the amount invested in each asset will be set according to the share of that asset in the global financial market. For example, if the total outstanding value of Intel's stock represents 0.008 percent of all global financial assets, 0.008 percent of the personal security fund would be invested in Intel stock.

Notice that this system is fully funded. Moreover, the accounts are private insofar as the assets are invested primarily in securities issued by private companies and households (e.g., mortgages) and the size of each person's account balance will depend on what she contributes over time as well as how the global personal security fund performs.

Providing a Guarantee

Anyone who was invested in the stock market in recent years knows that stocks can be a very wild ride. But there are three important points to bear in mind in considering investments in the personal security fund.

First, the fund would be invested in globally diversified stocks; it would hold stocks issued by companies around the world, including those in developing countries. This is not a fantasy. As you will see in chapter 12, two funds of this type already exist as exchange traded funds (ETFs) that track an index of global equities. All that needs to be added is a similar index of global debt issues. Clearly the personal security fund's trustees, which would consist of the chairman of the Federal Reserve, the secretary of the treasury, and the director of the personal security system, would need to decide whether to include illiquid stocks issued in emerging countries, but such decisions are being routinely and reasonably made by major investment companies that manage global stock index funds. By spreading its stock investment across all major stocks throughout the world, the fund will reduce the chances of major losses.

Second, the fund would not be invested solely in stocks. It would also be investing in corporate and government bonds issued by companies and governments around the world. Indeed, since bonds represent three-fifths of the world's financial assets, the fund would be invested primarily in relatively safe bonds.[6]

Third, the government would guarantee that each participant's account balance at the time it is converted to inflation-protected annuities would be no less than what the participant had contributed, adjusted for inflation. In other words, the government would provide a guarantee of a zero real return on the fund's performance. No one would lose, in real terms, her contributions.

Converting to Annuities

Between ages sixty and seventy, each worker's balances would be sold off at the prevailing market prices and be used to fund inflation-indexed annuities organized on a cohort basis by the government. Those dying before age seventy would bequeath their account balances to their heirs.

As with the investing of the personal security fund, Wall Street plays no role in the conversion of account balances to annuities. "Wall Street" in this context refers to the life insurance industry.

The conversion to annuities would work like this. All the proceeds of the sale of fund balances for people in a given cohort (born in the same year) would be pooled to purchase U.S. Treasury Inflation Protected Securities, known as TIPS. TIPS are designed to maintain their real value regardless of the rate of inflation. The principal and interest earned on the TIPS would be paid out to surviving cohort members as annual payments in proportion to the amounts that they had at the time of conversion. Thus, Joe Smith (and everyone else born in the same year) would have some of his personal security fund holdings converted in the year he hits age sixty-one, some in the year he hits sixty-two, and so on though the year he hits age seventy. When the conversion occurs, the proceeds would be used to purchase TIPS.

Joe and other surviving members of his cohort would receive payments from the TIPS pool starting at age sixty-two. The amount Joe would receive would be in proportion to his share of his cohort's total personal account balances as of age sixty. As each year passes through age seventy, more of the cohort's fund balances are converted to TIPS and more is paid out to survivors.

Note that only survivors receive payments. That's the nature of longevity insurance: those who die early pay those who die late. The personal security system does, however, provide extra protection for those who die young. If someone dies before having all of her personal security account balances converted to TIPS, the balance can be bequeathed to the personal security accounts of her heirs.

How much would be paid out in total to surviving cohort members from the TIPS cohort-specific account each year? The answer depends on how the TIPS performed in the market, how many members of the cohort survive, and how the cohort's future survival prospect change. The government would manage the payout with the goal of never having the payment per survivor decline in real (after inflation) terms.

The Personal Security System in Postcard Form

The postcard in box 11.1 conveys key features of the purple personal security system plan.

Box 11.1
The Purple Personal Security System Plan

1. Freezes the existing social security system by having Social Security enter zeros in workers' earnings records for years after the reform begins.
2. Requires all workers through age sixty to contribute 8 percent of their wages to their personal security accounts (PSAs).
3. PSA contributions are divided equally between spouses and legal partners.
4. The government makes matching contributions to PSAs on behalf of the poor, the unemployed, and the disabled.
5. All PSA balances are invested in a global market-weighted index fund of stocks, government bonds, corporate bonds, and real estate.
6. Between ages sixty-one and seventy, PSA balances for each cohort are gradually sold at market prices and converted to Treasury inflation-indexed securities.
7. The government guarantees that PSA balances at conversion equal at least what was contributed adjusted for inflation.
8. PSA participants who die prior to age seventy bequeath unconverted balances to their heirs.
9. Starting at age sixty-two, the cohort TIPS pool makes payout to surviving cohort PSA participants in proportion to their age sixty PSA balances.
10. Distribution from the TIPS pool is designed to ensure real (inflation adjusted) payout to surviving cohort members does not decline through time.

12

Becoming Our Own Solution

In an ideal world, one inhabited by wise and compassionate human beings blessed with flexibility and foresight, our postcard solutions might become a reality. We'd have a broad consensus on our social contract. Government would be the primary instrument for having that contract work. The problems we face would be solved.

But that isn't our world.

Since 1935 the budget of the U.S. government has been in surplus (and you've seen how unreal that is) a total of eight years. Other than 1999 and 2000, you have to go back a half-century, to 1960, to find another year of surplus. And the 1960 surplus was trivially small—a mere $3.9 billion in today's dollars. Over the long sweep of seventy-five years, the evidence is clear: balanced budgets are un-American. We do deficits.

Unfortunately, as discussed above, official deficits—changes in the stock of federal debt—represent less than the tip of the iceberg when it comes to the growth in our overall liabilities. While federal debt held by the public is now approaching an entire year of U.S. output, our nation's true debt—the fiscal gap, which includes all of Uncle Sam's unofficial spending commitments, net of all the taxes he'll likely collect to cover these commitments—is a gargantuan 14 times GDP.

We're broke beyond broke. But like General Motors before its bankruptcy, we're lumbering on because of our enormous size and borrowing capacity. And given our long history of dumping both formal and informal debts in the laps of youngsters, while legislating greater and greater benefits for oldsters, don't hold your breath awaiting a rational solution. The most likely scenario is the simultaneous and colossal fiscal, financial, and economic meltdown portrayed in the prologue.

This raises the question you have, no doubt, been asking since page 1: *How can we protect ourselves?*

We're all asking this question, and the answers are getting more and more unusual. A visit to a bookstore is instructive. While Barnes and Noble saw the vampire romance trend early and created an entire section devoted to "teen paranormal romance" novels, it has yet to create an "American Armageddon" section.[1] But the books are there, mixed in with the ever-growing shelf of survivalist tomes. So if you think the future will require having emergency food and water supplies that you defend with your newly purchased AK-47 or assault rifle, there are a lot of instruction manuals you can buy.

Our personal salvation advice is far less extreme. There are lots of straightforward small steps you and your family members can take that will leave you in a safer position for facing what's coming. So there's no need to join freedom fighters in Montana, new age groupies in California, or defiant religious cult members in Texas.

Let's start with a mental reboot—an understanding that we can change our personal fate far more readily and quickly than government policy.

Trust Yourself, Not Short-Lived Institutions

Most of us have years of conditioning telling us that we are small and temporary while the institutions around us are big and permanent. Nothing could be further from the truth. The notion of small and temporary versus big and permanent persists in spite of some obvious realities. It is a good bet, for instance, that regardless of your age or marital status, you've had your name longer than your current bank has had its name. One banker Scott knows likes to tell people about having worked at the same desk, in the same office, for thirty years while the bank he works for has been taken over, digested, and renamed four times.

With Americans now living an expected eighty years, few things or institutions have our duration. In the material world, we're outlasting our computers, our cars, our home appliances, our household goods, even some of our homes, and certainly the tenure of whatever political party is in office.

Only one of the original twelve companies in the Dow Jones Industrial Average still has the same name: General Electric. The other eleven companies have been sold, renamed, liquidated, or otherwise become something else since 1885. According to Jeremy Siegel's classic *Stocks for the Long Run,*[2] 987 new names were added to the Standard & Poor's 500 Index (an index of large-capitalization stocks that accounts for about 74 percent of all stock market value in the United States) between its creation in 1957 and 2006. In its single greatest year of change, 1976, a whopping sixty new stocks were added to the list and sixty were displaced. However you slice it, most of us will be around longer than a typical large American enterprise whose average life expectancy is less than fifty years, about the life span of the average American more than a century ago.

As individuals we are a lot stronger and more durable than we think, and we are likely to become more so. In futurist Alvin Toffler's prescient 1970 book *Future Shock,* his driving theme was accelerating change in technology, information, knowledge, products, and businesses. In addition to the idea of the information economy, much the same was predicted in Fritz Machlup's classic 1973 book, *The Production and Distribution of Knowledge in the United States.*[3] Both authors were incredibly prescient about a growing truth—*things don't last.*

In the last chaotic decade alone we've seen the decline of the newspaper industry, a revolution in the distribution of music that has now spread to movies and books, a need to dramatically shrink the U.S. Post Office because people aren't using traditional mail, and the familiar list of big corporate failures. We're not talking about the constant change in small retail stores or restaurants. We're talking about the institutions that define our world. And the fact that they are relatively short-lived makes their long-term promises inherently untrustworthy.

Think about it. Thirty years from now, today's politicians and all their lofty promises will be gone. Many of today's banks and insurance companies will be gone. Many of today's investment advisors will be gone. Many of today's employers will be gone. Many of today's pension funds will be gone. Many of our tax breaks and benefits will be gone. Much of our good climate may be gone. Our two-party political system may be gone (amen), and the list goes on.

They'll be gone, but we'll, for the most part, still be here. It's an uncomfortable mind reset, but the truly durable institutions in society are people—that is, us. We generally outlive the supposedly eternal institutions that we rely upon so heavily. And we have no option but to make careful long-term plans for ourselves. That's a big responsibility, and most of us aren't prepared for it because we are beset by thinking traps, unrecognized cognitive failures.

Fixing Our Cognitive Errors

One indication that an idea has come a long way is the attachment of a Nobel Prize to its originators, like the 2002 prize Daniel Kahneman received for his pioneering work in behavioral finance.[4] Since then, we've all learned that our financial decisions are often irrational because we suffer from a variety of thinking distortions that bias our decisions away from the lucid calculations of self-interest that Adam Smith thought guided our behavior. Through Kahneman and his deceased coauthor, Amos Tversky, we've learned about:

• Anchoring—relying too much on a single piece of information, often unrelated to the question at hand

• Focusing effect—putting too much weight on a single aspect of a question

• Loss aversion—attaching excessive importance to avoiding losses rather than seeking gains

• Framing—assessing choices based, in potentially very large part, on how they are presented

Those are just a few of a growing array of cognitive errors being explored in the burgeoning literature of behavioral economics. The only thing these errors share is our felt need to economize on observing and thinking.

We don't think; therefore we err.

Our greatest cognitive errors are far beyond the narrow world of personal economic decision making. We also have a painful tendency to make ourselves miserable in every aspect of our lives. Here, for instance, is a short list of cognitive errors offered by David D. Burns, M.D. (no relation to Scott), in his popular 1980 book, *Feeling Good: The New Mood Therapy*. Rather than offering a possibly therapeutic long-term exhumation of the past or a quick pharmaceutical fix, Burns focused on the immediate habits of thought and perception that regularly lead people to despair, depression, and indecision:

- All-or-nothing thinking
- Overgeneralization
- Mental filter
- Disqualifying the positive
- Jumping to conclusions
- Magnification or minimization
- Emotional reasoning
- Should statements
- Labeling and mislabeling
- Personalization

Each one of these cognitive errors can be found in abundance when you examine the public discourse on the economic decisions and the reality we face as individuals, as a nation, and as a planet. One of the most common cognitive errors is the first on Burns's list: all-or-nothing thinking. It is our tendency to look for binary, yes/no answers to problems that usually have calibrated solutions.

Rather than deal with the actual problems of Social Security, for instance, many Americans choose to "believe in" Social Security, while others dismiss it altogether. Either way, they don't have to take responsibility for fixing it. Or they will use mental filters to put the blame for all Medicare problems on illegal immigrants, welfare mothers, phony disabled people, greedy doctors, or some other group that is tiny compared to the number of retirees and their growing demand for income and unlimited medical care. Others, learning that Medicare benefits will have to be cut in the future, quickly assume that benefits will disappear altogether. You have to admit, these kinds of responses offer great economy and a kind of instant comfort when it comes to thinking.

So let's ask a question: Is there a root cause—some common element—to the cognitive errors in our personal lives, our political lives, and our economic lives?

There is. In all three cases, our cognitive errors begin with anxiety about having any control or influence over the outcome of an event, something external that is important to us. We can minimize these errors and maximize ourselves as the new and durable institutions if we focus our attention on things we can do entirely by ourselves—things that don't require the permission or acceptance from others that causes so much anxiety. We can empower ourselves and clear our thinking just by doing what we can do rather than worrying about all the things we can't do and can't control.

When we ask what we can do, financially the answers turn out to be a very long list. It's a list that can offset much (but not all) of the peril in the unending growth of federal debt and government spending. The list has two main themes, which we explore in this chapter and the next.

The first theme is that we can take our futures back from the financial services industry. We can realize that most of what is offered by the financial services industry costs more than it's worth, if, indeed, it has any positive value. In truth, the financial services industry is an unending source of inadvertently induced maladies—what doctors call iatrogenic illnesses. Wall Street routinely offers financial cures that can be far worse than the financial problem they are marketed to solve. As we have recently seen, these iatrogenic illnesses can be nearly fatal. They can put the entire economy into intensive care.

Here are two specific steps we can take to become our own institution:

• Save and invest with the lowest-cost tools available.

• Find better paths to investment return than brilliant Wall Street management.

Not possible? Too simple? Not really that easy? Well, we beg to differ. We'll tell you how and why shortly.

The second theme is, if anything, even more down home: we can make decisions about how we live that can mean as much, or more, to our long-term financial security as saving adequately and getting an adequate rate of return on what we save. Here are some of the specific steps we can take to replace financial capital with life decision capital.

• We can understand the unexpected benefits of the human life cycle.

• We can make powerful positive decisions that will benefit our economic future.

• We can cultivate our ability to adapt to change.

• We can revel in the benefits of natural aging.

• We can comprehend that even the death of a partner has a small benefit for the survivor.

Let's start with the area now burdened with the greatest skepticism and pessimism: how we can save and invest for our futures.

The Investment Nirvana Hiding Inside Investment Hell

If you are pessimistic about your investing future, it's not surprising. In the first ten years of the new century, we've gone from enjoying investment returns that were far above average to investment returns that are far below average. In the twenty years from 1980 to 1999, the S&P 500 Index provided an annual compound return of 17.9 percent. That return multiplied $1,000 of equity investment nearly twenty-seven times to $26,932 over the period.

In the ten years from 2000 to 2009, the same index returned an annualized loss of 0.9 percent. For most people, it was a decade that went nowhere. For others, it was a good reason to refer to their 401(k) plans as 201(k) plans.

Investors lost money in four of the ten years. They lost money in only one year of the 1990s and only one year of the 1980s. The losses of the first decade were greater, in total, than the three years of loss during the 1970s, a period widely regarded as devastating. Only the six years of losses in the 1930s were worse. Except for the Great Depression, no period in living memory has been worse.

Meanwhile, more damage was being done in the housing market. After decades of steady price increases and a few years of spectacular increases, home values started to fall in 2006. Today, five years later, they are still well below their peak values. While losses suffered depend on how long you have owned your house and where it is located, Federal Reserve consumer balance sheet figures show that $6.6 trillion of home value has vaporized since 2006, a decline of 29 percent.[5]

More specific measures, such as the National Association of Realtors median home prices, show that where you live could make the difference between modest appreciation and devastating loss. Spurred by job and population growth, home values in Texas have been relatively stable. In some areas, such as Austin, prices have actually risen. During the same period, the national median home price fell sharply, and home values in the most distressed areas of the country fell as much as 60 percent (Cape Coral–Fort Myers, Florida).[6] The losses have been so great that some home owners are doing strategic foreclosures, figuring that it is better to take the wipeout than hang on for years of mortgage payments based on values that no longer exist.

Since homeowner equity has routinely been the largest component of net worth for the majority of Americans, it would be difficult to overstate the impact of falling home prices. For some people, owning a home was their entire retirement plan. Many who lived in high-price and high-appreciation areas like California or the Northeast, for instance, could sell their old home for $1.5 million, pocket the appreciation, and retire to a lower-cost area like Arizona or Florida.

That's not going to happen now. Much, if not all, of the appreciation has been lost. Even at lower prices, many homes aren't selling. Scott recalls visiting friends in the Fort Myers area and learning that a local continuing care community had a rising vacancy rate because would-be residents in their eighties were trapped in their unsalable homes.[7]

So where is there an investment advantage if asset returns recover?

It is right under our noses: *the cost of saving and investing has been dropping.* It has now reached levels no one could imagine as recently as 2000.[8] While large companies like Exxon Mobil, IBM[9] and Texas Instruments[10] are blazing this path, more and more companies are introducing low-cost index funds to their 401(k) menus. Index funds are managed to duplicate a given list of stocks, such as the S&P 500 Index. The cost of managing such funds is very low, with really large funds having costs as low as 3 basis points, or 0.03 percent. As a consequence, the average cost of investing in 401(k) plans is dropping. The impact can be dramatic. You can understand how dramatic by comparing the hypothetical lifetime accumulations of workers in 401(k) plans at several different cost levels. Assuming identical wages that rise with 3 percent inflation, annual contributions of 6 percent of income for thirty-five years, and a gross return of 8 percent before expenses from a balanced portfolio, here are the differences in what employees will accumulate:

• A schoolteacher in an expensive insurance-based 403(b) plan with annual costs of 2.25 percent will accumulate 3.5 years of final salary. The expenses reduce the potential accumulation by 36 percent.

• A worker in a typical small company plan with expenses of 1.5 percent will accumulate 4.05 years of final salary. The expenses reduce the potential accumulation by 26 percent.

• A worker in a typical large company plan with expenses of 1 percent will accumulate 4.47 years of final salary. The expenses reduce the potential accumulation by 18 percent.

• A worker in a new index fund–based plan with expenses of 0.15 percent, such as those at Texas Instruments, will accumulate 5.3 years of final salary. The expenses reduce the potential accumulation by only 3 percent. A worker in a 1 percent cost plan would need to have a 20 percent employer match to equal the accumulation of the Texas Instruments worker.

Losing 28, 36, or more percent of the return on your investment is yet another indication of the predatory nature of large portions of the financial services industry. To put the loss in terms of taxes, an average-income school teacher who makes a bit over $50,000 a year loses as much to the financial services industry in a typical 403(b) plan as the Internal Revenue Service would take from a worker in the highest-income tax bracket. That's someone with taxable income over $372,950. Slightly less than 1 percent of all households have income taxed at the top 35 percent rate.[11]

In a typical small company plan where the charges of the financial services industry consume about 26 percent of the investor's return, the costs still loom large compared to the top income tax rate most workers pay. In 2008, for instance, IRS statistics tell us that only 5 percent of households had adjusted gross incomes over $159,619, and only 1 percent of all households had adjusted gross incomes over $380,354. On a joint tax return, those workers would be facing marginal tax rates of 28 percent and 35 percent, respectively. Most workers pay at substantially lower marginal tax rates.

While the industry routinely points to how much you can build your savings through tax-deferred accounts, it never points to how much is removed by the industry itself. Escaping this "tax," like avoiding actual income taxes, is a major step that workers can take to improve their futures. Fortunately, it is a step that is increasingly easier to take.

Today anyone with an IRA can save and accumulate with virtually no expense drag simply by taking advantage of the low-cost, no commission exchange traded funds (ETFs) now available from firms like Vanguard, Fidelity, Schwab, TD Ameritrade, and other brokers. Unlike conventional mutual funds whose shares are issued or redeemed by the managing company, ETFs are traded on stock exchanges, much like the shares of closed-end funds. Significantly, the costs can even be slightly lower than the 0.15 percent cost of the Texas Instruments 401(k) plan.

At Charles Schwab, for instance, you could build your retirement IRA using Scott's "Margarita portfolio" which is invested in equal portions of the U.S. total equity market, the foreign developed economies market, and U.S. Treasury inflation-protected securities.[12] The three Schwab ETFs to use in this portfolio are:

• Charles Schwab U.S. Broad Market ETF (ticker: SCHB, expense ratio 0.06 percent)

• Charles Schwab International Equity ETF (ticker: SCHF, expense ratio 0.13 percent)

• Charles Schwab U.S. TIPS ETF (ticker: SCHP, expense ratio 0.14 percent)

The portfolio would have an average expense ratio of 0.11 percent. That's about one-ninth the cost of typical plans in large companies. Workers in typical large corporation plans with expenses of 1 percent a year can, in effect, have the benefit of a 20 percent match by opting for a low-cost IRA.

Schoolteachers saddled with expensive insurance product–based 403(b) plans can, in effect, have the benefit of a 50 percent match by opting for a low-cost IRA. An employer would have to put up a 50 percent match to offset the damage done by many of these high-cost plans. Since most teacher plans have no employer match and most teachers would have difficulty saving the $5,000 IRA contribution limit ($6,000 for those age fifty and over), we see no reason for any teacher to participate in a typical variable annuity based 403(b) plan when they can do far better in a low-cost IRA.

The opportunity here is enormous, and it is available to everyone. Better still, the opportunity may get larger and easier. One of the recommendations in the 2010 report from the National Commission on Fiscal Responsibility and Reform is that all existing tax-deferred savings plans should have the same limit of $20,000 a year.[13] While this is a reduction from the current maximum of $49,000 for defined contribution plans and $22,000 for 401(k) plans for those age fifty and over, many upper-middle-income workers who are trapped in expensive 401(k) or 403(b) plans would be able to move to lower-cost IRA accounts if the contribution limit for IRAs was increased from $6,000 to $20,000.

Will it happen? We don't know.

Why the Opportunity Isn't Visible

If this is such a great opportunity, you might be asking, Why doesn't everyone know about it? Why aren't more people doing it?

The primary reason is that many people in the financial services industry are in it to do well for themselves first. Your welfare and benefit are entirely secondary. This may sound harsh and cynical, but you can understand it if you imagine that you are in financial services trying to make a living. You have these choices:

Choice A: You can sell mutual funds or insurance-based investment products and can collect anywhere from 1 percent a year to over 3 percent a year on each dollar of client investment.

Choice B: You can sell low-cost index mutual funds or ETFs and collect less than 0.20 percent for your most popular funds.

Question: Which path will pay your mortgage fastest? The easy choice is A. It would take five to fifteen years to make as much money in fees in choice B as you would make in a single year in choice A. The difference here isn't a percentage; it is a multiple, and a large multiple at that.

That multiple also supports an enormous volume of advertising that in turn supports lots of media coverage based on hope for superior returns from brilliant minds on Wall Street. Check any of the major glossy personal finance magazines—*Money, Smart Money, Kiplinger's*—and you'll find pages and pages of advertisements for large fund firms, large insurance companies, and large brokerage houses. You'll find less advertising and less article content on low-cost index funds. This relative lack of coverage is important.

Behavioral economics researchers have found that there is a menu effect in 401(k) plans: employee portfolios will tend to parallel the choices they have in each asset category. Much the same happens with the larger public menu of what we see from day to day. When a 401(k) plan menu has twenty equity fund choices and five bond fund choices, plan participants are likely to have an asset allocation that is 80 percent equities and 20 percent fixed income. They selected from the menu.

So it is in the larger world of financial communications. We invest in what we see most of. That's high-cost managed mutual funds and insurance products offering "special" lifetime benefits. The menu is good for the financial services industry but terrible for people who need to save for retirement and other reasons.

Today, even after a national and global economic disaster that was massively magnified by the financial services industry, claims are still being made of superior securities selection skill. Beyond that, there are claims of great strategic decision making. These are supposed to be beyond the capabilities of ordinary human beings.[14] At the same time, claims are made that diversification didn't work during the crisis (because virtually everything fell in value) and that this is a time for careful stock and bond picking, avoiding dangerous "buy and hold," and special strategies that involve the purchase or sale of options and other short-term tools. Global disaster notwithstanding, it's the same old, same old.

All this comes from an industry that clearly can't manage its own risks. Remember that we are still recovering from the failure of the world's largest insurance company, the failure of major brokerage houses, and the near death of our largest banks. The only reason they still exist is that our government provided an enormous rescue, whose cost remains to be totaled.

Only one thing is certain: whatever the cost, regular people will be paying it, not top-dog bankers. Thanks to Federal Reserve policy, our banks now pay virtually nothing for their raw material, money. As a consequence, banks are making money that otherwise would be paid as interest to depositors. With nearly $5.5 trillion in savings deposits in our banking system, savers would have an additional $220 billion in interest income if they were paid an average of 4 percent on those deposits.[15] As you might expect, this cost is not labeled as a tax on savers and is not included in the cost of the (ongoing) rescue of banking.

Even if you don't fall for the continuing claims of wisdom and investment savvy from these failed institutions, it remains that millions of other investors—most other investors—still do. We call it tooth fairy investing: believing that someone has a special ability and will devote himself to our financial betterment.

Sadly, this continues at every level of investing. Wealthy investors, who we would like to think are pretty smart about money, continue to invest in hedge funds whose basic charges (2 percent annually for management plus 20 percent of profits) are a formula for manager enrichment and investor loss magnification. Average investors at the other end of the risk spectrum seek certainty and security. They continue to commit new billions to variable annuities with "living benefit" clauses. Since these products generally have annual insurance and management costs in excess of 3 percent and guarantee lifetime payouts of 5 percent from a portfolio that is a mixture of stocks and bonds expected to return about 8 percent, the inevitability of bad market years virtually guarantees major erosion or outright loss of the original investment over the long investment periods for which they are intended.

The Actual Performance of Managed Funds

Every six months Standard and Poor's updates its SPIVA Report, short for Standard and Poor's Indices Versus Active.[16] First published in 2002, the report examines what percentage of managed funds failed to beat the index for their category over trailing time periods up to five years. So far there have been twenty-four of these reports. Although there has been some variation in the results, one finding is consistent: a large majority of managed funds fail to beat the index for their category.

A mid-2010 report shows these results for the percentages of managed funds that fail to beat their category index:

- U.S. large capitalization, 63.76 percent
- U.S. midcapitalization, 76.65 percent
- U.S. small capitalization, 65.18 percent
- U.S. multicapitalization, 65.08 percent
- U.S. real estate, 59.21 percent
- International equity, 84.56 percent
- Emerging markets, 85.95 percent
- Long term government bonds, 82.98 percent
- Intermediate term government bonds, 72.92 percent
- Short term government bonds, 74.42 percent
- Investment-grade long term bonds, 71.57 percent
- Investment-grade intermediate term bonds, 67.92 percent
- Investment-grade short term bonds, 94.20 percent
- High-yield bonds, 92.68 percent
- Mortgage bonds, 86.04 percent

Are there any bright spots in this research? Yes, from time to time. In this particular report, for instance, managed funds in several relatively narrow market sectors were able to beat their assigned index slightly more than 50 percent of the time. So there are glimmers of hope, but the blunt reality is that the probability any professional manager will beat his assigned index is small. This is not a new or recent finding. Researchers have been finding that managed money generally fails to beat an index for more than half a century. That's a long time, but just as *Cosmopolitan* magazine has been discovering new sex tricks every month since the early 1970s, money managers keep making claims of new and better ways to win high returns.

It's also important to note that you'd have to win two bets, not one, for the selection of a successful fund manager to make much difference. Emerging market stocks accounted for only 10 percent of global market capitalization at the end of 2009. Domestic small capitalization value stocks and international small capitalization stocks don't account for much of global market capitalization, either. So unless you put a lot of money into a relatively obscure market area and picked a good fund manager, it wouldn't make much difference to your total portfolio.

Worse, the odds are still smaller that you'll be able to pick a winning portfolio of funds on your own or with professional help.

Suppose, for instance, that you or your advisor builds a simple three-part portfolio that is equal parts domestic large capitalization, international equity, and intermediate government bonds. On average there is only a 26.25 percent chance that these choices will beat passive index funds. The probability of selecting three funds that beat their indexes is 1.5 percent. Either way, these are not good odds. Still worse, financial professionals don't select funds for free. They often charge 1 percentage point a year over and above the cost of the underlying funds. So you are giving up a significant portion of your portfolio return in exchange for a small chance that the manager will be able do better than you (or a monkey) would do throwing darts at a list of funds.

Needless to say, although these performance figures are readily available, free, on the Internet, they are not common knowledge. You won't learn them by watching the talking heads on CNN. Indeed, you won't even learn them by visiting a first-rate information source like Morningstar.

The S&P research adjusts results for something called "survivor bias"—the fact that not all funds survive for three or five years. In every time period, there are funds that don't survive, usually due to poor performance and loss of assets. We're not talking statistical piffle here. For the five years ending in mid-2010, only 72 percent of all domestic funds survived. Only 78.5 percent of international funds survived. Survivorship was better among emerging markets funds at 92.2 percent. In fixed income, survivorship ranged from a low of 80.4 percent for long-maturity investment-grade bond funds to 94.2 percent for mortgage-backed securities funds. Survivorship among emerging markets bond funds was 100 percent. (This was not due to brilliant management. It was due to a broad public realization that many emerging market countries were better credit risks than most countries in the industrialized world, including the United States, so net new money was constantly flowing from developed world bond funds to emerging markets bond funds.)

Survivorship figures change with money flows. There have been periods in which survivorship of fixed income funds was relatively low and survivorship of equity funds was relatively high. Whatever is happening, the regular disappearance of funds and their track records has a material effect on the apparent performance of the surviving funds. We hear about the funds that live and grow. Unsuccessful funds are quietly interred in unmarked graves.

Visit the Morningstar Web site and enter FINFX, the ticker for the Vanguard 500 Index fund, and click on "performance," and you'll read numbers that indicate that the mother of all index funds has provided a higher return than the majority of surviving domestic large-capitalization funds.[17] On our visit this morning, for instance, the fund ranked above 61 percent of all competing funds over the previous twelve months, 55 percent over the previous three years, 54 percent over the previous five years, and 62 percent over the previous fifteen years. It trailed 54 percent over the previous ten years. These figures, by the way, are among the worst we've seen since the Morningstar data became available. Since Morningstar presents surviving funds and does not adjust for the funds that are quietly taken out, these figures understate the long-term advantage of index investing.

Another way to examine performance is to see where a fund ranked against its competition in each year. Over the twenty years beginning in

1991, the Vanguard 500 Index fund was in the top 25 percent in six years. It was in the top 50 percent in sixteen years. It was never in the bottom 25 percent and was in the third quartile for only four years. The track record for Vanguard's Total Bond Market Index fund is nearly as good: it was in the top 25 percent for seven years and the top 50 percent for fourteen years, and it spent only one year in the bottom 25 percent and six years in the bottom 50 percent.

Underperformance of Managed Funds Isn't a New Thing

Standard and Poor's may have begun its reporting in 2002, but underperformance and overpricing isn't news. The failure of professional management has been well researched and well documented for about fifty years. But if the financial services industry ever learns this, it is forgotten every year. As a result we have an entire well-compensated industry that repeats the experience of actor Bill Murray in the 1993 movie *Groundhog Day*, magically starting each year with no memory of past embarrassments. We are regularly amazed at the idea of an entire industry existing to sell us on the idea of using a low-probability tool—managed investing—as the solution for something that is 100 percent likely—retirement. That's why we think it's really important to tell you more than a little history. The more you clearly understand the history of financial management failure, the less likely you'll be to waste money on Wall Street's snake oil.

One of Scott's favorite research exercises was done by a newspaper publishing company, Media General, in the early 1970s. Under the guidance of its chairman at the time, a statistics expert, the company created a unit that computerized the fabled monkey portfolios where portfolios were constructed by throwing darts at the stock listing page. The Media General CEO had a computer programmed to randomly select thousands of stock portfolios from stock universes of three different sizes ranging from a few hundred of the largest-capitalization companies to a much larger universe of about a thousand companies. Then the performance of each portfolio was calculated and rank-ordered so a percentile score could be developed. For a period of time, the results appeared as full-page displays in the *Wall Street Journal*.

And how did professionally managed mutual funds do when measured against a scale of randomly selected portfolios? Below the fiftieth percentile. This was a consistent finding across all universe sizes. As you might expect, this research was not greeted with enthusiasm by the investment community. They were routinely being beaten by a crew of virtual monkeys. So this finding drew little financial support from investment management companies. Media General eventually abandoned the effort. Today it could be done on a laptop, so we are wondering why similar research hasn't been conducted.

The problem here isn't a lack of brain power among portfolio managers. They are bright, articulate people, and they have access to information and tools well beyond anything a small investor has. The problem is that managing money is difficult because no one knows the future. It is comforting to believe that someone has insight into the future, but the reality is that few predictions are even remotely accurate. Whether the market is efficient or inefficient, no one knows what future prices will be. Worse, in spite of this reality, managers and financial service firms routinely incur expenses and charge fees as though they were capable of adding value when decades of results say they are not.

Someday this reality will be as obvious to people as the idea that the world is round, not flat. But it will take time for the news to spread because there is an army of 317,000 brokers and commissioned salespeople selling stocks, bonds, mutual funds, and insurance products, all sharing a single marketing ploy: "We'll charge you 1, 2, or 3 percent a year but, like luxury shampoo, 'we're worth it.'"[18]

They aren't. There are many things in life that we can overpay for and not be harmed. Shampoo comes to mind, as does coffee, but expensive asset management is a nearly certain recipe for not being able to overpay for shampoo when you retire.

Access to Low-Cost Investing Is Spreading and Easing, and Costs Are Dropping

It wasn't long ago that index investing was only a concept. It couldn't actually be done. While Wells Fargo offered the first index investment accounts to institutions in the early 1970s, index advocate John Bogle didn't start the Vanguard 500 Index until August 1976.[19] By current standards it wasn't even that cheap to run, with an expense ratio of 0.46 percent according to Morningstar.

Today there are nearly 2,000 index funds. About half of them are exchange-traded index funds. While many are expensive enough to be silly (the ProFunds group has many funds with expenses approaching 3 percent a year), the trend has been to lower and lower expense ratios. Today, for instance, the Vanguard 500 Index mutual fund has an expense ratio of 0.18 percent, while the Admiral shares (minimum purchase $10,000) have an expense ratio of only 0.07 percent. Schwab offers its Schwab Broad Market Index ETF at only 0.06 percent, the SPDR S&P 500 Index ETF is priced at 0.09 percent, and the Fidelity Spartan 500 Index is priced at 0.10 percent.

Late in 2009 Schwab announced its own basic ETFs, available with no commission. Fidelity followed suit a few months later, offering a group of twenty-five iShares ETFs at no commission, and Vanguard eliminated ETF commissions after that. TD Ameritrade joined the fray in late 2010 with 100 commission-free ETFs. Today a careful index fund investor can build a portfolio with all the basic asset classes for an average expense ratio of less than 0.15 percent and with virtually no commission expenses.

Here's an example, using Vanguard ETFs:

• Vanguard Total Stock Market Index ETF, 0.07 percent expense ratio
• Vanguard Total Bond Market ETF, 0.12 percent expense ratio
• Vanguard REIT Index ETF, 0.13 percent expense ratio
• Vanguard Europe Pacific ETF, 0.15 percent expense ratio
• Vanguard Emerging Markets ETF, 0.27 percent expense ratio

The same portfolio can be built at similar low expense on the brokerage platforms offered by Fidelity, Schwab, and TD Ameritrade.

The ultimate in low-investing expenses is the Federal Thrift Savings Plan (TSP), a 401(k) plan for federal employees with investment expenses of only 0.03 percent a year. This is virtually frictionless, costless investing. The Investment Company Institute, the lobby for the mutual funds industry, has been quick to point out that the TSP could achieve such low expenses only because government agencies did the plan record keeping and assumed other expenses that are part of most commercial 401(k) plans.[20] That said, an increasing number of large company 401(k) plans, such as Exxon Mobil, IBM, and Texas Instruments, offer employees a menu of index fund options that cost 0.15 percent a year or less.

If you work for a small company whose plan costs more due to record keeping and other costs, you should give serious thought to not participating and saving through an IRA account with a major discount broker. You'll face a lower contribution limit—$6,000 for those age fifty and over versus $22,000 for those age fifty and over in 401(k) plans—but many workers can't save more than $6,000 a year.

The bottom line here is very simple. Today it is possible to save for your retirement and have almost every dime of the return on *your* money stay in your account rather than being paid out to people in the financial services industry who are working on owning houses in Palm Beach *and* Jackson Hole. The cost difference—at least 1 percent a year for most employees in 401(k) plans and 2 percent a year for employees in the most common 403(b) plans—means a lot more money in your account when you retire.

The Birth of Lazy Portfolios

Behavioral finance psychological research has shown that most of us have trouble making choices, and the more choices we have, the more trouble we have. This has not escaped the financial services industry, which continues to proliferate the number of investment choices we face and the number of distribution channels in which we can buy them.

It's small wonder that so many people throw up their hands and despair at being able to manage their own money. If it's vexing to decide between eight brands of strawberry preserves, how can one ever decide between the offerings of just the top eight mutual fund firms? Not knowing where to start or what to choose, millions of people put themselves in the hands of a friendly, well-compensated salesperson whose primary mission is to rack up commissions and do enough dollar volume to get the free trip to Hawaii. Helping the customer may also be a motive, but it can be well down the list of motivating factors. The cost to the customer may be a long-term accumulation that is as much as 50 percent lower than it would have been in low-cost passive index funds.

Investors need a do-it-yourself way to invest that requires virtually no thought, effort, or time that will still produce attractive returns. In fact, there is such a method. The Couch Potato Portfolio, which Scott introduced in 1991, is one way to do it.[21] If you can fog a mirror and divide by the number 2 with the help of an electronic calculator, you can manage your own money and be proud of the results.

Here is how it is done.

1. Take your money and divide it in half. Put half in a domestic total market index fund and the other half in a domestic bond index, preferably one of intermediate maturity. Then go back to watching the latest installment of *The Young and the Restless*. When done, watch *All My Children*, as recorded on your DVR.

2. Continue watching daytime soap operas for the next twelve months. Avoid newspaper financial news; don't read anything written about the Federal Reserve, its chairman Ben Bernanke, or the ongoing problems in Greece, Ireland, Portugal, Spain, or Italy. Indeed, avoid reading anything that might cause you to worry. Don't worry; be happy. After a year, return to your portfolio with a profound knowledge of daytime soap operas. Find the total amount in your portfolio somewhere on your monthly statement. Divide that number by 2 using your calculator. Then move money from the fund with more money in it to the fund with less money in it until they are equal.

3. Rinse, and repeat at yearly intervals.

If you had done this from 1973 through 1991, a period that includes a long bear market (1973–1981) and a roaring bull market (1982–1991), you would have done quite nicely, producing good returns with nearly half the risk of an all-stock portfolio. During the full period, a simple Couch Potato portfolio would have returned 10.9 percent annualized, while the S&P 500 would have returned 11.5 percent, a difference of only 0.6 percent. Since the raw index provides a higher return than the majority of managed funds and the return difference is about equal to the cost of running a managed fund, you would have enjoyed a somewhat superior return with about half the risk. You would also have avoided a major source of angst for the entire eighteen years.

The standard deviation of the S&P 500 during the period was 17.9 percent. (Standard deviation is a statistical measure of portfolio volatility.) The Couch Potato portfolio had a standard deviation of 10.7 percent. The simple combination of an equity index fund and a fixed-income index fund worked to provide you with a higher return for the amount of risk you took. This has been called the free lunch of diversification.

If you had invested only during the long bear market (1973–1981), the return on your Couch Potato portfolio would have been 6.3 percent while the S&P 500 would have returned 5.2 percent. If you had invested only during the long bull market (1982–1991), the Couch Potato return was 15.2 percent annualized, trailing the all-equity portfolio return of 17.6 percent.

The second Couch Potato portfolio, created in 2004, was called the Margarita portfolio in honor of the Buffett named Jimmy. You know, the one wasting away:[22]

Wastin' away again in Margaritaville
Searching for my lost shaker of salt

Like the drink, the Margarita portfolio consists of three equal parts: a broad domestic equity index fund, a broad international equity index fund, and a TIPS index fund. (We'll leave it to you to decide which one is tequila and which one is lime juice.) While dividing by the number 3 may pose a greater challenge for some than dividing by the number 2, remedial arithmetic can be practiced by making traditional margaritas, which are made with equal parts tequila, triple sec, and lime juice. (Practice in making this drink is yet another advantage of living in the Southwest.)

Readers who aren't interested in daytime soap operas or the weight gain and liver damage that comes from active margarita drinking can become more active investors by using the Couch Potato Building Block portfolios.[23] These portfolios use anywhere from two to ten asset class building blocks to create broad, diversified portfolios that include international bonds, REITs, energy stocks (as a proxy for commodities), value slices of large- and small-capitalization stocks, and emerging markets.

Needless to say, the Couch Potato portfolios aren't the only way to build what many now call "lazy portfolios." Other entries in the good-performance-comes-from-being-cheap-and-slothful crew include Bill Schultheis's Coffee House portfolios, Bill Bernstein's Coward's Portfolio, Ben Stein's portfolios, Dan Solin's portfolios, Ted Aronson's portfolios, Andrew Tobias's portfolios, Rick Ferri's Core Four portfolio, Frank Armstrong's Ideal Index portfolio, John Bogle's Tax Sheltered Portfolio, the Ultimate Buy and Hold portfolio, David Swensen's Yale portfolio, Jim Lowell's Sowers Growth portfolio, and Craig Israelsen's 7Twelve Balanced portfolio. MarketWatch columnist Paul Farrell provides regular coverage on the performance of many of these portfolios.

Although the construction of all these portfolios is different and each portfolio has a different return and risk level from the others, they share something very important: all are easy to build. They are all built with low-cost index mutual funds or ETFs.[24]

A hefty number of lazy portfolios already exist, and we can be sure that more are coming. We doubt, however, that their numbers will ever come anywhere close to the number of mutual funds (6,974) or ETFs (1,254) that cause people to cringe in indecision.[25] While some may find it difficult to choose among any of more than thirty lazy portfolios, it is certainly an easier task than choosing among the 287 funds categorized as "moderate allocation" by Morningstar, not to mention the 119 categorized as "world allocation" and the 174 categorized as "conservative allocation."

When in doubt, we'll put ease of construction and rebalancing at the top of our preferences. That means we'll go for the Couch Potato Portfolios or Craig Israelson's 7Twelve balanced portfolio. All are built with equal-sized commitments to each investment category or asset class. It means you'll never have to deal with percentages and funny little slices. Like a carefully cut pizza, all investment slices are the same size but with different asset class flavors.

One complaint here is that if there are many solutions to a problem, maybe the problem hasn't been solved. The answer to that is that solution proliferation is less abundant with lazy portfolios than with portfolios offered by the financial services industry. The fact that the industry can afford to offer so many "solutions" is just an indication that it is a very profitable business. They will continue creating "solutions" until it is no longer profitable (for them). At the end of 2010, the Morningstar Principia database recorded 7,950 unique fund portfolios that, when combined with different distribution systems, offered 27,306 ways to be purchased. The choice proliferation was even worse in variable annuities. The same database showed a stunning 103,157 subaccount choices offered through 2,129 variable annuity or life insurance contracts.

This is an area where less is more. The lazy portfolios are a step in the right direction.

More important, returns for the lazy portfolios are attractive. Whatever lazy portfolio you select, it has a good shot at beating the majority of its higher-cost managed competitors. Table 12.1 compares the five-year trailing performance of lazy portfolios with similar broad asset allocations (equities versus fixed income) to both a category average and the twenty-five largest and most successful funds in the category for the period ending May 31, 2011.

The average annualized return of these twelve lazy portfolios was 5.62 percent. The highest was 6.56 percent, and the lowest was 4.49 percent. All had between 60 and 70 percent equity, the typical range for moderate-allocation funds. Yet the average return of all managed funds in this category was only 4.30 percent, a full 1.32 percentage points a year lower. The worst of the dozen lazy funds provided a higher return than the average of the managed funds.

Table 12.1
Comparing lazy portfolios with managed portfolios

Portfolio	Percentage equity	Five-year annualized return
Couch Potato—6 Ways from Sunday	67	6.56%
Yale	70	6.10
Coffeehouse Vanguard	60	6.06
Couch Potato—5 Fold	60	5.96
Aronson Family Taxable	70	5.86
Ultimate Buy and Hold	60	5.86
Frank Armstrong Ideal Index	70	5.48
William Bernstein's Coward's Portfolio	60	5.37
Coffeehouse ETF	60	5.26
Couch Potato-Margarita	67	5.24
Andrew Tobias Lazy	67	5.24
Coffeehouse 3 ETF	67	4.49
Largest 25 Moderate Allocation	63	4.95
Category Average Moderate Allocation	60	4.30

Source: Morningstar Principia, May 31, 2011.

The lazy portfolios don't have quite as large a margin of superiority when we examine the twenty-five largest (and most successful) moderate-allocation funds. This group provided an average annualized return of 4.95 percent. Success, massive assets, and relatively low expenses notwithstanding, this group still trailed the average lazy portfolio by an annualized 0.67 percent a year.

Will the lazy portfolios always perform in this order? No. The same exercise using other trailing time periods will produce a different top dog and a different bottom fund. The only thing we can be reasonably confident about is that you'll get a higher return with one of the lazy portfolios than with a managed portfolio. You certainly won't be penalized for being a do-it-yourself investor who takes slothful investing seriously.

One indication is the long-term performance of a very basic indexed portfolio, the Vanguard Balanced Index fund (VBINX). Over the same time period, the five years ending May 31, 2011, this fund returned an annualized 5.40 percent, a better return than 81 percent of its managed competitors. Over the past fifteen years, this fund, which is a typical 60/40 mix of a domestic stock index and bond index, has provided a higher return than 76 percent of its surviving competitors. Over the past ten-and three-year periods, it has beaten 68 percent and 82 percent, respectively, of its competitors. Over its past eighteen years of operation, the fund has been in the top 50 percent for thirteen years, or 72 percent of the time.

Not convinced? Well, if there ever was a good time for managed funds, it had to be the disaster of 2008 followed by the recovery of 2009 and 2010. That was when adroit, savvy, and egregiously well-paid fund managers would have earned their keep by dodging the bullet of 2008 and bravely recommitting in the next two years. They would have achieved the Holy Grail of investing: selling high and buying low.

Alas, the track record indicates they didn't. While the average moderate-allocation mutual fund provided an annualized return of 0.16 percent over the three years, the average return of twelve lazy portfolios with a similar broad asset allocation was 1.44 percent. That average return would have placed in the top twenty-fourth percentile of funds. Also important, a large majority of the lazy portfolios provided higher returns than the category average, so the odds were with you even if you selected your lazy portfolio randomly, because you liked its name, maybe, or because your tarot cards said it was a winner.

What we have here is the investment version of the race between the tortoise and the hare. The hare is clever, fast, and prideful, but the tortoise is consistent, cheap, and humble. The tortoise, in due course, beats the hare. Needless to say, you won't hear this from Merrill Lynch, Morgan Stanley, UBS, or any other firm that wants to sell you a brilliant service that costs 2 percent a year and is likely to help high-placed strangers build palaces in the Hamptons.

Are we agnostic about which lazy portfolio will be the best one for the coming ten or twenty years? No. We urge readers to be as diversified as possible. We suggest that investors should tilt their portfolios toward investments that would hedge both future inflation and a declining dollar. For us, that means favoring TIPS over traditional coupon Treasury obligations. It means having a commitment to international bonds. It also means owning international stocks. It means owning REITs because they own real estate that inflation would make more valuable. (It doesn't hurt that they also produce an above-average yield.) It means owning a proxy for commodities. For us, the simple way to do that is to own an index fund that invests only in energy companies.[26]

Although many will argue that an energy stock is still a stock, not a commodity, we like the liquidity of these stocks. We know they go up and down with oil prices. We also know that energy is the largest single component of every commodity index. As curmudgeon investor Jim Rogers pointed out in his 2004 book *Hot Commodities*,[27] a whopping 72.5 percent of the Goldman-Sachs Commodity Index is different forms of oil and gas energy. Equally important, every other commodity requires large energy inputs for its growth or extraction. Environmentalists are quick to point out that whether we are eating corn, wheat, or soybeans, we wouldn't be eating anything without the oil- and petrochemical-based products used in farming. Basically the real currency of the industrial world isn't the dollar, the yen, the pound, or the yuan.

It is the British thermal unit.

Would we add anything else to these six pieces? Only if you really like managing your own investments. If that's the case, we'd add "value" slices of the different equity asset classes: U.S. large-capitalization value, U.S. small-capitalization value, and international value. Research has regularly shown that buying low price-to-earnings-ratio stocks provides better long-term returns than buying high price-to-earnings-ratio stocks. This may seem perverse, since we all hope for growth, but that may be part of the reason: the high price-to-earnings ratio stocks carry an optimism premium while the low price-to-earnings ratio stocks carry a pessimism discount.

Is there a lazy portfolio that has all the basic pieces? Yes. It is the Couch Potato Six Ways from Sunday portfolio. It has all six of the important elements; it is 67 percent equities and 33 percent fixed income. You'll find in table 12.1 that its annualized return of 5.96 percent was well ahead of the 4.30 percent annualized return of the average managed moderate allocation fund.

The message here is very simple and relentlessly affirmed by work from different researchers over different time periods in the past half-century. The purported smart money on Wall Street can't get in the ring with simple, low-cost index investing. Ignore the calls to superior returns by people in the know, keep your expenses down, let overwhelming indecision spread your investments around, and you are on your way to a happy investment success.

One of the most interesting lazy portfolios was created by Craig Israelsen, an associate professor at Brigham Young University. Searching for an updated, global version of the traditional balanced fund—something that would reflect our increasingly global economy—Israelsen selected a dozen basic indexes and put them together in a portfolio. Investing equal amounts in each asset class, he used eight equity indexes and four fixed income indexes. This made the portfolio two-thirds equities and one-third fixed income, similar to the traditional 60/40 balanced portfolio of domestic equities and bonds.

For his building blocks Israelsen used these indexes:

- Large-capitalization domestic stocks
- Midcapitalization domestic stocks
- Small-capitalization domestic value stocks
- Non-U.S. developed stocks
- Non-U.S. emerging markets
- Real estate
- Natural resources
- Commodities
- Domestic bonds

- U.S. inflation-protected securities
- Non-U.S. bonds
- Cash

Over the ten years ending December 31, 2010, a portfolio based on indexes that track these asset classes returned an annualized 8.49 percent while the Vanguard Balanced Index fund returned 4.13 percent, as shown in table 12.2.[28] Since, as we've shown, the Vanguard Balanced Index fund has put in a better performance than the majority of all managed balanced funds, it is reasonable to conclude that a lazy portfolio like this would have trounced the active funds.

Sadly, it would have been difficult to create an actual 7Twelve Balanced portfolio back in 1999. Although there are over 1,000 ETFs today, there were only 29 at the beginning of 1999. There were no fixed-income ETFs, no real estate ETFs, no emerging market ETFs, and no broad international ETFs. Only two of the twelve ETFs needed were available to complete the recipe. It would have been easier with regular index mutual funds, but you still would not have had a natural resources fund, a commodities fund, an international bond fund, or an inflation-protected securities fund. To fill each of the missing categories, it would have been necessary to choose a managed fund.

But that was then. Today, as Israelsen's book points out, you may have multiple choices of ETFs to fill each category.[29]

Equal Investment Amounts Don't Mean Even-Handed Investing

Most lazy portfolios, like professional portfolios, have different allocations to different asset classes. Some, like the Couch Potato portfolios and the 7Twelve Balanced portfolio, put equal amounts in each asset class, so it is tempting to view them as even-handed. But they are not. A truly neutral index investor—one who wanted to participate in the broad growth of global wealth—would invest in each asset class in proportion to its value in the total of all global wealth.

Eugene Fama Jr. is the son of the University of Chicago professor who, along with Professor Kenneth French, did the research that has created so much interest in small-capitalization and value stocks. Fama has a talent for graphic displays. One of his best is a map of the world in blocks of different size, with each block representing the total market capitalization

Table 12.2
A diversified global balanced portfolio versus a traditional balanced portfolio

Measure	7Twelve Balanced Index	Vanguard Balanced Index
2010	14.28%	13.12%
Three-year-annualized return	2.48	1.85
Five-year-annualized return	6.65	4.48
Ten-year-annualized return	8.49	4.13
Number of negative years	3	3

Note: This table compares the annualized performance of an index fund portfolio with twelve asset classes with a traditional balanced portfolio that is 60 percent equities and 40 percent bonds.
Source: Craig L. Israelsen, "Building a Better Balanced Fund," January 2011, http://www.7twelveportfolio.com/Downloads/A-Better-Balanced-Fund.pdf.

of each nation—figure 12.1. It's a picture that gives a quick and visceral sense of where the wealth is around the planet.

At the end of 2009, the biggest block was the United States, with 42 percent of world capitalization. The United Kingdom and Japan tied for second, with 9 percent each. Canada, France, Germany, Switzerland, and Australia followed at 3 to 4 percent each. Every other market was 2 percent, or less, of the global total. For all that we hear about China, it accounted for only 2 percent of global capitalization—the same amount as Brazil, South Korea, Taiwan, and Spain.

If we divide the world into large blocks—domestic, international, developed, and emerging markets—the split is 42 percent for the United States, 46 percent for the other developed economies, and 10 percent for the emerging markets. (The missing 2 percent represents markets in which investing is extremely difficult or impossible.) The size of the blocks changes every year, and it is widely anticipated that the emerging markets capitalization will eventually grow to equal or exceed the wealth of the developed economies.

Inside the U.S. market, you can also participate in finer slices; witness the well-known Morningstar tic-tac-toe matrix of nine boxes representing large-capitalization, midcapitalization, and small-capitalization crossed with growth, blend, and value. If Eugene Fama Jr. drew the Morningstar matrix, however, it would have very different size squares because

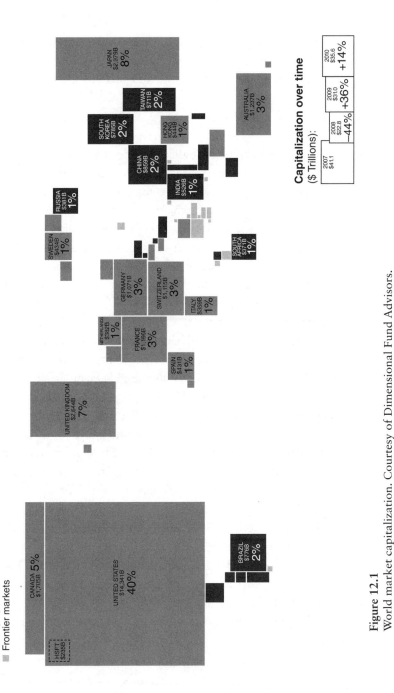

Figure 12.1
World market capitalization. Courtesy of Dimensional Fund Advisors.

the large-capitalization portion of the U.S. market accounts for about 74 percent of its total market capitalization. That leaves only 26 percent to be divided between midcapitalization and small capitalization.

When Is an Index an Index?

If it was difficult to build an index fund portfolio twenty years ago because of so few fund choices, today it is difficult to build an index fund portfolio because there are so many choices. This is particularly true in the burgeoning world of ETFs, where over 1,000 funds now hold over $1 trillion in assets, many of them pushing the limits of what most people think an index fund is. Some are so specific and specialized that they aren't remotely close to representing an asset class. Others were designed as speculative vehicles, creating opportunities to profit from (and multiply) a major bear (or bull) market move.

This proliferation worries some. In his book *The Power of Passive Investing,* index investing researcher and investment advisor Richard A. Ferri writes, "What qualifies as an index has broadened over the years as more ETFs come to market that follow highly customized non-standard index methods. Today, it seems as though anything can be called an index. An index provider merely creates a mechanical set of rules for security selection, security weighting, and trading, and publishes their back-tested results."[30] Ferri's firm, Portfolio Solutions LLC, creates and manages index fund portfolios at very low cost, representing a challenge to the much higher costs of legacy brokerage and management firms.[31]

Ferri isn't alone. More recently Don Phillips at Morningstar commented that indexing had developed true believer extremists.[32] He noted that one ETF provider had declared that active fund managers were akin to big tobacco companies because active management was as dangerous to investor wealth as tobacco is to our health. The reality is that Wall Street has seen that ETFs are an opportunity for trading and fees. So it is proliferating offers that have no connection to the basics of indexing.

Skeptics should consider the names of a few ETFs:

- Proshares UltraShort MidCap 400
- Powershares DB Gold Double Short ETN
- Rydex Inverse 2X S&P 500
- Direxion Daily Financial Bear 3X Shares

So what defines a real index fund? Ferri and others argue that it is a portfolio that holds stocks in proportion to their market capitalization and that it is unambiguous, measurable, and specified in advance. After that, it represents an identifiable asset class, such as domestic, international, or emerging market equities (for broad strokes) or domestic large capitalization or domestic small capitalization for finer (but distinct) strokes.

Sadly, the requirement for market capitalization weighting excludes what we believe is the most interesting new effort at index construction, Rob Arnott's Fundamental indexes. Frustrated by traditional indexes because of their capitalization weighting, the former editor of the *Financial Analysts Journal* developed a variety of indexes based on factors that are more fundamental than market capitalization, such as sales, growth of book value, and dividends. Although some dismiss his method as nothing more than brilliant marketing for his firm, Research Affiliates, which now manages $75 billion, it can also be argued that fundamental weighting works to avoid the distortions of over- and undervaluation that routinely happen in bull and bear markets, such as the information sector stocks.[33] Morningstar, which combines computer hardware, software, telecommunications, and media stocks to create what it calls "the information sector," notes that the combined value of these stocks soared to a peak of 43.5 percent of the entire S&P 500 index early in 2000. That was the peak of the Internet bubble. From there, the value of the sector plummeted to a low of 19.3 percent of the index in September 2002. As we write this, it has recovered to 22.75 percent of the index. If you slavishly follow market capitalization, Arnott argues, any index you create will systematically buy high and sell low.

Using Arnott's fundamental indexing method, the Powershares RAFI US 1000, an index of the largest publicly traded domestic stocks, provided a return of 2.51 percent annualized for the three years ending November 2010. That may not sound very good, but it beat the Russell 1000 Value index by 4.60 percent a year. Other Research Affiliates Fundamental Index vehicles, such as the Schwab International Large Company Index ETF, have also provided superior performance over the same period. Back testing over longer periods indicates performance that is significantly better than that of traditional capitalization-weighted indexes.

Below, for instance, are some trailing period returns for a variety of Research Affiliates Fundamental Indices compared to their traditional capitalization-weighted competitors. As you can see, Arnott's method may be against conventional indexing rules, but the returns that follow from this method are more than enough to gain our interest. If capitalization-weighted index funds trump managed funds about 70 percent of the time and fundamental weighted-index funds trump capitalization-weighted funds, it is possible that the indexing purists and indexing pragmatists will part company.

The performance differences, at least over the past ten years, are significant. Here are some examples:

• The FTSE RAFI All World 3000 index returned an annualized 9.67 percent over the period, while the MSCI All World index returned only 5.13 percent.

• The FTSE RAFI 1000 index of the largest U.S. stocks returned an annualized 5.76 percent compared to the 3.16 percent of the Russell 1000 index.

• The FTSE RAFI Developed World ex US index returned 8.34 percent while the MSCI World ex US large cap index returned 5.58 percent.

• The FTSE RAFI Emerging Markets index returned 23.33 percent compared to the 16.48 percent of the MSCI Emerging Markets index.

As you can see, these are significant differences, at least for this time period.

Is There a Better Way Than the Lazy Portfolios?

While the evidence supports the simple, "naive" asset allocation of most of the lazy portfolios (remember that the managed portfolios, on average, provided a lower return than the built-for-ease lazy portfolios), readers who want to do more than make equal investments in different areas may be wondering if there is some way to figure out an asset allocation that might improve returns or reduce risk.

One way is avoid any asset class bets. This means having your portfolio constructed so that each market or asset class is represented in proportion to its role in the real-world global portfolio. That would mean a 42 percent allocation to domestic stocks, a 9 percent allocation to both the United Kingdom and Japan, and only 2 percent to China, because those are their relative sizes in the real global portfolio.

Having done that, your wealth would grow, or shrink, with the ups and downs of the world economy. Rather than increase your standing in the world by superior investment decisions, you could increase your share of global wealth by superior personal saving, that is, investing more new money. That's pretty neutral. We think it's a good way to go, and you may make some contribution to ending the American saving famine. The worst that will happen is that you go down with everyone else. The best that will happen is that you'll work your butt off to add to your savings and rise above steerage on the *S.S. Global Wealth*.

Unfortunately, that's also a complicated way to go if you are trying to do it country by country. It can also be a little silly if you are a small investor, since your small-country investments will be tiny, which is neither easy nor efficient.

The only practical solution for small investors is to buy shares in a fund that puts it all together for you. Fortunately, such funds now exist. Since its launch in June 2008, the Vanguard Total World Stock Index ETF (ticker: VT) has allowed investors to buy the entire world market with an annual expense ratio of 0.25 percent. They put all the pieces together for you and do all the necessary rebalancing. The iShares MSCI ACWI Index ETF (ticker: ACWI), launched in March of the same year, indexes the world for 0.35 percent.

After that, you simply make the Panglossian assumption that this is the best of all possible worlds and that whatever happens was meant to happen, because your "my world, like it or not" portfolio is about as good as it gets. As a practical matter, it probably is.

Another approach uses a technique called mean variance optimization, which is not something you can do in your spare time at home. Based on work by Nobel laureate Harry Markowitz, the idea is to seek risk efficiency rather than maximum return. This isn't a portfolio that beats the market. It is a portfolio that is constructed so that it gets the maximum return for a given level of risk. Since most portfolios aren't constructed with this in mind, effort made to achieve risk efficiency may be rewarded with a better "ride" than most people experience: more return for a given amount of risk.[34]

Will low-cost passive investing alone save our butts in a world full of irresponsible governments that make, and pay, their promises with printing presses? No, but it will help. It's a big step toward protecting ourselves from Wall Street and its asset-destroying fees. Think of it as swimming with the tide rather than swimming against it.

As you will soon see, there are other steps we can take. These have nothing to do with investing and everything to do with how we live our lives. Many of them are entirely natural, some are obligatory, and all can work to protect us from both Wall Street and government. These decisions can also be worth as much as, or more than, every dime we ever save in our 401(k) accounts.

13

The Power of Ordinary Living

Certain things in life are highly predictable. Talk to a suburban mom, for instance, and there is a high probability that she drives a minivan or an SUV. She might want to drive something else, but kids have stuff and friends, so a vehicle with a large carrying capacity is essential. That little Miata will have to wait.

We could get dark about life's predictability. We could sum up all human existence with, "Life's a bitch, and then you die." There are moments, such as watching the evening news, when this seems like a pretty good summary. But when it comes to personal finance, there are predictable things about our life cycle that make our lives a lot easier than the financial services and retirement complex would have us believe.

The greatest myth we face is based on something called the replacement rate, the amount of income we will need as percentage of our preretirement income to sustain our standard of living in retirement.[1] The conventional wisdom puts this at 70 to 85 percent, depending on household income level. Although this may be close to true if you live your entire life as a single person, never have children, and always rent rather than own, most of us marry, have children, and educate them. More often than not, we also borrow to own a home and slowly pay off the mortgage.

Each of these very common actions has the same impact on our lives: each reduces the amount of money we have to spend on ourselves during most of our working years. We spend lots of income that doesn't need to be replaced because we won't be raising children when we are seventy-five years old. That means we don't need to replace 70 to 85 percent of our preretirement income because we've never had that amount to spend on ourselves. And since we need less income to sustain ourselves in retirement, we also don't need to save as much or accumulate as big a nest egg as that 70 to 85 percent industry rule-of-thumb requires.

Skeptical? We don't blame you. After all, the financial services industry has been pounding these high replacement rates into our brains. But the industry just happens to derive its income from our savings. And the higher they set our retirement income target, the more money we're told to save. We need to remember that our long-term saving is their short-term lunch money.

The intentional error of the conventional wisdom becomes visible when you examine the cost of creating and supporting a household from its creation, from being young and single to being old and widowed. Table 13.1 shows an exercise done with a Department of Labor tool for estimating the differences in cost of living for households of different sizes and ages.[2] As you can see from the table, two may not be able to live for the price of one, but there is an economy of shared living: the cost index changes from 71 to 100 on marriage, not 142. The consumption index figure tracks the relative cost of sustaining a household at each stage of development and age.

Observe how the cost changes with each change in family age and structure. It more than doubles in real cost until the children start to leave the nest. (These figures, by the way, don't include the cost of a college education for the children, orthodontics, or family trips to Disney World.) When the kids leave the nest, the cost of supporting them also leaves. By the time the couple is retired, their cost of living is about the same as it was when they were young marrieds. Creating a family is a very expensive project. We probably didn't have to tell you that.

Now suppose we presented these figures another way. Suppose we graphed household cost of living against age.[3] Then we'd see an expense mountain. The cost of living from marriage would rise sharply as children were born, and it would peak at they matured enough to leave home. It's a pretty intimidating mountain, and we are climbing it, or descending it, most of our adult lives.

The important observation, however, is that the cost of living for the newlyweds on one side of the mountain is about the same as the cost of living on the other side of the mountain as the couple approaches retirement. Everything in between represents income the couple was spend-

Table 13.1
Consumption through the life cycle

Household status	Years married	Age	Consumption index relative to 100 for young marrieds
Single	NA	24	71
Young marrieds	0	25	100
Young marrieds with one child	3	28	127
Young married with two children	5	30	147
Married, older child age 6–15	10	35	204
Married, older child age 16–17	19	44	231
Married, older child 18 or over	21	46	196
Married, one child at home	25	50	186
Empty nest couple	30	55	120
Retired couple	40	65 or over	104

Note: How the cost of living varies with your age and household size, expressed as an index. A young couple represents a base index of 100.
Source: Carolyn A. Jackson. "Revised Equivalence Scale for Estimating Equivalent Incomes or Budgets Costs by Family Type." Bureau of Labor Statistics, 1968. http://openlibrary.org/books/OL5389004M/Revised_equivalence_scale_for_estimating_equivalent_incomes_or_budgets_costs_by_family_type.

ing on the kids, not on itself. As you can see in figure 13.1 it's a lot of spending, over many years.

Climbing the Mountain of Family Expenses

These are not exact numbers. We are simply representing a positive side of the reality of human reproduction, and one that is largely overlooked in conventional financial planning. Typically we are told of an intimidating expense such as college tuition (*Here, buy our 529 plan!*). We are never told that we won't have to replace all that income we spend on

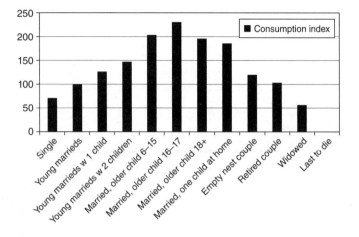

Figure 13.1

Consumption index. *Source*: Carolyn A. Jackson. "Revised Equivalence Scale for Estimating Equivalent Incomes or Budgets Costs by Family Type." Bureau of Labor Statistics, 1968. http://openlibrary.org/books/OL5389004M/Revised_ equivalence_scale_for_estimating_equivalent_incomes_or_budgets_costs_by_ family_type.

or put aside for the kids. All of that income is income we don't need to replace when we retire.

We could also change the profile of expense by adding or subtracting a child. And we could move it in time by delaying marriage, as many do. But it would still be a steep mountain, and every couple with children must climb it. This is why most couples don't need to replace 70 to 85 percent of their total income when retired: much of its past income has been spent on children and their education. Additional income has been committed to debt repayment, such as a home mortgage. None of this income needs to be replaced in retirement.

This is not what we hear from the insurance industry, the brokerage industry, or most of the research organizations that study retirement and retirement income adequacy. Indeed, media reports regularly tell us of surveys and studies showing that our savings are inadequate, that we will need a small fortune to cover our medical expenses in retirement, that we won't be able to afford the nearly inevitable cost of long-term care, and so on, all grounded on the assumption that people need to replace about 80 percent of their preretirement income.

While it is true that all of these things—retirement savings and income, medical expenses in retirement, and long-term care—are serious issues because most of us don't save enough or get a high enough return, after investing costs, on the money we save, the reality is that it is all overstated by an amount that makes a big difference.

To see the difference between economics-based financial planning, called consumption smoothing, and conventional financial planning, you can use ESPlannerBASIC for free and with no login at www.esplanner .com/basic. Economic Security Planning, Inc. (Kotlikoff's company) provides this simplified, top-rated financial planning program as a public service. You can also read the extensive case studies posted at www.esplanner.com under Learn More and at Scott's website, www.assetbuilder.com.

Will everything be hunky-dory thanks to procreation and consumption smoothing? Maybe. Maybe not. But if you start to pay attention to expenses that you have today that you won't have at some future date, you'll be taking the first steps to explore what you can do beyond active worry about public policy. You'll be able to play with actions you can take to protect, maintain, or improve your standard of living through the rest of your life. Note that most of this has nothing to do with investing per se. Yet we're talking about tweaks and personal decisions that are likely to have a big impact on your long-term security.

Rearranging the Investment Sock Drawer

While most investment advice focuses on how you can maximize the return on your savings by picking savvy managers, capturing big dividends, or bagging big capital gains in the next big start-up, you may be able to find an effective fortune by making better decisions about how you manage the resources that you have. Here's an example using ESPlannerBASIC.

With $1.2 million in financial assets and a debt-free house in Alabama, Bill and Belinda, age sixty, figured they could afford to retire, even if they weren't yet eligible to take their Social Security benefits.[4] Their shelter costs are $5,500 a year, and they have the good fortune to have $400,000 in taxable accounts, $200,000 each in 401(k) accounts, and another $200,000 each in Roth IRA accounts. They also make fairly conservative assumptions about the earning power of their savings: 3 percentage points over inflation.

So how should they proceed? If they do what most people do, they'll take Social Security benefits at age sixty-two, allow their 401(k) plans to continue growing tax deferred, and draw down their Roth IRA accounts. That will feel good because it will virtually eliminate a tax bill in their first years of retirement. If they do that, consumption smoothing says they will be able to sustain spending of $71,089, in today's dollars for each of the next forty years until they die at age 100. They figure that gives them some margin for error since the odds are they won't live that long. That $71,089 a year, by the way, is what they have to spend after income taxes, Medicare premiums, and shelter expenses.

Can they do better? You bet. If they take their 401(k) assets first and exhaust these funds before tapping their Roth accounts, their lifetime spending will rise slightly to $72,236. But if they also delay taking 401(k) withdrawals until age sixty-five, their sustainable spending will be $73,516. This is not magic. It reflects their ability to lower their lifetime taxes by withdrawing from their 401(k) when they have less taxable income and, therefore, face a lower marginal tax rate.

They can do even better by not taking Social Security benefits until they are seventy years old instead of sixty-two. This will increase their sustainable spending to $78,282: a 10.1 percent increase over the path most people take. To have $78,282 a year in spendable income from their first plan of withdrawals, they would have needed an additional $225,000 in assets!

How does additional income come from what seems like nothing? Three things. First, they benefit from deferring taking Social Security benefits because the increase in benefits from deferral is worth a lot more than the assets they have to spend while they are deferring. Second, by deferring their Social Security benefits, they avoid some of the higher taxes they would pay due to the taxation of Social Security benefits when their income from other sources exceeds certain thresholds. Those thresholds aren't inflation adjusted. Third, they benefit from the receipt of some additional spousal benefits thanks to a wrinkle in Social Security regulations few people know about. Belinda can receive spousal benefits between ages sixty-six and seventy thanks to Bill's filing for his retirement at full retirement age but suspending its collection. We won't bother you with all the details of this and other options, but this case study (http://www

.esplanner.com/case-when-should-i-take-social-security) provides a clear summary.[5]

If you are tempted to sniff at the 10.1 percent increase in their retirement standard of living, remember that we're talking about a period of forty years, so they are gaining $7,193 a year in real purchasing power every year—from age sixty to one hundred, if they live till then. However you slice it, the increase is worth more than every dime one of them saved in a 401(k) plan over a lifetime of work.

Another way to view that $7,193 annual gain in real spending power is to think about how difficult and chancy it would be to squeeze that amount of income from a portfolio in the current low-yield market.

It can also help to annuitize some of your assets. You can do this by giving a sum of money to an insurance company in exchange for a guaranteed lifetime income, no matter how long you live. You can buy an annuity for the length of your life or your spouse's life. You can also buy a joint annuity that will provide a lifetime income until both of you die. William and Alice, for instance, are both sixty-five years old and have no children; they have $300,000 each in 401(k) accounts, $500,000 in taxable investments, a modest home, and $17,000 in Social Security benefits.[6] If they invest their 401(k) money in Treasury Inflation Indexed Securities (TIPS) that earn 2.4 percent over the rate of inflation, consumption smoothing says they can spend $59,692 a year until they die at age 100. If they buy inflation-adjusted life annuities with their 401(k) assets, however, their lifetime consumption will rise by 15.4 percent to $68,884 a year.

These are decisions that require nothing. No effort. No behavior change. No additional savings. It's all gain, no pain.[7] We can also improve our long-term spending by making lifestyle decisions that entail less pain than it seems.

Benefits from Big Decisions 1: The Five-fold Benefit of Working Longer

The Social Security Administration reports that nearly 70 percent of all retirees take their Social Security benefits at the earliest possible age, sixty-two. Some do this out of necessity. Others do it because they have the resources to retire then. Retiring at that age was a lot easier in the America that has largely disappeared since 1970. That's the America where workers had lifetime jobs at large, profitable corporations that created generously funded pensions and retiree health insurance benefits. In that America, companies offered buyouts that bridged the gap until full retirement age. In a typical "5 and 5" staff reduction plan, the corporation would offer employees a year or more of severance pay. Then it would calculate their pension as though they had five more years of service and were five years older. As a consequence, it was possible to retire at age sixty with essentially the same income as if they had worked the additional five years. But you could move to Florida instead.

Today very few offers are as generous. Worse, with employer-provided retirement health insurance disappearing, many would-be early retirees compare their severance offer to the cost of health insurance until they are eligible for Medicare. They quickly decide that early retirement isn't for them. They can't afford to finance the cost gap.

Working longer has a quintuple payoff.

1. Initial Social Security retirement benefits rise for each year you delay taking benefits. They rise at between 7 and 8 percent a year in real terms for everyone born in 1953 or later.

2. Those additional years of work are likely to be at relatively high income. Those high-income years may replace lower-income years, and the benefit is calculated based on your highest thirty-five years of earnings during your entire work life, increasing the benefit still more.

3. Any savings you already have will be allowed to grow for as many years as you defer retiring. Decide to delay retiring eight years, from sixty-two to seventy, and your 401(k) plan savings could double even if you don't add a dime in new savings. Doubling would require an annualized return of about 9 percent, not something you could count on but close to historical averages.

4. You may be able to save big chunks of new money over the additional years of working. While few young workers can afford to salt away the $16,500 a year contribution maximum for 401(k) plans, let alone the $22,000 maximum for workers who are at least fifty years old, many workers in their sixties can do it and are eager for the additional tax deductions. Many couples, for instance, replace their dependent child deductions with deductions for higher qualified plan contributions. It is the only way to prevent an increase in taxes.

5. Every additional year you work is a year gone. It won't reduce your life expectancy by a full year, but it does reduce the number of years you'll be living in retirement. According to the United States Life Tables from the National Vital Statistics Reports, for instance, a typical American has an expectancy of 20.5 years at age sixty-two and 14.6 years at age seventy, a reduction of nearly 6 years during the 8-year period.[8] The difference will allow some retirees to safely make larger withdrawals from their retirement savings.

The combination of these five factors can be extraordinary.

Take the case of Island Guy George. If he could, Island Guy George would be a model for Tommy Bahama. Unfortunately, he is more like the Margaritaville version of the Big Lebowski, so he has had to keep a regular day job to pay the bills. George is wondering what delaying retirement will do for him. At the moment he is sixty-two, divorced, and single, earning $50,000, a year and renting at $1,000 a month. He has $25,000 in taxable savings and $100,000 in his company 401(k) plan. Social Security tells him that his benefit, at age sixty-two, would be $1,500 a month. He is hoping to earn 6 percent on his financial assets and plans to live to 100, sustained by a daily vitamin-rich margarita. How will that work?

Not too well. Consumption smoothing says he will have $8,509 a year to spend after rent and other expenses. But if he keeps working through age seventy, his Social Security benefits will increase by roughly 70 percent, and his 401(k) assets will increase nicely even if he saves only enough (6 percent of income) to capture his employers' 3 percent match. His sustainable consumption spending, however, will rise to $22,916, an increase of 216 percent even if he lives to 100.

Does he need that much? Maybe not. Island Guy George is a shorts and flip-flops kind of guy, so he plans to play it by ear, knowing he can quit anytime and take fifty-two rather than just three weeks of vacation. If he works another five years, for instance, he knows his after-rent, after-taxes, and after-Medicare premium spending money can rise to $18,472 a year. So in only five years, he can more than double his remaining lifetime spending power.

Figuring out how to double your retirement spending money is difficult if you are forty or fifty, but one of the really big advantages of the sixties is that each year of additional work is a powerful lever on what you'll have when you don't work. George also has a backup plan: trade his flip-flops for dance shoes and start a new career as a cruise ship tango instructor.

Benefits from Big Decisions 2: Renting or Hitting the Open Road

The most valuable asset many Americans own is their home. It may have gone down in value, but long-term owners are likely to have built equity from both paying off their mortgage and seeing some increase in value since they bought their house many years ago. Lou and Linda Homebody, for instance, are about to retire. They own their $250,000 home outright. Lou has been what the Social Security trustees call a high earner, earning about $65,000 in 2010, or about 60 percent more than the average wage earner. Linda is Lou's age and has worked on and off during their marriage, so she'll enjoy a Social Security benefit that is about half of Lou's benefit of $17,000, providing them with total Social Security benefits of $25,500 a year.

They also have $250,000 in Lou's 401(k) account, but no pension and other financial assets of only $25,000. Although their home has no mortgage, its annual tax, insurance, and operating expense bill is rising, and they are facing years of major replacements that are likely to bring the out-of-pocket cost of shelter to about $15,000 a year—if they are careful and avoid doing a kitchen remodel that will use enough granite to build a mausoleum. But if they do avoid trendy excesses and they can hold their shelter expenses at that level, consumption smoothing says they will have $15,132 a year available to spend after income taxes, Medicare premiums, and shelter expenses.[9] (All of this assumes they will earn 7 percent on their financial assets, slightly less than the 8 percent average of a balanced portfolio, and that inflation will run at 3 percent a year.)

Lou and Linda would like to do more in their retirement than mow their lawn, so that $15,132 of income available for consumption spending doesn't look very attractive.

"Gee, Linda, what should we do? What are our options?"

"It all depends on how adventurous we are."

"What do you mean?"

"Well, suppose we gave up lawn care and became renters? I don't really want to spend the next twenty years staying at home because we need to replace the roof, the heating and air-conditioning system, the appliances, and whatever else comes up."

"That's radical."

"Think about it. My 'honey-do' lists would get real short."

"And what's the other option?"

"Let's be extreme retirees. Let's buy an RV and a good truck to haul it and hit the road. If you're going to have a short honey-do list, I want to go minimalist on housekeeping. That's what happens when you live in less than 300 square feet."

"Wow. We could see everything we want to see, drive the open road for years, and then settle in one of those RV resorts in Florida. Or Texas. Or Arizona!"

Renting or living in an RV is not for everyone, but the reality is that some alternative to traditional home ownership may be the way that millions of boomers solve the retirement equation.[10]

How much will either path change their consumption spending? Lots.

If they sell their house and net $250,000 that they invest for the same 7 percent return they get on their other retirement assets and limit their shelter expenses to the same $16,000 a year they were expecting to pay to support their house, their sustainable real consumption rises to $28,611. That's nearly double the $15,132 they would have by holding on to their house. In addition, both of them will gain personal freedom, and they'll be able to travel with fewer worries.

Their spending power will rise still more if they become full-timers in an RV. Selling their cars and house, they take $50,000 from the sale of the home to buy a complete truck and RV. They could spend lots more, but they take advantage of the depressed economy to buy a fifth wheel (a type of trailer) that is a few years old in case they discover that the open road isn't what they hope it will be.

They also figure on spending $400 a month for slots at different RV parks through the year. They know some are less expensive and some are more expensive (or much more expensive in high season), but it ought to even out with some free nights when they visit children and friends or enjoy free stays in WalMart parking lots. The result is $38,838 a year of money to spend. That's an enormous change from the $15,000 they would have by staying put in their aging traditional house.

Is there a similar but more conventional choice? You bet. They can instead buy a manufactured home in an RV park where larger units are allowed. This will get them a unit with about 1,100 square feet, two bedrooms, two baths, and long-term ground rent in a manufactured home community or an RV park. A prime example is Monte Vista in Mesa, Arizona.[11]

Will the numbers actually work out this way? We have no doubt that there will be surprises. But there are also surprises in owning an aging house. Lou and Linda could also decide to sell their house and downsize to a condo, knowing that many are available in Florida, Arizona, and Nevada at reasonable prices. The inventory of unsold houses is so great in some areas that it is possible to find modest houses and condos for $40 to $50 a square foot—well under replacement cost. Whatever they do, getting out of their existing house and trying something else will give them more spendable income—something more than $15,132 a year but probably less than $38,838 a year.

That's a big range. Creating it has absolutely nothing to do with their investment returns. It has everything to do with their adaptability and personal decisions that add significant freedom to their lives. Those decisions are the equivalent of new investment. As we write this, Lou and Linda would need to invest $160,000 in an inflation-adjusted life annuity to gain $10,000 a year of lifetime income, before taxes.[12]

Yes, We Are Free to Move around the Country!

Our shelter decisions are probably the biggest single lever we have on our cost of living. Shelter figures prominently in the consumer price index. Whether owning or renting, we spend more on shelter than we spend on anything else. The fact that shelter is our biggest lever doesn't mean it is our only one, though. We can do a great deal simply by "repotting" ourselves from a high-cost-of-living area to a lower-cost-of-living area.

The best-known data for comparing the cost of living in different U.S. urban areas are those developed by the Council for Community and Economic Research. The council develops data on specific spending areas from participating cities to produce relative cost-of-living figures. Their data include not only the cost of housing but the cost of food, insurance, fuel, clothing, medical care, and everything else people commonly buy.

(You can access this information, for a fee, by visiting the council's Web site, www.coli.org, to get full reports comparing one city with another.)

But we have a quicker way to get a broad overview of the economic benefits or liabilities of moving: pick up a copy of *Where to Retire* magazine. The newsstand price is $4.95. Each issue contains a chart that will help you compare the cost of living in 100 cities. What you will see very quickly is that some places are good to be from and other places are good to be moving to. Needless to say, your actual moving decision won't be just about money. There are places in this country where people will happily move to be poor. That, at least, is what many people say in Santa Fe, New Mexico, where income is scarce and prices are high.

If you live in a high-cost area—just about anywhere in the Boston-to-Washington corridor or the West Coast—you have a lot of choices for places you can move to and enjoy a substantial drop in your cost of living. A resident of Philadelphia, for instance, would cut his cost of living by 24 percent moving to Austin; 22 percent to Charleston; 25 percent to Colorado Springs; 28 percent to Florence, Arizona; 28 percent to Knoxville; 30 percent to Palm Coast, Florida; or 10 percent to Portland, Oregon.

Indeed, the fastest way to improve your standard of living is to move almost anywhere else from some of our most expensive cities. If you live in Manhattan, for instance, you can reduce your cost of living by 20 percent by moving to Honolulu, another very expensive location. But you could also cut your cost of living by 37 percent moving to San Diego; 46 percent by moving to Bellingham, Washington; Fort Lauderdale; or Hilton Head. As a practical matter, Manhattanites can move almost anywhere else in the country and cut their cost of living by more than 50 percent according to Council for Community and Economic Research data.

Some cities are so expensive that you will be able to upgrade your shelter even as you cut your cost of living. You can see the possibilities by using the National Association of Realtors median home price figures to compare housing costs in different cities. Recently, for instance, the median home price in the Boston/Cambridge area at the end of the first quarter of 2011 was $322,100, down from $361,100 in 2008, while the median home price in Austin, the most expensive urban location in Texas, was $188,200, down only slightly from $188,600 in 2008. Switch from urban living to a slower pace, and the same people could move to Cape Coral/Fort Myers, Florida, and buy a median price house for only $91,800.

There are differences, of course. The Cape Coral/Fort Myers area would probably be the poster child for the housing bust if there wasn't such heavy competition from places like Las Vegas, Stockton, California, and Phoenix. Beyond that, it isn't likely that your grandchildren live and work in Cape Coral or Fort Myers—if only because there are so few jobs there. Many boomers are discovering, however, that cities with strong job growth—cities like Austin and Dallas in Texas and Phoenix in Arizona—are where their grandchildren live, so the draw is even greater. It is possible to move from an expensive area and be closer to adult children and grandchildren at the same time.

Reducing your cost of living has a direct impact on the amount you need to have saved to finance your retirement. Suppose, for instance, that your Social Security and investment income put you into the nasty little tax trap that David Stockman set in 1983 with the reform of Social Security. Suppose some of the dollars withdrawn from your IRA rollover account are taxed at 15 percent. This is the highest rate most Americans are likely to pay in retirement since a couple filing a joint return can have up to $88,000 of income and be in the 15 percent bracket. Unfortunately, some of that income may also trigger the taxation of an additional 50 cents of Social Security benefits. That means you are, in effect, paying taxes at a marginal rate of 22.5 percent. Suppose also that you feel safe making IRA withdrawals at 4 percent. As a consequence, it takes $25,000 to provide $1,000 of pretax income and $775 of spendable income. Cutting your cost of living by $10,000 a year by moving, then, is the equivalent of "finding" over $300,000 in retirement savings. Some readers may sniff at $300,000, but it is more than most boomers have. To put it in another perspective, if you made the maximum 401(k) contribution allowed for people age fifty and over, $22,000, that $300,000 is nearly fourteen years of maximum contributions and you can create the equivalent by making a single personal decision—a carefully planned move to a lower-cost location. Very, very few workers make maximum contributions to their 401(k) plans.

Personal Decisions versus Investing

The Employee Benefit Research Institute (EBRI), a Washington, D.C., nonprofit, has a massive database on 401(k) plans and participant accounts. The database includes 42 percent of participants and 44 percent of all plan assets, so it is a good tool for looking at participation, savings rates, investment choices, asset allocations, and account balances. Its most recent report, issued late in 2010, shows that only 7.1 percent of plan participants had an account balance greater than $200,000. Another 9.5 percent had balances between $100,000 and $200,000.[13]

As you might expect, older workers with more years of participation in any given plan tended to have higher balances than younger workers with fewer years of participation. Workers in their sixties with thirty years of job tenure (very rare birds!) had average account balances of $197,472 at the end of 2009, down from $227,070 at the end of 2007, but nicely recovering from their $175,890 value at the end of 2008. The average account size for workers in their sixties, regardless of job tenure, was significantly lower: only $144,004. Most of us should make an effort to keep our jobs.

The more important observation here is that our personal decisions about where and how we live truly are powerful levers on our retirement security. Valued in portfolio terms, it is pretty easy to make personal living decisions that have a greater impact on our lifetime standard of living and security than a lifetime of savings in a 401(k) plan. (Then again, if 401(k) costs were lower, these average account sizes would be larger.) This applies for people who have been renters all their lives, moving to areas where rents are lower. It applies in spades to people who have owned a home and built equity in it.

If there is a caveat here, it is this: changing your asset allocation is a lot easier than picking up and moving. One change is removed. The other is up close and personal. Many people are constrained by the proximity of family. Others are constrained by community engagement and a long history with friends. These are real constraints because they embody meaning as well as personal finances.

Many, however, simply assume that everywhere in America is the same when it is not. Readers of Scott's syndicated column, for instance, regularly send notes protesting the reality of the rent or housing cost figures cited in his question-and-answer column. They are from people who live in less expensive places such as Houston or San Antonio in Texas, older communities in Florida, or the suburbs of Nashville, Tennessee. Readers in Boston, Chicago, or Seattle can't believe that it is possible to rent an apartment for $500 a month, that gas and electricity prices can be lower, or that income and real estate taxes can be lower. But they are, and every $100 of cost-of-living difference means at least $117.65 in pretax income not needed. It also means you can get by with $3,000 less in account assets.

You won't find much attention to this from the financial services industry. It isn't their business. Their business is encouraging us to use their financial products to provide for our security when we can no longer work for a living. But the reality is that we make decisions every day that have a significant impact on our need for financial assets. While moving or downsizing is a dramatic example of such decisions—one that ranks up there with the lifetime savings of most workers—we are also faced with an increasing number of health care decisions where some amount of personal adaptation can be the equivalent of a small fortune.

The Investment Value of Taking an Extra Pill

When your doctor prescribes a medication for a chronic condition, it amounts to a long-term lien on your retirement savings, perhaps a lifetime lien. As long as the prescription is for a generic drug, such as a statin drug that is off patent or older blood pressure medications, for example, your out-of-pocket cost is likely to be $4 to $7 for a month's supply. A newer drug that is still on patent, however, is likely to cost much more. You can, for instance, pay $110 a month retail for Lipitor, which will be off patent when you read this, but as little as $7 for a generic statin. What you'll pay on your Medicare Part D plan will be somewhere in between, but the out-of-pocket difference between the on-patent form and the generic form is likely to run about $50 a month, or $600 a year.[14]

This is not a small sum. To provide a painfully absurd example, if you hoped to earn that amount in a checking account with any of the nation's largest banks (Bank of America, Chase, Wells Fargo) where the recent highest rate was an annual percentage yield of 0.05 percent, you'd need to keep $120,000 on deposit. Even at a more reasonable rate of 4 percent, you'd need to have $15,000 invested to provide the income. And that makes no allowance for income taxes you'd have to pay before getting your prescription filled.

When drugs come off patent, some pharmaceutical companies change the formulation, looking to extend the period of premium pricing. One break-the-bank example is Rythmol SR, the newer sustained-release version of generic propafanone, a drug used to treat heart arrhythmias such as atrial fibrillation. Doctors will casually prescribe Rythmol SR because time release means patients need only take the drug twice daily. Patients on the generic form of the drug need to take their pills three times a day.

The out-of-pocket cost difference between the two drugs is roughly $200 a month (the actual difference will depend on how your particular Part D insurance plan treats the drug). In effect, this means that you can save nearly $7 a day, every day, by remembering to take a third pill in the middle of the day. Think of the difference as premium pay for sentience.

So here's the question: How many retirees have so much retirement income that they can afford to pass up an opportunity to save $7 a day? This $2,400 a year is the same as doing just that. Now consider that the average Social Security retirement benefit check for a male worker is $1,325 and $1,025 for a female worker.[15] The average male with atrial fibrillation would save nearly two months of Social Security benefits a year. The average female with atrial fibrillation would save more than two months of benefits—and just for using a prescription that requires taking an extra pill a day. Atrial fibrillation, by the way, is not a rare condition. It has been estimated that about 5 percent of all people age sixty-five and over have it, and the percentage rises with age.

The investment value of taking an extra pill a day is equally impressive. If the retiree is in the 15 percent income tax bracket, he would need $2,823 of withdrawals from an IRA rollover account to net $2,400.[16] This means he would need to have $70,500 in his 401(k) plan. That's more than most people in their sixties have in their retirement plans according to the EBRI data. We could go on, but it should be abundantly clear that personal decisions and personal actions are as important for your long-term security as the amount of dough you have saved.

Going, Going, Gone

Anything can, and will, be done to extremes. Television confirms this daily. So if you can make a personal decision to move from the Rust Belt to the Sun Belt that will do as much for your retirement standard of living as your lifetime savings, what about going further? How about leaving the country?

Few other topics get more response from a newspaper column. Scott knows this because he has been writing about Americans living in Mexico for years. The largest-known American retiree expatriate colony is in Lake Chapala, not far from Guadalajara. Although there are regular reports of rising prices, it remains that an American seeking a relaxed and low-cost lifestyle can live there for far less than it costs almost anywhere in the United States. And for all the highly publicized stories of cartel-based murder and carnage along the border, there are few to none stories coming from Lake Chapala and other American enclaves such as Puerto Vallarta, San Miguel Allende and Playa del Carmen, not to mention smaller beach towns such as Sayulita and San Francisco, just north of Puerto Vallarta.

Can you go to such places and live like a king for next to nothing?

No. The closer you are to a tourist spot, the higher and more U.S.-like the prices are likely to be, right down to your evening margarita. But if you move from the market most vacationers live in, you'll dramatically reduce the cost of rent and, over time, dramatically reduce your other expenses as you shed imagined necessities such as having a car. One of the advantages of living in a foreign country is that it frees you of what might be called ambient status baggage—the unconscious consumption choices we make to create or preserve who we think we are or want to be.

Is this for you? Maybe; maybe not. We're not going to presume, and we think there are so many variables to consider that there is no way to say one place or another is the best possible place to retire. One indication is from International Living, a Web site that reports on living abroad; its most recent report lists the twenty-five top places in the world to retire—in rank order, Ecuador, Panama, Mexico, France, and Italy. The United States ranks fifteenth, behind Malta (seventh), Uruguay (sixth) and Colombia (twelfth). Go figure.

Whatever the nuances of place—and we think there are more than a few nuances separating France and Colombia—what it all comes down to is a gigantic arbitrage of domestic living expenses versus living expenses in other countries. In much of the world, a combined Social Security check income of $2,350 a month, or $28,200, a year will support a higher standard of living than it will in most of the United States. Some of those places are near beaches or other amenities that are nearly priceless in this country. In Panama, for instance, you can obtain a *pensionado* residency permit simply by demonstrating that you have a pension of $1,000 a month.[17] You can obtain a "person of means" visa to stay by bringing $300,000 into the country and using it in several ways, such as buying real estate or keeping funds on deposit.

What most people living overseas learn very quickly is that duplicating the American standard of living, making a carbon copy, is very expensive. But creatively adapting to local practices is relatively cheap. The more you adapt, the further your money will go. We'll leave discussion of whether adaptation is really a decline in living standard to the philosophers.

What we are confident about is that an increasing number of Americans will be thinking about retiring somewhere outside the country. They will do this for adventure. They will do this to have a higher living standard. They will do this to renew themselves. They will do it because they are frustrated that our political process has broken down so entirely and are fearful of the long-term results. For them, leaving the country will be a positive way to take action.

While the number of Americans who become retiree expatriates may rise dramatically in the future, it will still be a small minority. Most of us like where and how we live, have deep attachments to family and friends, and enjoy the security of being familiar with the tasks of everyday life. It's also possible to dramatically cut your cost of living by avoiding the most expensive aspects of the American lifestyle and taking advantage of our very low-cost distribution system.

When the dollar dips against the euro or the pound, hordes of Brits and Europeans get on chartered planes to come to the United States. Some come to New York or Boston. Others go to Florida. Wherever they go, they come to shop because we have the most competitive retail distribution system in the world. It makes clothing and other goods cheap relative to comparable (or identical) goods in other countries.

With that in mind, a careful retiree could retire to an older home in a low-cost area of the United States, such as the more remote parts of Texas Hill Country or communities in Florida that are a few miles inland. This would take housing costs down well below the costs in the areas regularly covered in *Where to Retire* magazine. Require also that the house was convenient to a Walmart, preferably a superstore, and the retiree could be assured of having access to the lowest possible retail costs in the United States and possibly the world. This would not be difficult because a large majority of Americans live within fifteen minutes of a Walmart, which sells more food than any other store in the world although it has been selling food only for fifteen years.

We have many choices ahead of us, but our choices will do a lot to solve the problems we face.

Yes, There Is a Kind Part to the Economics of Aging

The marketing view of aging—and that's the one we see most often—is harshly split between two images. One is of a benign ageless old age, one where our hair turns Classic Wise White but we can still play singles tennis or golf eighteen holes a day if we aren't too busy on our jet skis, or driving the Boxster. In that image, our task is to save like mad now so we'll have the money we'll need for that luxury African safari later. This is good for those in financial services because their income is directly proportional to the money we put in their care.

The other view is equally extreme. It reminds us that we could live a really, really long time and run out of money, so we should save more today. The proverbial poster child for this future is someone with Alzheimer's disease. Doomed to spend the last five years of their lives not knowing the names of their children or even themselves, they are locked in a secure facility and condemned to eating from a menu designed for people with no teeth. Without long-term care insurance, we are warned, our life savings will be spent, our spouses will be impoverished, and the family homestead will be sold to pay a portion of the Medicaid bill.

Reality, it turns out, is kinder. We don't face two polar opposites. Although few will enjoy living full and expensive lives from the day they retire until the day they die, neither will everyone draw the nasty Alzheimer's card (or any other major disability) that will cause a long and impaired life, spending their fortunes on medical care.

For most of us, real life is different. It is neither eternal active youth nor eternal impaired old age. While the demographers once lumped everyone sixty-five or older into a single group, they now designate three distinct groups of older people. The differences between them are instructive.

Those sixty-five to seventy-four are the "young old." They generally lead far more active lives than was thought possible only a generation ago. It is their smiling faces that we see in *Where to Retire* magazine, accompanied by their spending comparison group, the fifty-five- to sixty-five-year-old early retirees. These are the people you see in the brochures for Princess and Royal Caribbean cruise lines: trim, elegantly white haired, and comfortably seated at a table with an infinite ocean view. And don't forget the delicate glow of bubbles in the champagne glass.

This age, the ads would have us believe, is as playful and carefree as the world of Peter Pan, except that you don't have to give up sex to live there. Indeed, it is a world of sexual abundance either by nature or with the sublime aid of a regular supply of Viagra and K-Y Intense.

Those seventy-five to eighty-four years old are the "old." We don't see them very much except in advertisements on the TV channels that cater to the old folks demographic. There, Robert Wagner will tell us of the benefits of reverse mortgages, Sally Field will remind us of the dangers of unrelenting bone loss, and Jamie Curtis will encourage us to eat yogurt to restore the soothing peristalsis of youth. Less-well-known spokespeople will tell us about Medic Alert and the possibility of a spiffy Medicare-paid electric wheelchair that seems to corner faster than a Lotus. We will also be reminded that it is never too late to buy life insurance—at least enough to pay for our burial. Advertisements to this group are about retaining or recovering diminished capabilities—taking steps to stay in the world of the once-young.

Today those eighty-five and over are what used to be old, but they are called the "old-old." They are the pariahs of advertising, the nasty secret of aging. They are the disturbingly quiet people with concerned relatives in the ads for drugs dealing with cognitive disorders. Advertising is not directed to them. It is directed to their caretakers, and for good reason. While we'd all love to think that we age without disability and that modern medicine will save us from the afflictions of old age, the brute reality is that the age of disability may have been deferred, but it has not been eliminated.

As we get older, our capacities decline. We may all have somewhat different glide paths, but we all get to a decrepit place sooner or later (unless we die early). This is existentially scary, but it is good news for financial planning. It means that our ability, capacity, and interest in consuming decline as we age. It does not remain constant or increase. This means that our retirement nest egg can be smaller because it won't need to produce as much income over our remaining lifetimes. This should not be confused with poverty or even with the lower consumption spending of the previous generation. It is simply less consumption than you were inclined to do ten, twenty, or thirty years earlier.

Table 13.2 is based on an examination of the Consumer Expenditure Survey. It shows that our consumer spending declines in all areas except health care as we age. More important, the declines are large. Spending on personal insurance and pensions, as you might expect, plummets as we age from fifty-five to sixty-four to seventy-five and older. Spending on apparel and services, entertainment, and transportation all declines by 60 percent. Spending on food and alcohol and housing declines by at least 40 percent. Only health care spending rises, increasing by 19 percent.

"I've been teaching and working in the retirement field a long time and I can see the deficiencies in the accumulation models," researcher Kenn Tacchino told Scott. "It just isn't true that people consume at the same rate all of their lives. At some point, usually in their eighties, the retiree settles into a sedentary life. Put it this way: next time you are on a plane, look around for 80 year olds."[18]

Kenn Tacchino and Cynthia Saltzman, the academics who did this research, also found that lower spending wasn't a result of lower income. People in their mid-seventies spent less in each category even when they had the same income as people a decade younger.

"It's always been assumed that medical expenses would increase to offset any decline in consumption spending. But that isn't so. The out-of-pocket [medical] expenses of retirees are significant but not overwhelming. . . . Retirees who are properly insured with medi-gap insurance, etc. can be most confident about future medical expenses," Tacchino observed.

Senior Spending: Transcending Consumption

Ty Bernicke, a Wisconsin-based financial planner, examined these figures and used them to create what he called "reality retirement planning." Writing in the *Journal of Financial Planning*, Bernicke showed that a couple retiring with an $800,000 nest egg would be broke by age eighty under conventional assumptions of constant consumption.[19] Using nature's

Table 13.2
Most spending declines as we age

Spending category	55 to 64	65 to 74	75 and over	Percentage change
Apparel and services	$ 1,791	$ 1,252	$ 674	(62%)
Entertainment	$ 2,297	$ 1,371	$ 896	(61%)
Food and alcohol	$ 5,979	$ 4,803	$ 3,446	(42%)
Housing	$13,831	$10,052	$ 8,252	(40%)
Transportation	$ 8,449	$ 5,731	$ 3,178	(62%)
Personal insurance and pensions	$ 4,838	$ 1,853	$ 696	(86%)
Miscellaneous	$ 4,138	$ 3,593	$ 3,028	(27%)
Health care	$ 3,007	$ 3,588	$ 3,584	19%
Total average expenditures	$44,330	$32,243	$23,759	(46%)

Note: This table shows the decline in each of the major categories of consumer spending as households move from retirement age to midretirement.
Source: Ty Bernicke, "Reality Retirement Planning: A New Paradigm for an Old Science," *FPA Journal*, 2005.

glide path, however, the same couple would have a much larger nest egg by age eighty-five—about $2.4 million. He found that the couple would exhaust their assets before death 87 percent of the time under constant consumption. Using nature's glide path, he found a 0 percent fail rate.

That's quite a difference: 87 percent broke versus 0 percent broke. It's a strong indication that nature is on our side. More important, it's another indication that there is a lot more to our financial futures than the return we get on our savings. Just as personal decisions about whether we rent or buy and whether we live in Seattle or Phoenix can be as important as a lifetime of 401(k) contributions, the kind side of aging works to reduce our spending and increase the probability that we won't run out of money.

That's good news. So this might be a good time to ask an awkward question: Why did you have to read it here? Tacchino and Saltzman published their research in the April 1999 issue of the *Journal of Financial Planning*. While a lone certified professional planner in Wisconsin has incorporated it into his financial planning process, we don't know of a single financial institution that has incorporated personal decision making or natural spending reductions into the financial planning models they purport to use to "help" their clients. Instead, they continue to use the reliable carrot and stick that have served *them* so well: lust for future luxury and fear of future health care costs to sell financial products.

While this ongoing intellectual dishonesty doesn't inspire trust in the financial services industry, it may turn out to have a perverse and unintended benefit for the rest of us. It has created a significant fudge factor that we can use to adapt in a future of broken or, more likely, finagled government promises. The facts of real life may turn out to be a major hedge against future inflation.

A Saving Grace: Death

Even death has its benefits.[20] For one thing, it brings the ultimate drop in the cost of living. While the benefit of that drop may be moot for the person who died, it can be a boon for the decedent's surviving spouse. That's important because most of us make an effort to have a long-term relationship with another human being. We also make our financial plans based entirely on our shared lives. We seldom give the lives we will lead as widows or widowers much thought because that's not the life we want to imagine.

In America today a sixty-five-year-old man can be expected to live another 16.8 years, to 81.8 years. A sixty-five-year-old woman can be expected to live another 19.5 years, to 84.5 years. Their life expectancies will be longer if they are white and rich, shorter if they are black and poor.

The life expectancy of a couple holds some surprises.[21] While neither is expected, as an individual, to live more than 19.5 years and neither is expected to live less than 16.8 years, one of the two is expected to live 26.2 years and both of them are expected to be alive for 15.8 years. They need to plan for one of them to be alive longer than either's life expectancy. Now take a second look at those numbers: the period that both of them can expect to be alive is shorter than either of their life expectancies.

It turns out that across all couples, the second to die spouse will, on average, live alone for about ten years. We can change the starting ages for the couple and play a bit with starting age differences, but we will consistently find that in most couples, the last to die will be a widow or widower for about a decade. (Importantly, few couples confronted by this morbid aspect of morbidity opt for the *Thelma and Louise* option. In that 1991 movie two desperate women solve an impossible problem by driving over a cliff into the Grand Canyon.)

Since men tend to marry younger women and women live longer than men, wives will generally be the one to go it alone for ten years.

This bad news is good news, in a way; the deceased hubby is no longer spending up the couple's remaining assets. Suppose, for instance, that we assume that the second person in a household does not double the couple's cost of living but instead increases it by only 60 percent. Suppose also that the couple expects to need $16,000 a year for its expected joint life or $419,200 ($16,000 times 26.2).[22]

By putting this amount aside in a no-yield inflation-adjusted investment, they would have provided for living together no matter how long they live.

Their actual need, however, will be lower. Their real need is for 15.8 years of joint income (15.8 × $16,000 or $252,800) plus 10.4 years of income ($10,000) for the survivor or $104,000. That's a total of $356,800. This reduces their lifetime money need by about 15 percent. The actual figure could be much smaller if both happened to live nearly 26.2 years, or larger if one dies before 15.8 years. But its probable value is a 15 percent reduction from planning for both to live to joint expectancy.

This is not money you take to the bank. It is simply another fudge factor that is weighted in our favor when it comes to planning our future finances. Most of the time, most couples will need less money than conventional lifetime planning suggests. What's important here is that every factor we've discussed is likely to make any given amount of retirement savings go further than financial planners are saying.

The Five Factors

Whether we read newspapers, read the glossy personal finance magazines, scan the Internet, or pay attention to the regular communications from our 401(k) provider, we face a singular emphasis on how much we should save and how clever people will manage it for maximum return. All of this information ignores rude questions about how much the clever manager is being paid for his service and the impact of that payment on our retirement nest egg. The most unstable and irresponsible sector of our economy, the financial sector, regularly tells us that we are uncertain, undependable, and incapable so American workers should rely on financial services.

The two of us see things differently. We see the span of human life as well beyond that of most of our businesses and institutions. We also see five opportunities in that span to improve our security throughout life. Those opportunities, in sum, are far greater than anything we can do through the usual workings of the financial service industry. They may even be sufficient to offset some of the damage coming our way from two political parties that have only one thing in common: addiction to the ultimate form of "taxation without representation"—promising big benefits today that will be paid for by the young and the yet unborn. Here, in summary, are those five factors.

• *Major reduction in investment expenses*   As we pointed out earlier, simple cost reduction for a typical 401(k) participant can increase his lifetime accumulation by 18 to 32 percent, or more. For workers in expensive plans, such as most schoolteachers, a move to low-cost plans can increase lifetime accumulations by 50 percent. Note that these figures are just for the years of contribution. Extended for another fifteen years in retirement, the same lower costs would mean a further material increase in retiree income. Nothing reveals this dilemma more clearly than a comparison of current investment yields with current investment management expenses. As we write this, the average moderate allocation mutual fund has a yield of 1.27 percent. The expense ratio for this category is slightly larger, 1.34 percent. The financial services industry, in other words, is getting all the income from our money while we get all the risk. What a deal!

• *Life cycle spending*   For all those who choose to marry and have families, a large portion of consumption spending goes to the care and education of children rather than to the parents. Like it or not, none of that spending is income that needs to be replaced in retirement because it was always spent on someone else. This reduces the amount of income we need to continue our adult living standard in retirement, which means we can save less or tolerate a lower return on our savings.

• *Personal decisions*   The largest lever on our financial futures is not our mutual fund choices. It is our personal decisions about the size and expense of our shelter, whether we own or rent it, and where it is located. Our decisions about how we manage our resources have a larger impact on our retirement standard of living than a lifetime of 401(k) contributions.

• *The natural glide path of spending*   As surveys have shown, the older we get, the less we are inclined to spend. Spending that was important at age twenty-five, thirty-five, or fifty-five becomes less important, unwise, or unnecessary. The net effect is to make hitting our goal of a secure retirement easier to do.

• *Death's saving grace*   Since most of us choose to live life in close relationships with another and plan for the same, the fact that we seldom die at the same time (however we might wish it) creates yet another reduction in lifetime income need.

These factors can be combined in an infinite number of ways. What is important is that all have a positive impact on our ability to cope with the major problems we face: increasing life expectancies, rising healthcare costs, a financially overcommitted government, and financial institutions that use our resources as their lifeblood.

What about buying gold and silver rather than counting on your spouse to die? The major problem with precious metals collection is that when, and if, they come into routine circulation, bullets are likely to be the most powerful currency. The exchange rate between a 357 Magnum and a trove of Canadian Gold Leaf has always favored the 357, whatever the price of gold.

As dismal as the future looks, it can be changed if we continue to be social and political creatures. That means realizing that the clash of generations is not a battle to be won by the old or the young. Instead, it is an opportunity to bring as much passion to the problem of the "nows" versus the "laters" as the "haves" versus the "have-nots." And if you look at the condition of our economy it's also very clear that both sides have everything to gain, and nothing to lose, by working to achieve generational equity.

Becoming a survivalist, which an increasing number of people are advocating, is an admission of defeat and a withdrawal from the human community that has, for all its faults, built a world where life is no longer "nasty, brutish and short."

14

The ~~Coming~~ Generational Storm

Our country's problems are real, and they aren't going away on their own or by saying, "Yes, we can." We're $211 trillion in debt, saving nothing, investing next to nothing, in most cases experiencing no real wage growth, suffering high unemployment, growing more unequal, getting older, refusing to die, balancing a phony budget, fighting wars of pride rather than purpose, dumping massive liabilities on our kids, and sustaining a "trust-me" banking system poised to redetonate.

We are, in short, totally screwed. Yes, that's strong language. But in thinking about the state of the economy and what we've done and are doing to ourselves and our children, it is the only honest description. It's loud and offensive, but when a house is on fire, screaming "FIRE" is the only responsible way to warn its occupants.

We've watched our generational firestorm for decades. When we saw the first flames, we wrote *The Coming Generational Storm* to raise the alarm. Others, particularly former commerce secretary Pete Peterson, now-deceased senator Paul Tsongas, former director of the Office of Management and Budget David Stockman, and former comptroller general of the United States and head of the Government Accountability Office David Walker, started shouting "FIRE" as well.

But the politicians, trained in the Donnie Brasco School of Language, said "Fugetaboutit. You're exaggerating. We'll outgrow the problem. Oh, and by the way, would you like a tax cut or a benefit hike?"[1]

Today they are singing a different tune. Today the fire is high and bright enough for even their constituents to see.

Much Ado About Next To Nothing

As we write, the Reds and Blues just waged a battle royal over the official debt ceiling. The president pushed a $4 trillion ten-year deficit reduction deal. The House Republicans wanted a $6 trillion package. They compromised on just under $2.5 trillion. A congressional "super committee" met for four months to save more but disbanded in utter failure. Even $2.5 trillion sounds like a lot of money. It's not. Our fiscal gap is $211 trillion. And it grew by $6 trillion last year alone.

Part of this huge growth reflects the fact that we're one year closer to having the huge baby boom cohort collecting roughly $40,000 per head, measured in today's dollars, from Social Security, Medicare, and Medicaid. Part reflects last year's payroll tax cut. And part reflects last year's 10 percent increase in Medicare and Medicaid outlays—one of the largest such increases on record.[2]

The purple health plan outlined here would cut our $211 trillion fiscal gap by $127 trillion, reducing it to $84 trillion. The purple Social Security plan would cut another $59 trillion from the fiscal gap, leaving it at $25 trillion. And the purple tax plan would shave off $36 trillion, closing the gap with $11 trillion to spare! There is a way forward. We can do this. We're totally screwed only if we refuse to make the radical reforms needed to end fiscal child abuse once and for all.

Too Little, Too Late

The big problem, though, is that the president and Congress are focused on budget balance. This, as we've demonstrated, is entirely inadequate. What's needed is *generational* balance, equity between the nows and the laters. We can only get this by eliminating the fiscal gap. Doing so requires a roughly $20 trillion fiscal adjustment over this decade, not $2.5 trillion. What's being argued about is classic too little, too late. Stated differently, we need to run huge official surpluses to deal with the long-term fiscal and demographic problems we're facing.

The goal of generational balance is not only fiscal policy that's sustainable but fiscal policy that's generationally equitable. Running policies that require hitting up successive generations for larger and larger shares of their lifetime earning in net taxes (taxes paid net of transfer payments received) is neither sustainable nor generationally equitable. We can't take away more than 100 percent of what our children earn and spend it on ourselves. They don't have that much to give. And as we start getting close to that limit, they will start finding other places to live much as second sons did in Victorian England because they had no birthright. Nor is it fair to ask future generations to pay a bigger share of their lifetime earnings—to face a higher lifetime net tax rate. Our goal is to give our children a better life, not show them this enduring American dream and then take it away with one hidden provision after another in the inordinately complex travesty we call our tax-transfer system.

Balancing the Wrong Books

Of course, few in Washington are focused on generational balance. Budget balance is the goal of those most worried about our kids. But the two have no connection. Taking more money in "taxes" from the young year after year, decade after decade, and giving it to the old in "transfer payments" is consistent with budget balance, but represents a Ponzi scheme that will blow up in our kids' faces.

In continuing to balance the wrong books (the government's annual budget rather than the fiscal gap, which economists call the government's intertemporal budget), the president and Congress are trying yet again to stick our kids with a bigger bill. But they are also leaving all of us in the lurch—not knowing for sure whose ox will ultimately get gored. This man-made production of risk is also a cost to society that is not properly measured by government accountants. But gauging by the number of conversations we've had of late with people about the country's fiscal affairs and the future of their children, we know the anxiety costs are real, very large, and rising.

The question, though, is not where we stand in terms of the size of the bills we're leaving behind or the neuroses we're producing. Anyone who looks carefully at the Congressional Budget Office's long-term spending and tax projections can see the fiscal gap in broad relief and start to worry. The real question is, Why did we do this? Why did we spend the postwar era taking from the young and giving to the old? Why did we use fraudulent deficit accounting to hide our generational theft? Why did we shirk our educational responsibilities and let our kids take on so much college debt? Why did we sacrifice our children in losing wars? And why did we leave Wall Street free to prey on them—and everyone else?

Other People's Children

We think the answer can be found in how people feel about other people's children: "They aren't my kids. They're somebody else's. I worry about my own. Let *their* parents worry about them. They aren't my responsibility." Maybe this generational selfishness reflects America's tremendous racial, ethnic, and religious heterogeneity. We're a melting pot, for sure, but one that's never fully melted. Consequently no one recognizes himself in his neighbor's child, let alone a child he's never met who lives halfway across the country.

Whatever the explanation, we're engaged in child abuse, social, economic, fiscal, and, when it comes to our ill-conceived adventures overseas, physical. No gloss can cover this up. And this is the moral issue of our times.

Our decision to take from our kin and promise them, with our fingers crossed, more than we could deliver has permeated our culture. It's not just Uncle Sam that's played Charles Ponzi's reckless and deceitful game. For decades, states and local governments made massive pension and health care promises—promises they knew couldn't be met and would land in the lap of those coming behind. They made these promises in exchange for current services from teachers, firefighters, police, and other public servants. They pocketed something real and handed back something fake in exchange. Corporations and labor unions did the same. And like Uncle Sam, they used phony accounting to hide their crime. We're now seeing the fallout, be it in Minnesota, which shut down the entire state government in summer 2011 to limit its bills, or Wisconsin, which has cut back on pension cost of living increases, or in California, which has resorted to paying its expenses in IOUs, or in General Motors, which went bust paying retiree benefits.

Wall Street watched this behavior and started copying it—selling claims to securities it knew were toxic in order to make a fast buck. What penalty has that sector paid for selling snake oil? What lesson has it learned about the consequences for financial malfeasance? What rules have really been changed to make Wall Street truly safe for Main Street? None.

"Take the money and run" has become our national pastime and "To hell with the American dream, I'm taking the cash" our national motto. Unfortunately, there are only two ways this problem can end. Either this will all end very badly with the Fed printing more and more money to meet Uncle Sam's ever growing bills, leading prices to shoot through the roof. Or it will end with the government reforming our fiscal and financial systems along the radically sensible lines we have outlined in the previous chapters.

Co-opting the Young

Which outcome prevails will depend on America's youth. It's time for them to stand up and be counted. The most depressing thing we see is the extent to which today's young people are being co-opted by the two parties into choosing sides—become one of them, a liberal or a conservative, as if these distinctions were meaningful. The parties' major purpose is to perpetuate a distracting side show, namely a fight over words. The fight distracts attention from the real policy underway: generational expropriation.

The fight over meaningless words has led us to stop thinking about what we're saying. This point is well captured by a letter President Obama recently received from a very angry constituent, saying "Don't socialize my Medicare."[3]

People are venting because they are angry. They are angry because they are under lots of economic pressure. They are terribly scared. Our can-do spirit seems lost. We've turned into a worried, anxious country for good reason.

We're in an extremely deep hole. But we have plenty of shovels and just enough time to dig out. The simple reforms we've outlined can jump-start the economy and put us back on top.

American Spring

We start digging in the right direction by talking, at long last, about fundamentals, not words—by recognizing our shared values, seeing our problems for what they are, and fixing them for good. The young don't need to turn on their parents and grandparents. But they do need to make their parents and grandparents understand in no uncertain terms what's really going down. It's time for the young to draw a line in the sand, to say, "Enough!" It's time for the young to declare, with their votes, their feet, and their capacity to engage that they aren't going to sit back and watch their futures disappear.

There are about 70 million Americans between eighteen and thirty-five years old. Imagine they all march on Washington. Imagine they let their elders know they aren't happy with their treatment. Imagine they join together in a party—the Generational Equity Party—and start voting for candidates who represent the interest of today's *and* tomorrow's young generations. Imagine how that would change the conversation.

And imagine those older than sixty seeing their faces and hearing their voices and saying *Yes, they're right*. These are our children and grandchildren. We need to protect them. They are on earth, if not in heaven, our only true future.

Notes

Chapter 1

1. Nor do they have to begin with oil contracts. Recently the Chinese have dramatically increased their purchases of U.S. corn. A future breakdown could easily begin with a run on food deposits. See Scott Kilman and Brian Spegele, "Chinese Hunger for Corn Stretches Farm Belt," *Wall Street Journal*, August 17, 2011, http://online.wsj.com/article/SB1000142405311190355490457646030015568 1760.html.

2. Laurence J. Kotlikoff and Scott Burns, *The Coming Generational Storm* (Cambridge, MA: MIT Press, 2004).

3. This references debt held by the public.

4. The CIA World Fact Book, Country Comparison: Public Debt, accessed October 18, 2011, https://www.cia.gov/library/publications/the-world-factbook/rankorder/2186rank.html.

5. Elliott Gotkine, "Uruguay Fights Emigration Wave," *BBC News*, January 12, 2005, http://news.bbc.co.uk/2/hi/americas/4120905.stm; U.S. Department of State, "Background Note: Uruguay," June 23, 2011, http://www.state.gov/r/pa/ei/bgn/2091.htm.

6. "Immigration Statistics," NationMaster.com, 2008, http://www.nationmaster.com/red/graph/imm_net_mig_rat-immigration-net-migration-rate&int=-1.

Chapter 2

1. The march to Moscow and back to Paris was graphically depicted by Charles Joseph Minard, an engineer who pioneered modern data presentation. The graphic can be seen at: http://en.wikipedia.org/wiki/File:Minard.png.

2. Central Intelligence Agency, *The World Factbook*, Country Comparison: Life Expectancy at Birth, https://www.cia.gov/library/publications/the-world-factbook/rankorder/2102rank.html.

3. Futurist Ray Kurzweil has estimated that we are approaching "the singularity" when life can be infinitely extended, http://en.wikipedia.org/wiki/The_Singularity_Is_Near.

4. James F. Fries and Lawrence M. Crapo, *Vitality and Aging: Implications of the Rectangular Curve* (New York: Freeman, 1981).

5. John Abramson, *Overdosed America: The Broken Promise of American Medicine* (New York: HarperCollins, 2004), 49.

6. http://www.cdc.gov/mmwr/preview/mmwrhtml/00056796.htm.

7. Central Intelligence Agency, *The World Factbook,* https://www.cia.gov/library/publications/the-world-factbook/fields/2102.html. We collected these data in summer 2011, but *The World Factbook* is updated weekly.

8. Frank McCoy, "Where Did All the Centenarians Go?", *AARP Bulletin*, November 2010, p. 10. Some of the fabled longevity in Japan may be a bit exaggerated. The November 2010 issue of the *AARP Bulletin* reported that many of the countries' 234,354 centenarians couldn't be found, suggesting the possibility of major pension fraud.

9. Kathleen Fackelmann, "Centenarians Increase in Age and Numbers," *USA Today,* October 24, 2005, http://www.usatoday.com/tech/science/2005-10-23-aging-centenarians_x.htm.

10. "Living to 100 May Be Easier Than Counting Those Who've Made It," *Wall Street Journal,* April 11, 2008, http://online.wsj.com/article/NA_WSJ_PUB:SB120787019819506391.html.

11. U.S. Census Bureau, "State and County Quick Facts." October 18, 2011, http://quickfacts.census.gov/qfd/states/11000.html.

12. Federal Reserve, "Balance Sheet of Households and Nonprofit Organizations," June 9, 2011, http://www.federalreserve.gov/releases/z1/current/z1r-5.pdf.

13. And research is being done to make sure there is: Nicolas Wade, "Longer Lives for Obese Mice, With Hope for Humans of All Size," *New York Times,* August 18, 2011, http://www.nytimes.com/2011/08/19/science/19fat.html?_r=1&hp.

14. W. Somerset Maugham's short story "The Lotus Eater" details one attempt at solving the ultimate coming to the end of the money before the end of the month problem, http://maugham.classicauthors.net/lotuseater/.

15. Here is the Wikipedia description of the original Richard Matheson story, http://en.wikipedia.org/wiki/I_Am_Legend_(novel).

16. In 2007 about 17 percent of the population of Florida was 65 or older, http://www.mineful.net/Florida/State/state_population.html. But projections from the census department indicate that the entire country will have 17.88 percent of its population 65 or older by 2025, http://www.census.gov/population/www/projections/files/nation/summary/np2008-t3.xls.

17. "The Falling Fertility of Europe," *Rickety,* January 16, 2009, http://www.rickety.us/2009/01/the-falling-fertility-of-europe/.

18. United Nations, "World Population to 2300" (New York: United Nations, 2004), http://www.un.org/esa/population/publications/longrange2/WorldPop2300final.pdf.

19. Dmitry Orlov, *Reinventing Collapse: The Soviet Experience and American Prospects* (Gabriola Island, British Columbia: New Society Publishers, 2011).

Chapter 3

1. These figures are calculated based on the CBO's alternative fiscal scenario projection and the U.S. Census's population projection. The $30,000 and $40,000 figures do not include Social Security, Medicare, or Medicaid benefits paid to those under age sixty-five. They also exclude Medicaid payments made to those over age sixty-five by state governments. The source for the CBO assumptions is Congressional Budget Office, "The Long-Term Budget Outlook," August 2010, http://www.cbo.gov/ftpdocs/115xx/doc11579/06-30-LTBO.pdf. The CBO projections are posted at http://www.cbo.gov/ftpdocs/115xx/doc11579/LTBO-2010data.xls.

2. U.S. Social Security Administration, "Social Security Basic Facts," May 17, 2011, http://www.ssa.gov/pressoffice/basicfact.htm.

3. FICA references the Federal Insurance Contributions Act.

4. "2011 Annual Report of the Boards of Trustees of the Federal Hospital Insurance and Federal Supplementary Medical Insurance Trust Funds," 2011, https://www.cms.gov/ReportsTrustFunds/downloads/tr2011.pdf.

5. "U.S. Heading for Financial Trouble?" *60 Minutes,* October 8, 2009, http://www.cbsnews.com/stories/2007/03/01/60minutes/main2528226_page2.shtml?tag=contentMain;contentBody.

6. *60 Minutes,* "Is the U.S. Heading for Financial Trouble?," October 8, 2009, http://www.cbsnews.com/stories/2007/03/01/60minutes/main2528226_page2.shtml.

7. Scott Burns, "Yes, the Rich Have (Still) More Money," *AssetBuilder,* March 12, 2006, http://assetbuilder.com/blogs/scott_burns/archive/2006/08/13/Yes_2C00_-the-Rich-Have-_2800_Still_2900_-More-Money.aspx.

8. John F. Dickerson, "Confessions of a White House Insider," *Time,* January 10, 2004, http://www.time.com/time/magazine/article/0,9171,574809,00.html.

9. Scott Burns, "April 15th and the Rising Prices of Civilization," *AssetBuilder,* April 21, 2007, http://assetbuilder.com/blogs/scott_burns/archive/2007/04/21/April-15th-and-the-Rising-Price-Of-Civilization.aspx.

10. Scott Burns, "The $43 Trillion Surprise," *AssetBuilder,* June 1, 2003, http://assetbuilder.com/blogs/scott_burns/archive/2003/06/01/The-_2400_43-Trillion-Surprise.aspx.

11. Department of Health and Human Services—Chief Actuary's Communications with Congress, U.S. Government Accountability Offices, B-302-911, September 7, 2004, http://www.gao.gov/decisions/appro/302911.pdf.

12. Check succeeding reports from the trustees, and you'll see he was right.

13. See table IV.B6 in U.S. Social Security Administration, "2011 OASDI Trustees Report," May 11, 2011, http://www.ssa.gov/oact/TR/2011/IV_B_LRest.html#267528.

14. Scott Burns, "Future Medicare: Cheap, But Not Available," *AssetBuilder,* August 13, 2010, http://assetbuilder.com/blogs/scott_burns/archive/2010/08/13/future-medicare-cheap-but-not-available.aspx.

15. The fiscal gap is calculated using the CBO's alternative fiscal scenario released June 2011. This scenario is the CBO's most realistic long-term budget forecast. In forming the fiscal gap, we first assumed that annual noninterest spending and taxes (both measured in today's dollars) would grow indefinitely by 2 percent a year beyond 2075, the point at which the CBO's estimates end. We then discounted the entire stream of noninterest spending net of taxes at a 3 percent real discount rate and added in the 2011 value of debt in the hands of the public.

16. See Alan J. Auerbach and Laurence J. Kotlikoff, *Dynamic Fiscal Policy* (Cambridge: Cambridge University Press, 1987).

17. U.S. Government Accountability Office, "State and Local Governments' Fiscal Outlook: March 2010 Update," March 2010, p. 8, http://www.gao.gov/new .items/d10358.pdf.

18. Congressional Budget Office, "Long-Term Budget Outlook," August, 2010, http://cbo.gov/ftpdocs/115xx/doc11579/LTBO-2010data.xls.

19. Census Bureau, Population Estimates, 2009, http://www.census.gov/popest/national/asrh/NC-EST2009-asrh.html.

20. Peter Grier, "Health Care Reform Bill 101: Who Gets Subsidized Insurance?" *Christian Science Monitor,* March 10, 2010, http://www.csmonitor.com/USA/Politics/2010/0320/Health-care-reform-bill-101-Who-gets-subsidized-insurance.

21. One mitigating consideration is that employer-paid insurance premiums are exempt from income taxes, so the worker's taxes will rise when he or she moves to the health exchange. Competition by employers to hire workers, who are now cheaper to employ, is likely to end up with the worker in this hypothetical family receiving some, if not all, of the $11,800 net subsidy in terms of higher wages.

22. Executive Office of the President of the United States, "Economic Report of the President: 2010 Report Spreadsheet Tables," February 22, 2011, http://www .gpoaccess.gov/eop/tables10.html.

23. This is no different from what happened with Medicare, which over time has crowded out employer-provided retiree health care.

24. The change in language appears to have helped economists within the Chilean government engage in a substantive change in policy: keeping the Chilean Navy from purchasing a used aircraft carrier from the United States. By pointing to the larger deficit (actually, smaller surplus at the time), the economists, as Kotlikoff understands it, were able to tell the military that the ship was not affordable.

25. The CBO ignores debt owed by one branch of government, like the U.S. Treasury to another, like the Federal Reserve.

26. Carmen Reinhart and Kenneth Rogoff, *This Time Is Different: Eight Centuries of Financial Folly* (Princeton, N.J.: Princeton University Press, 2009).

27. Indeed, were we to form official debt-to-GDP series for each country in their sample using alternative, internally consistent, but nonetheless arbitrary labels for

receipts and payments, we could make all countries' official debt-to-GDP ratios look really large or really small prior to economic downturns. In other words, we could choose whatever ratio of "official" debt to GDP we wanted to call critical and adopt labels to make every country have that ratio just before it tanked. Here's the bottom line. What's official is only what someone calls official. The fact that governments choose a particular set of words to characterize receipts and payments does not prevent others from using their own set of labels and making up their own official historical times series for deficits. So as much as we'd like to say that the U.S. debt-to-GDP ratio is becoming critical, we can't. Once you understand the labeling problem, you understand that U.S. debt, as conventionally measured, is a number in search of a concept. Hence, the 90 percent official debt-to-GDP threshold is important only because Rogoff and Reinhart take governments' inherently arbitrary fiscal labeling as meaningful and have persuaded themselves and others that 90 percent is *the* threshold. It isn't.

28. In 2003 the fiscal gap we mentioned in our book *The Coming Generational Storm* (Cambridge, MA: MIT Press, 2004) was $45 trillion, as calculated by Kent Smetters and Jagadeesh Gokhale in their work for the President's budget, figures that were cut from the document when Snow replaced O'Neil as Secretary of the Treasury.

29. As shown in Laurence J. Kotlikoff, *Generational Policy* (Cambridge, MA: MIT Press, 2003), and Jerry Green and Laurence J. Kotlikoff, "On the General Relativity of Fiscal Language," in *Key Issues in Public Finance: A Conference in Memory of David Bradford*, ed. Alan J. Auerbach and Daniel Shaviro (Cambridge, MA: Harvard University Press, 2009), the labeling problem arises in all neoclassical models, which includes models with distortionary policy, time-inconsistent policy, incomplete markets, adverse selection, moral hazard, uncertainty, and agency problems. The reason is intuitive and immediate. Any such model can be discussed with or labeled with different words, and it won't change any agent's or government's behavior since they aren't making decisions on the basis of what things are called, but on the basis of fundamentals, such as their budget sets, preferences, and production opportunities, and information.

30. See Hans Christian Anderson, *Fairy Tales,* ed. Jackie Wullschlager and trans. Tina Nunnally (New York: Viking Press, 2005).

31. Green and Kotlikoff, "On the General Relativity of Fiscal Language."

32. A corollary of this statement is that economic theory cannot, and therefore does not, distinguish capitalism from socialism.

33. The estimate for Greece was made by economists Bernd Raffelhüschen and Christian Hagist of the University of Freiburg and communicated to Kotlikoff in a private conversation in July 2010.

34. Organization for Economic Development and Cooperation, "Economic Outlook—Interim Report 106," March 24, 2009, http://www.oecd.org/data oecd/3/62/42421337.pdf.

35. "List of Countries by Military Expenditures," *Wikipedia,* http://en.wikipedia .org/wiki/List_of_countries_by_military_expenditures.

36. Some economists would argue that as an equilibrium proposition, the fiscal gap must be zero, that is, that the government's intertemporal budget constraint must be satisfied. Furthermore, they'd argue that since this constraint constitutes a balance sheet, the current market value of official debt must equal the current market value of the net cash flows of all the nonofficial government programs. They then proceed to infer the risk characteristics of these net cash flows by considering the risk characteristics of their balance sheet equivalent: official debt. At one level, it's hard to argue with this approach, since equilibrium requires the intertemporal budget constraint to hold, or, more generally, it requires that the government pay its bills along any path taken by the economy. But saying, in effect, that policy will inevitably have to adjust to make the realized fiscal gap zero provides no measure of the extent of the adjustment needed along any path of the economy, let alone, on average. See Dale F. Gray, Robert C. Merton, and Zvi Bodie, "New Framework for Measuring and Managing Macrofinancial Risk and Financial Stability," NBER working paper 13607 (Cambridge, MA: NBER, 2007).

37. See Deborah Lucas and Robert McDonald, "An Options-Based Approach to Evaluating the Risk of Fannie Mae and Freddie Mac," *Journal of Monetary Economics*, 53 (2006), 155–176; Alexander Blocker, Laurence J. Kotlikoff, and Stephen A. Ross, "The True Cost of Social Security," NBER working paper 14427 (Cambridge, MA: NBER, October 2008); and John Geanakoplos and Steven P. Zeldes, "Market Valuation of Accrued Social Security Benefits," in *Measuring and Managing Federal Financial Risk*, ed. Deborah Lucas, 213–233 (Chicago: University of Chicago Press, 2010), for initial attempts at risk-adjusting government programs. This research does not, by the way, necessarily suggest using a common discount rate for all the government's net cash flows. The lifetime net tax treatment of particular current and future agents may be more certain than that of others and therefore differentially discounted.

Chapter 4

1. To be precise, we're eating all the income we produce from working and investing our national wealth, whether at home or abroad.

2. Some economists argue that we earn more, on average, from our investments abroad than foreigners earn in the United States on their investments here and that the difference is not properly captured by our national income accounts. In this case, our national saving rate would be somewhat underestimated and our current account deficit somewhat overestimated.

3. W. W. Rostow, *The Stages of Economic Growth: A Non-Communist Manifesto* (Cambridge: Cambridge University Press, 1969).

4. Ian Dew-Becker and Robert Gordon, "Where Did Productivity Growth Go? Inflation Dynamics and the Distribution of Income," *Brookings Papers on Economic Activity*, no. 2 (2005), 67–150.

5. As long as China plays by market rules, we have no legitimate economic beef against it. The major concern with Chinese competition involves allegations that

China is stealing intellectual property developed in the United States and other countries (e.g., violating patents and ignoring copyrights). Such violations need to be vigorously addressed. But whatever advantage the Chinese are receiving from such behavior cannot explain why China is saving at such a high rate and we are saving at such a low one. These differences essentially dictate the pattern of current account deficits and surpluses we observe.

6. Paul Krugman, "China, Japan, America," *New York Times*, September 12, 2010, http://www.nytimes.com/2010/09/13/opinion/13krugman.html.

7. "U.S. Delays Report on Alleged China Currency Manipulation," *CNN*, April 4, 2010, http://articles.cnn.com/2010-04-04/world/us.china.treasury_1_currency-manipulation-china-delay?_s=PM:WORLD.

8. Jackie Calmes, "Geithner Hints at Harder Line on China Trade," *New York Times*, January 22, 2009, http://www.nytimes.com/2009/01/23/business/worldbusiness/23treasury.html.

9. Were the Chinese to revalue their exchange rate as so many advocate, they would do so printing fewer yuan and buying up fewer dollars. This would reduce the yuan money supply, leading prices in China, measured in yuan, to fall.

10. The household saving rate is $1 - C/(Y - G)$, where C stands for household consumption, Y for national income, and G for government consumption.

11. Flow of Funds Accounts of the United States, Federal Reserve, Statistical Release, September 16, 2011, http://www.federalreserve.gov/releases/z1/current/data.htm. To arrive at this figure, we added household and nonprofit and government sector net wealth.

12. Jagdeesh Gokhale, Laurence J. Kotlikoff, and John Sabelhaus, "Understanding the Postwar Decline in U.S. Saving: A Cohort Analysis," *Brookings Papers on Economic Activity*, no. 1 (1996), 315–371, http://www.kotlikoff.net/sites/default/files/Understanding%20the%20Postwar%20Decline%20in%20US%20Saving%20A%20Cohort%20Analysis,%20%20Brookings%201996.pdf. These consumption propensities may seem unusually low, but they are measured by forming the ratio of the cohort's annual consumption to its remaining lifetime income, where lifetime income is measured as the present value of the cohort's future labor earnings plus its wealth, less the present value of its future taxes, plus the present value of its receipt of future transfer payments.

13. "The First Social Security Beneficiary," Social Security Online, http://www.ssa.gov/history/imf.html.

14. Real wages depend not just on the amount of capital per worker but also the state of the technology. So less investment may not mean falling real wages if the rate of technological change is sufficiently high. But it will certainly spell slower growth in real wages.

15. Peter A. Diamond, "National Debt in a Neoclassical Growth Model," *American Economic Review* 55 (1965), 1126–1150, http://www.hss.caltech.edu/~camerer/SS280/DiamondAER65.pdf.

16. See, for example, Alan J. Auerbach and Laurence J. Kotlikoff, *Dynamic Fiscal Policy* (Cambridge: Cambridge University Press, 1987), and Hans Fehr, Sabine

Jokisch, and Laurence J. Kotlikoff, "Dynamic Globalization and Its Alarming Implications for Wage Inequality," mimeo., Boston University, 2011.

17. See, for example, Joseph G. Altonji, Fumio Hyashi, and Laurence J. Kotlikoff, "Parental Altruism and Inter Vivos Transfers: Theory and Evidence," *Journal of Political Economy* 105 (1997), 1121–1166, http://www.kotlikoff.net/content/parental-altruism-and-inter-vivos-transfers-theory-and-evidence.

18. Ronald Lee and Andrew Mason, *Population Aging and the Generational Economy: A Global Perspective* (Cheltenham, UK: Edward Elgar Publishing, 2011).

19. See table 2 in Congressional Budget Office, "The Long-Term Outlook for Health Care Spending," November 2007, http://www.cbo.gov/ftpdocs/87xx/doc8758/MainText.3.1.shtml.

20. Roni Caryn Rabin, "With Expanded Coverage for the Poor, Fears of a Big Headache," *New York Times*, April 25, 2010, http://www.nytimes.com/2010/04/27/health/27landscape.html. Medicaid now covers close to half of all children and almost one in five Americans. Henry J. Kaiser Family Foundation, "Distribution of Medicaid Enrollees by Enrollment Group, FY 2007," statehealthfacts.org, 2007, http://www.statehealthfacts.org/comparemaptable.jsp?ind=200&cat=4.

21. National Bureau of Economic Research, "Social Security and elderly Poverty," accessed July 2011, http://www.nber.org/aginghealth/summer04/w10466.html.

22. National Poverty Center, University of Michigan, "Poverty in the United States: Frequently Asked Questions," accessed July 2011, http://www.npc.umich.edu/poverty/.

23. Food Insecurity, Table 1, Child Trends Data Bank, October 1, 2011, http://www.childtrendsdatabank.org/.

24. Charles Oberg, "The Impact of Childhood Poverty on Health and Development," *Healthy Generations* 4 (2003), http://www.epi.umn.edu/mch/resources/hg/hg_childpoverty.pdf.

25. Christine Haughney, "To Reach Simple Life of Summer Camp, Lining Up for Private Jets," *New York Times,* July 24, 2011, http://www.nytimes.com/2011/07/25/nyregion/to-reach-simple-life-at-camp-lining-up-for-private-jets.html?_r=1&hp.

Chapter 5

1. U.S. Department of Health and Human Services, Administration for Children and Families, "Fourth National Incidence Report of Child Abuse and Neglect," NIS 4 Report, January 2010, http://www.acf.hhs.gov/programs/opre/abuse_neglect/natl_incid/reports/natl_incid/nis4_report_congress_full_pdf_jan2010.pdf.

2. Mark Mather and Diana Lavery, "In U.S., Proportion Married at Lowest Recorded Levels," Population Reference Bureau, September 2010, http://www.prb.org/Articles/2010/usmarriagedecline.aspx.

3. Charles Martel, "The End of Marriage," *Spearhead,* January 8, 2010, http://www.the-spearhead.com/2010/01/08/the-end-of-marriage-2/.

4. Centers for Disease Control, "Marriage and Cohabitation in the United States: A Statistical Portrait Based on Cycle 6 (2002) of the National Survey of Family Growth," February 2010, http://www.cdc.gov/nchs/data/series/sr_23/sr23_028 .pdf.

5. Robert Rector, "Marriage: America's Greatest Weapon against Child Poverty," Heritage Foundation, September 16, 2010, http://www.heritage.org/Research/Reports/2010/09/Marriage-America-s-Greatest-Weapon-Against-Child-Poverty.

6. D'Vera Cohn and Richard Fry, "Women, Men and the New Economics of Marriage," *Pew Social and Demographic Trends,* January 19, 2010, http://pewsocialtrends.org/2010/01/19/women-men-and-the-new-economics-of-marriage/.

7. Brenda Luscombe, "Workplace Salaries: At Last, Women on Top," *Time,* September 1, 2010, http://www.time.com/time/business/article/0,8599,2015274,00 .html.

8. Gretchen Livingston and D'Vera Cohn, "Childlessness Up Among All Women; Down Among Women with Advanced Degrees," Pew Research Center, June 25, 2010. http://www.pewsocialtrends.org/2010/06/25/childlessness-up-among-all-women-down-among-women-with-advanced-degrees/

9. Bureau of Labor Statistics, "Household Data Annual Averages, Employment Status of the Civilian Non Institutional Population 16 Years and Over by Sex, from 1973 to date, 2010," http://www.bls.gov/cps/cpsaat2.pdf.

10. Elizabeth Warren and Amelia Warren Tyagi, *The Two-Income Trap* (New York: Basic Books, 2004).

11. "In Deep: Underwater Borrowers," *Wall Street Journal,* November 24, 2009, http://s.wsj.net/public/resources/documents/info-NEGATIVE_EQUITY_0911 .html.

12. Anya Kamenetz, *Generation Debt: How Our Future Was Sold Out for Student Loans, Credit Cards, Bad Jobs, No Benefits, and Tax Cuts for Rich Geezers—and How to Fight Back* (New York: Riverhead Books, 2006, p. ix).

Chapter 6

1. "Homeownership in the United States," *Wikipedia,* http://en.wikipedia.org/wiki/Homeownership_in_the_United_States.

2. U.S. Bureau of the Census, "Median and Average Sales Prices of New Homes Sold in United States," 2010, http://www.census.gov/const/uspriceann.pdf.

3. Single and joint life annuity quotes can be obtained at www.immediateannuities.com. When we obtained the quote, the joint life annuity for a couple ages sixty-five and sixty-two was priced to provide an annual income of about 6 percent of the original investment.

4. Tara Siegel Bernard, "Two Big Banks Exit Reverse Mortgage Business," *New York Times,* June 17, 2011, http://www.nytimes.com/2011/06/18/your-money/mortgages/18reverse.html.

5. "Student Loans," *FinAid,* 2011, http://www.finaid.org/loans/.

6. Robert Longley, "Most Americans Still Drive to Work Alone," About.com, June 15, 2007, http://usgovinfo.about.com/b/2007/06/15/most-americans-still-drive-to-work-alone.htm.

7. M. G. Siegler, "Peter Thiel Has New Initiative to Pay Kids to 'Stop Out' of School," *Disrupt,* September 12–14, 2010, http://techcrunch.com/2010/09/27/peter-thiel-drop-out-of-school/.

8. Bill Gates, "Why MIT Matters," *Boston Globe*, May 15, 2011, http://www.boston.com/news/education/higher/specials/mit150/Gates/.

9. The software is Economic Security Planner (ESPlanner), marketed by a company that one of us (Kotlikoff) founded, at www.esplanner.com.

10. Laurence Kotlikoff, "Study This to See Whether Harvard Pays Off: Laurence Kotlikoff," *Bloomberg,* March 8, 2011, http://www.bloomberg.com/news/2011,-03-09/study-hard-to-find-if-harvard-pays-off-commentary-by-laurence-kotlikoff.html.

11. Unemployment figures for different groups were drawn from the U.S. Bureau of Labor Statistics, "Databases, Tables and Calculators by Subject," in mid 2011, http://www.bls.gov/data/home.htm#unemployment.

12. Craig Copeland, "Labor Force Participation Rates of the Population Age 55 and Older: What Did the Recession Do to the Trends?," February2011, p. 8, http://www.ebri.org/pdf/notespdf/EBRI_Notes_02_Feb-11.HCS_Part-Rts.pdf.

13. Executive Summary, "Rising Above the Gathering Storm: Energizing and Employing America for a Brighter Economic Future, 2007, http://www.ppinys.org/innovation/nas-gatheringstorm-sum.pdf.

14. "Report: One in Four Who Try to Join Army Can't Pass Entrance Exam," *Austin-American Statesman,* December 22, 2010, p. A7.

15. U.S. Census Bureau," "U.S. Population Projections," 2008, http://www.census.gov/population/www/projections/summarytables.html.

16. Matt Zoller Seitz, "Life Lessons in a Global Marketplace," *New York Times,* September 28, 2007, http://movies.nytimes.com/2007/09/28/movies/28outs.html.

17. Hans Fehr, Sabine Jokisch, and Laurence J. Kotlikoff, "Dynamic Globalization and Its Potentially Alarming Prospects for Low-Wage Workers," NBER working paper no. 14527 (Cambridge, MA: NBER, December 2008).

18. Internal Revenue Service, "SOI Tax Stats: Individual Income Tax Rates and Tax Shares," 2008, http://www.irs.gov/taxstats/indtaxstats/article/0,,id=129270,00.html.

Chapter 7

1. Fourteen states do so.

2. For more on the taxation of benefits see Christine Scott and Janemarie Mulvey, "Social Security: Calculation and History of Taxing Benefits," Congressional Research Service, January15, 2010, http://aging.senate.gov/crs/ss24.pdf.

3. Economists will quickly and appropriately point out that the total number of jobs in the economy is not fixed. But more labor supply of oldsters puts more downward pressure on wages, which may discourage some younger people from looking as hard for work or working as hard to keep their jobs when they find work.

4. Suzanne M. Kirchhoff, "Economic Impacts of Prison Growth," Congressional Research Service, April 13, 2010, http://www.fas.org/sgp/crs/misc/R41177.pdf.

5. Casey Miner, "In Oakland, Prisoner Release Already the Norm," *Oakland-North*, February 20, 2009, http://oaklandnorth.net/2009/02/20/in-oakland-prisoner-release-already-the-norm/.

6. Adam Liptak, "Justice, 5–4, Tell California to Cut Prisoner Population," *New York Times*, May 23, 20111, http://www.nytimes.com/2011/05/24/us/24scotus.html.

7. Scott Burns, "Explore Your Unrecognized Borrowing Capacities," *AssetBuilder*, October 31, 2001, http://assetbuilder.com/blogs/scott_burns/archive/2004/10/31/Explore-Your-Unrecognized-Borrowing-Capacities_2100_.aspx.

Chapter 8

1. These reforms are posted at www.thepurpleplans.org. Please consider endorsing them and forwarding the URL to your friends, family, and colleagues. We solicited endorsements for only the financial and health care reforms.

2. "Bank Credit at All Commercial Banks," *Economic Indicators*, August 2011, http://www.gpo.gov/fdsys/pkg/ECONI-2011-08/pdf/ECONI-2011-08-Pg28.pdf.

3. The FDIC itself faces potential claims totaling roughly $6 trillion and at last check had negative assets to cover this potential claim.

4. One of us (Kotlikoff) presents limited-purpose banking in his book, *Jimmy Stewart Is Dead: Ending the World's Ongoing Financial Plague with Limited Purpose Banking* (Hoboken, NJ: Wiley, 2010).

5. C and S corporations as well as limited-liability partnerships.

6. Unlike Glass-Steagall, the banking law passed in 1932 and repealed in 1999, which drew a line between commercial and investment banks—LPB draws a line based on limited liability. Bank owners who want their banks to borrow must operate with unlimited liability, so if their banks borrow and invest in risky assets and then can't repay, the owners will have to surrender all their personal assets, including their villas, private jets, and yachts.

7. Switzerland has an active unlimited liability banking system. Indeed, Wegelin Bank, the oldest bank in Switzerland, operates with unlimited liability. But the owners of these banks are extremely cautious about borrowing money and investing it at risk. Indeed, and this is quite telling, they are, of late, focused on

marketing mutual funds, which present no liability to the owners' wealth to their customers.

8. In converting from their current form to LPB banks, today's banks would have to turn their investment banking operations into consulting services and their trading businesses into matching services. LPB banks would not be permitted to engage in any risky activities of any kind, including having open trading positions and engaging in proprietary trading.

9. We're currently earning very little, if any, interest on our checking accounts and are facing fees, so the new system wouldn't be much different with respect to the cost of having a checking account from the current system.

10. "25 People to Blame for the Financial Crisis," *Time*, undated, http://www.time .com/time/specials/packages/article/0,28804,1877351_1877350_1877339,00 .html.

11. "Food and Drug Administration," *Wikipedia,* http://en.wikipedia.org/wiki/ Food_and_Drug_Administration.

12. Treasury Secretary Timothy Geithner, Republican Congressman Scott Garrett, and Democratic Senator Charles Schumer have all made positive noises about covered bonds. Indeed, Garrett has introduced covered bond legislation. With a few changes, he could change his bill to one that would produce a mutual fund–based mortgage system and do it right. See "Covered Bond," *Wikipedia,* http://en.wikipedia.org/wiki/Covered_bond.

13. There are more LPB details in Kotlikoff, *Jimmy Stewart Is Dead*, including the use of tontines and parimutuel mutual funds by insurance companies to run their businesses.

Chapter 9

1. Congressional Budget Office, "The Long-Term Budget Outlook and Options for Slowing the Growth of Health Care Costs," testimony of Peter R. Orszag before the Senate Committee on Finance, June 17, 2008, http://www.cbo.gov/ ftpdocs/93xx/doc9385/06-17-LTBO_Testimony.pdf.

2. Andrew Harris, "Obama Health-Care Law Goes before Second of at Least Three Appeals Courts," June 1, 2011, Bloomberg.com, http://www.bloomberg .com/news/2011-06-01/obama-health-care-law-goes-before-appeals-court-in-cin-cinnati.html.

3. Sam Stein, "Obama Debt Speech: Tax Increases, Medicare Changes Included In President's Plan," Huffington Post, April 13, 2011, http://www.huffingtonpost .com/2011/04/13/obama-debt-speech-_n_848446.html.

4. Sarah Palin, "Lies, Damn Lies—Obamacare 6 Months Later, It's Time to Take Back the 20!" *Fox News*, September 24, 2010, http://www.foxnews.com/opin- ion/2010/09/24/sarah-palin-health-care-reform-obamacare-berwick-death-pan- els-facebook/.

5. "The 2010 OASDI Trustees Report," *Social Security Online,* undated page, http://www.ssa.gov/OACT/TR/2010/index.html.

6. U.S. Congress, Joint Committee on Taxation, "Estimates of Federal Tax Expenditures for Fiscal Years 2010–2014," December 21, 2010, http://www.jct.gov/publications.html?func=startdown&id=3718.

7. Marilynn Marchione, "$93,000 Cancer Drug: How Much Is a Life Worth?" *Austin American Statesman,* October 3, 2010, p. D1.

8. Dr. John E. Wennberg points out in his book *Tracking Medicine* (New York: Oxford University Press, 2010), that only 15 percent of health care is directly necessary, 25 percent is "preference sensitive," and 60 percent is "supply sensitive," that is, a greater supply of doctors means that more procedures will be done.

9. The CBO's June 22, 2011, long-term budget forecast shows Medicare, Medicaid, Child Health Insurance Program, and exchange subsidies rising to 19.4 percent of GDP in 2085 from 5.6 percent now. Add in about 4.4 percent of GDP being spent by governments on health care through other channels and you arrive at a value of 23.8 percent of GDP in 2085.

Chapter 10

1. The Alternative Minimum Tax, like the Minimum Tax before it, was passed to limit tax avoidance by high-income households. For a brief history and explanation, see Wikipedia: http://en.wikipedia.org/wiki/Alternative_Minimum_Tax.

2. Social Security Administration, "Medicare Premiums: Rules for Higher-Income Beneficiaries," January 2011, http://ssa.gov/pubs/10536.html#rules.

3. "2011 Part B Premium Amounts for Persons with Higher Income Levels," Medicare.gov, November 5, 2010, https://questions.medicare.gov/app/answers/detail/a_id/2306/~/2011-part-b-premium-amounts-for-persons-with-higher-income-levels.

4. Pelosi: "We have to pass the health care bill so that you can find out what is in it," video on youtube.com, 3/9/2010, http://www.youtube.com/watch?v=KoE1R-xH5To.

5. Laurence Kotlikoff and David Rapson, "Does It Pay, at the Margin, to Work and Save? Measuring Effective Marginal Taxes on Americans' Labor Supply and Saving," in *Tax Policy and the Economy*, vol. 21 (Cambridge, MA: MIT Press, 2008) and Jagadeesh Gokhale, Laurence J. Kotlikoff, and Alexi Sluchynsky, "Does It Pay to Work?" NBER working paper, no. 9096 (Cambridge, MA: NBER, 2002). The fact that there are only two such studies is itself very telling when it comes to assessing the complexity of our fiscal programs.

6. Scott Burns, "A Flat Tax, with Bumps and Potholes," *AssetBuilder,* January 27, 2007, http://assetbuilder.com/blogs/scott_burns/archive/2007/01/27/A-Flat-Tax_2C00_-with-bumps-and-potholes.aspx.

7. There are reasons, in the economics literature on optimal income taxation, for marginal tax rates to have this surprising U-shaped pattern. But we doubt Con-

gress is thinking along these lines because we doubt Congress has any idea what marginal tax rates it's actually setting.

8. A term coined by George McGovern.

9. The purple tax isn't identical to the FairTax, which replaces all federal taxes with a single federal retail sales tax, but it has some similar features. See Neal Boortz and John Linder, *The FairTax Book: Saying Goodbye to the Income Tax and the IRS* (New York, ReganBooks, 2005).

10. The Tax Foundation estimates this at 6.6 billion hours: http://www.taxfoundation.org/research/topic/96.html.

11. The IRS would need to set up a system to ensure proper withholding of FICA taxes for workers earning less than $40,000 on each job but more than $40,000 on their combined jobs.

Chapter 11

1. The 2011 Annual Report of the Board of Trustees of the Federal Old Age and Survivors Insurance and Federal Disability Insurance Trust Funds, p.66, http://www.ssa.gov/oact/tr/2011/tr2011.pdf.

2. Thomas Jefferson to James Madison, 1789. ME 7:455, Papers 15:393,http://www.pafamily.org/_files/live/FamilyUpdateFactSheet09-01.pdf.

3. Richard H. Thaler, "Getting the Most Out of Social Security," *New York Times,* July 16, 2011, http://www.nytimes.com/2011/07/17/business/economy/when-the-wait-for-social-security-checks-is-worth-it.html?ref=socialsecurityus.

4. Jagadeesh Gokhale and Laurence J. Kotlikoff, "Social Security's Treatment of Postwar Americans: How Bad Can It Get?" December 1999. This unpublished paper addresses some of these issues. http://people.bu.edu/kotlikof/HowBadfinal.pdf.

5. Solving this problem, in light of the fact that our future earnings are not known for sure (i.e., we face earnings uncertainty), requires using dynamic programming, a mathematical technique. In the dynamic program, what one would construct each of the past years of earnings enter as so-called *state variables*. For Social Security, all of one's past earnings matter because this year's earnings, if they are high enough, will replace a prior year's earnings for purposes of calculating Social Security benefits. This happens because Social Security considers our highest past 35 years of indexed covered earnings in calculating our benefits. (Note, the indexing is based on wage growth but is limited to earnings through age 60.)

For purposes of the requisite dynamic program, past earnings represent what are called state variables. *So what?* Here's the rub. There are no computers on earth, or any computers that are likely ever to be developed, that can do the computations required to solve a dynamic program with more than about fifteen state variables. Solving a dynamic program with thirty-five state variables is completely out of the question. The reason is that the solution to such programs requires considering all the different possible combinations of the state variables. If each state variable could take on, say, 1,000 values, then we need to consider 1,000 raised to the power 35 or 10^{105}, a number that exceeds all the atoms in the universe. The bottom line here is that Social Security's benefit formula is set up in such a way as to put labor economists out of business if they were honest with themselves.

6. Michael Fidora, Marcel Fratzscher, and Christian Thimann, "Home Bias in Global Bond and Equity Markets: The Role of Real Exchange Rate Volatility," European Central Bank, Working Paper Series, No. 685, October 2006. http://www.ecb.int/pub/pdf/scpwps/ecbwp685.pdf.

Chapter 12

1. Scott Burns, "The Wealthy Vampire," *AssetBuilder,* October 29, 2010, http//assetbuilder.com/blogs/scott_burns/archive/2010/10/29/the-wealthy-vampire.aspx.

2. Jeremy Siegel, *Stocks for the Long Run,* fourth ed. (New York: McGraw Hill, New York, 2008), 52.

3. Fritz Machlup, *The Production and Distribution of Knowledge in the United States* (Princeton, NJ: Princeton University Press, 1973).

4. "Daniel Kahneman," Wikipedia, http://en.wikipedia.org/wiki/Daniel_Kahne man.

5. "Balance Sheet of Households and Nonprofit Organizations," June 9, 2011, http://www.federalreserve.gov/releases/z1/current/z1r-5.pdf.

6. National Association of Realtors Median Sales Price of Existing Homes for Metropolitan Areas, updated quarterly, http://www.realtor.org/wps/wcm/connect/c290fd8046cb377a9c15bd93b050a879/REL11Q1T_rev.pdf?MOD=AJPERES&CACHEID=c290fd8046cb377a9c15bd93b050a879.

7. Scott Burns, "Slider-Land," *AssetBuilder,* January 25, 2008, http://assetbuilder.com/blogs/scott_burns/archive/2008/01/25/slider-land.aspx.

8. In *The Coming Generational Storm* (Cambridge, MA: MIT Press, 2004), we railed against the cost of investing, pointing to the enormous impact of investment costs on retirement accumulations. Today, most Americans can save and invest through IRAs at a cost that is a fraction of what they paid only ten years ago.

9. Mark Bruno, "IBM Raises the Bar with New 401(k) Plan," *Truth,* September 16, 2011, http://www.pionline.com/article/20080317/REG/950467789.

10. Scott Burns, "Take Your Pick: Low Cost or High Match?" *AssetBuilder,* October 15, 2010, http://assetbuilder.com/blogs/scott_burns/archive/2010/10/15/take-your-pick-low-cost-or-high-match.aspx.

11. "SOI Tax Stats: Individual Income Tax Rates and Tax Shares," IRS .gov, table 6, through tax year 2008, http://www.irs.gov/taxstats/indtaxstats/article/0,,id=129270,00.html.

12. Readers can get monthly updated trailing returns for this portfolio, executed in Vanguard funds, at http://assetbuilder.com/lazyportfolio/lazy_returns.aspx/couch_potato_portfolios/margarita.

13. National Commission on Fiscal Responsibility and Reform, "The Moment of Truth," December 2010, http://www.fiscalcommission.gov/sites/fiscalcommission.gov/files/documents/TheMomentofTruth12_1_2010.pdf.

14. This isn't remotely true, of course, and at least one examination has shown that the 401(k) returns of major financial service companies trail a simple index. Scott Burns, "Finding the Right Mix," *AssetBuilder,* April 22, 2001, http://assetbuilder.com/blogs/scott_burns/archive/2001/04/22/Finding-the-Right-Mix.aspx.

15. Council of Economic Advisors, "Consumer Price Index—All Urban Consumers," July 2011. The trailing inflation rate is 3.6 percent as we write this. http://www.gpo.gov/fdsys/pkg/ECONI-2011-08/pdf/ECONI-2011-08-Pg23.pdf.

16. Standard & Poor's, "Standard & Poor's Indices versus Active," http://www.standardandpoors.com/indices/spiva/en/us.

17. Morningstar, http://www.morningstar.com/.

18. Bureau of Labor Statistics, *National Outlook Handbook*, 2010–2011 edition, http://www.bls.gov/oco/005122.htm

19. John C. Bogle, *Common Sense on Mutual Funds*, 10th anniversary ed. (Hoboken, NJ: Wiley, 2010).

20. Investment Company Institute, "The Federal Thrift Savings Plan: A Model for the Private Sector?," 2008, http://www.ici.org/pdf/ppr_tsp.pdf.

21. Scott Burns, "On the Importance of Being a Dull Investor," *Dallas Morning News,* September 29, 1991.

22. Scott Burns, "The Margarita Portfolio," *AssetBuilder,* March 16, 2004, http://assetbuilder.com/blogs/scott_burns/archive/2004/03/16/The-Margarita-Portfolio.aspx.

23. Scott Burns, "Monthly 'Self-Managed Couch Potato Portfolio Returns,'" *AssetBuilder,* August 2011, http://assetbuilder.com/couch_potato/couch_potato_results.aspx.

24. Readers who want to see recent trailing performance and standard deviation figures on all of these portfolios can find a monthly update on Scott's Web site, http://assetbuilder.com/.

25. Morningstar Principia data, May 31, 2011.

26. Our suggestions in *The Coming Generational Storm* were the same. The fast, simple, and low-cost way to build such a portfolio is the "Six Ways From Sunday" Couch Potato Building Blocks portfolio.

27. Jim Rogers, *Hot Commodities: How Anyone Can Invest Profitably in the World's Best Market* (New York: Random House, 2004), 218.

28. Israelsen, "Building a Better Balanced Fund," http://7twelveportfolio.com/Downloads/A-Better-Balanced-Fund.pdf.

29. Craig L. Israelsen, *7Twelve: A Diversified Investment Portfolio with a Plan* (Hoboken, NJ: Wiley, 2010).

30. Richard A. Ferri, *The Power of Passive Investing* (Hoboken, NJ: Wiley, 2011).

31. See http://www.portfoliosolutions.com/.

32. Don Phillips, "Indexing Extremists," Morningstar, September 11, 2002, http://news.morningstar.com/articlenet/article.aspx?id=394139&t1=1317062025.

33. See http://researchaffiliates.com/about/index.htm.

34. Scott's firm, AssetBuilder, uses this method.

Chapter 13

1. For a more complete discussion of why the conventional replacement rate calculation is wrong, see Kotlikoff and Burns, *"Spend 'til the End": Raising Your Living Standard in Today's Economy and When You Retire* (New York: Simon & Schuster, 2008), 95–100.

2. The tool, called the Revised Equivalence Scale, was used in the late 1960s to estimate the expense differences for households of different ages and sizes through the life cycle.

3. Scott Burns, "Rethinking Retirement Income," speech to the Austin chapter of the Certified Financial Planners Association, February 9, 2010.

4. http://www.esplanner.com/case-timing-withdrawls.

5. Kotlikoff's software company has produced an inexpensive program at www .maximizemysocialsecurity.com. that helps you get the most benefits out of Social Security. It also explains, in simple terms, the highly complex choices people have about when to collect which benefits from the system.

6. http://www.esplanner.com/case_annuitizing_assets.

7. We're assuming the insurance company issuing the annuity is good for payment.

8. Elizabeth Arias, "United States Life Tables, 2006," *National Vital Statistics Reports,* June 28, 2010, http://www.cdc.gov/nchs/data/nvsr/nvsr58/nvsr58_21.pdf.

9. Calculation from ESPlannerBASIC.

10. Here's one real-life example: Scott Burns, "Unlocking the Secret of RV Living," *AssetBuilder,* April 13, 2004, http://assetbuilder.com/blogs/scott_burns/archive/2004/04/13/Unlocking-the-Secret-of-RV-Living.aspx.

11. Scott Burns, "A Vision Fulfilled in Mesa," *AssetBuilder,* April 10, 2004, http:// assetbuilder.com/blogs/scott_burns/archive/2004/04/10/A-Vision-Fulfilled-in-Mesa.aspx.

12. Principal Financial Group, "Income for Retirement," accessed in early 2011, http://www.principal.com/retirement/incomeannuity/elm/income.htm.

13. Employment Benefit Research Institute, *401(k) Plan Asset Allocation, Account Balances, and Loan Activity in 2009* (Washington, DC: Employee Benefits Research Institute, 2010), http://ebri.org/publications/ib/index .cfm?fa=ibDisp&content_id=4707.

14. Part D insurance plans can be compared on the Web site www.medicare.gov/ find-a-plan.

15. http://ssa.gov/cgi-bin/currentpay.cgi.

16. Scott Burns, "The Investment Value of Generic Drugs," *AssetBuilder,* January 8, 2010, http://assetbuilder.com/blogs/scott_burns/archive/2010/01/08/the-investment-value-of-generic-drugs.aspx.

17. "Panama Visa and Residency Information," *International Living,* http://internationalliving.com/Countries/Panama/Visa/.

18. Scott Burns, "In the Future You'll Need Less Money," *Dallas Morning News,* April 4, 1999.

19. Ty Bernicke, "Reality Retirement Planning: A New Paradigm for an Old Science," *FPA Journal,* 2005, http://spwfe.fpanet.org:10005/public/Unclassified%20 Records/FPA%20Journal%20June%202005%20-%20Reality%20Retirement%20Planning_%20A%20New%20Paradigm%20for%20an%20Old%20 Science.pdf.

20. Scott Burns, "The Sublime Benefits of Death," *AssetBuilder,* July 15, 2011, http://assetbuilder.com/blogs/scott_burns/archive/2011/07/15/the-sublime-benefits-of-death.aspx.

21. "Estimate Your Life Expectancy," 72t on the Net, http://www.72t.net/Calculators/LifeExpectancy.aspx.

22. This ignores discounting for interest to keep things simple.

Chapter 14

1. "Fugetaboutit—Donnie Brasco," YouTube, http://www.youtube.com/watch ?v=a8hchspIj8I.

2. Dennis Cauchon, "Medicare, Medicaid Tab Keeps Growing," *USA Today,* August 3, 2011, http://yourlife.usatoday.com/health/healthcare/story/2011/08/ Medicare-Medicaid-tab-keeps-growing/49776998/1.

3. Rachel Slajda, "Obama Pokes Fun at 'Don't Touch My Medicare' People," *TPM Live Wire,* July 28, 2009, http://tpmlivewire.talkingpointsmemo.com/2009/07/ obama-pokes-fun-at-dont-touch-my-medicare-people.php.

Index

Banks (cont.)
  Federal Reserve and, 178 (see also
    Federal Reserve)
  gambling and, 115–116
  gas stations as role model for,
    115–116
  limited liability and, 113–115, 121,
    245n5–7
  limited-purpose banking (LPB) and,
    113–121, 245n6, 246nn8,13
  purple plans and, 113, 121
Barnes and Noble, 168
Bear market, 186–187, 197
Bear Stearns, 1, 114
Belarus, 21
Bernanke, Ben, 196
Bernicke, Ty, 222–223
Bernstein, Bill, 187
Bill of Mortality, 10
Birth control, 19–20
Birthrate, 73–74, 106
Blue Cross Blue Shield, 134–135
Bogle, John, 183, 187
Bonds, 2
  covered, 246n12
  economic fallout and, 51–52, 56
  purple plans and, 109–112, 116,
    120
  retirement and, 162–163, 165
  self-management and, 177–187,
    190–194
Boskin, Michael, 113
Bosnia, 21
Bradley, Bill, 113
Brigham Young University, 192
Budweiser, 51
Buffett, Jimmy, 187
Buffett, Warren, 49
Bulgaria, 21
Bull market, 186–187, 196
Burden on children, 6
  capital and, 112
  Congressional Budget Office (CBO)
    and, 23–24, 33–34, 37–38
  debt and, 23, 26–32, 35–40, 43, 99
  fiscal child abuse and, 4, 26–28, 59–
    60, 154, 230

  fiscal gap and, 26–43 (see also Fis-
    cal gap)
  GDP measurement of, 23–24, 30, 32,
    34, 36–37, 40
  generational policy and, 24–25, 27–
    31, 43, 70–71, 99, 103
  health care and, 24, 33–36, 84, 107,
    109
  investment and, 24, 28, 32–33, 37
  Medicaid and, 23–24, 27, 31, 34,
    38, 40
  Medicare and, 23–28, 34, 38, 40–42
  Ponzi schemes and, 24–25, 29,
    57–62
  real wages and, 33
  savings and, 24, 32–33, 39, 95,
    105–107
  Social Security and, 23–24, 27, 31,
    34, 38, 40–42
  societal abuse and, 69–79
  taxes and, 24–41, 71, 79, 99–102
  U.S. Congress and, 26, 32–33, 38,
    42, 100
  voodoo economics and, 31–33
  zero-sum generational game and, 31,
    70, 158
Burns, David D., 170–171
Burns, Scott, 12, 222
  AssetBuilder and, 205, 250nn24,34
  cost of education and, 91
  Couch Potato Portfolio and, 185–
    189, 192–193
  entitlement and, 101
  housing and, 174
  living abroad and, 218
  longevity and, 14, 19
  Margarita portfolio and, 176, 187
  Media General study and, 182
  self-management and, 168, 170, 176,
    182, 185–189, 192–193
  syndicated column of, 215
Bush, George H. W., 31
Bush, George W., 25–26, 144, 162

Canada, 15, 124, 194
Cancer, 12, 118, 133
Capital, 5